The Definitive Executive Assistant & Managerial Handbook

Second edition

The Definitive Executive Assistant & Managerial Handbook

Leadership for PAs, executive assistants, senior administrators and office managers

Sue France

Publisher's note

Every possible effort has been made to ensure that the information contained in this book is accurate at the time of going to press, and the publishers and author cannot accept responsibility for any errors or omissions, however caused. No responsibility for loss or damage occasioned to any person acting, or refraining from action, as a result of the material in this publication can be accepted by the editor, the publisher or the author.

First published in Great Britain and the United States in 2012 by Kogan Page Limited
Second edition 2022

2nd Floor, 45 Gee Street
London
EC1V 3RS
United Kingdom
www.koganpage.com

122 W 27th St, 10th Floor
New York, NY 10001
USA

4737/23 Ansari Road
Daryaganj
New Delhi 110002
India

Kogan Page books are printed on paper from sustainable forests.

ISBNs
Hardback   9781398602489
Paperback   9781398602465
Ebook   9781398602472

British Library Cataloguing-in-Publication Data

A CIP record for this book is available from the British Library.

Library of Congress Control Number

2021947856

Typeset by Hong Kong FIVE Workshop
Print production managed by Jellyfish
Printed and bound by CPI Group (UK) Ltd, Croydon CR0 4YY

This book is dedicated to my two daughters,
Sara Reading and Samantha Lewis,
and my three wonderful grandchildren,
Bella, Theo and Sophie,
without whom my life would not be
so fulfilled and joyous.

It's a wonderful and overwhelming feeling to have the
opportunity to be a proud grandmother and I simply feel
blessed to have such a wonderful family.

I also dedicate this book to each and every proactive
professional assistant around the world for all the hard work
you do with such passion and enthusiasm. Thank you for
buying this book, which I hope gives you wisdom and
knowledge and helps motivate and encourage you to keep on
learning and aiming high.

CONTENTS

FOREWORD

Laura Schwartz, Professional Emcee, keynote speaker, author of *Eat, Drink and Succeed* and television commentator

I was delighted when Sue asked me to write a foreword for her latest book, *The Definitive Executive Assistant & Managerial Handbook* 2nd edition, as, just as in her first book, *The Definitive Personal Assistant & Secretarial Handbook* 3rd edition which complements this book, Sue understands the attitude, knowledge and skill set required of assistants in order to excel at their role and help themselves and their bosses shine.

I met Sue France on the speaking circuit when we were both speaking in three cities together in Australia in 2010 at conferences for assistants. We watched and admired each other's presentations and swapped signed books that we had written, and we have been friends ever since. I have spoken with many assistants and understand their needs and wants and I know Sue's advice in this book is paramount to being able to exceed in their roles.

Sue is highly qualified to write books for the professional administrators/ assistants as she was an award-winning assistant herself, has been a training manager for a global firm responsible for the development of assistants, and she has had her own assistants, so she understands the role from both sides. Sue started her own training company in 2009 and has since helped thousands of assistants worldwide through her books, her face-to-face workshops and also interactive webinars.

This 2nd edition includes Sue's knowledge of neuroscience and neuro-linguistic programming and how the brain works, so being able to understand yourself and why you act and behave the way you do and why others react the way they do. Sue has created her own 'Flock Personality Styles', which gives you a better understanding of how to influence and communicate well, negotiate for a win–win result, and be a true leader of yourself and the people you work with. Sue has written the book to allow the assistants to keep on evolving, stretch their abilities, grow confidence, have the ability to succeed at challenges and exceed in their career. This book has practical advice for all levels of assistants as well as office managers. It teaches you how to lead teams, and includes tips for virtual meetings, recruiting, manage performance and motivating yourself and others. There is also useful advice on successful remote working. You learn how to manage projects, and how to lead and manage through change, using emotional intelligence and coaching skills to help build strong relationships, defuse conflict and relieve stress. There are also some useful resources to download from Sue's website to complement this 2nd edition.

Reading Sue's book is like listening to her face-to-face and receiving friendly, well-researched and informed advice. Many people have commented that they keep Sue's book on their desks like a friend, so that they can dip in and out when advice is needed. I highly recommend Sue's work both in her training and her books as she is authentic and has extensive personal experience. She believes strongly in lifelong learning and continuous improvement – hence the 2nd edition of this book.

ABOUT THE AUTHOR

Sue France, FCIPD, INLPTA

After working in the secretarial field for over 30 years, Sue France set up her own training business for assistants in November 2009, which has taken her all over the world as well as conducting online webinars which have enabled her to train thousands of Assistants. Whilst working for a training and development company, Persuasion, in 2006, she won the prestigious title of 'The Times Crème/DHL PA of the Year.' Sue was also a finalist in the Smart European PA of the Year 2007 and since then she has been the judge of several PA of the Year awards.

Sue is an internationally renowned professional motivational speaker, coach and trainer and the author of the worldwide best-selling book *The Definitive Personal Assistant & Secretarial Handbook* – 3rd edition.

Sue is a certified Neuro-Linguistic Programming (NLP) Master practitioner and a qualified learning and development practitioner, as well as a Fellow of the Chartered Institute of Personnel and Development. Sue has created her own behavioural profiling system which she teaches both in person and online. Sue is a neuroscience enthusiast and has been learning about and is fascinated with behavioural science. Sue has updated this new edition with tips from neuroscience and how we can maximize our brains for excellence. Sue is an Editorial Board Member of the global *Executive Support Magazine for Administrative Professionals*, and regularly writes articles for this magazine and other publications.

Her career began as a shorthand typist/word-processing operator, becoming a senior secretary, team leader, events manager and executive assistant to the head of a global leading accounting firm. Whilst working full time, Sue attended university as a mature student two nights a week for three years and gained a postgraduate diploma in human resource management. She then became the UK training manager responsible for the development of 600 executive assistants in the UK.

From 2002 to 2009 Sue worked for Bill Docherty MBE of Persuasion, an international motivational speaker, as his PA, global marketing, training and events manager, trainer/coach for assistants as well as being Bill's co-presenter at PA conferences for administrative professionals worldwide. From 2009 to 2013 Sue was the UK National Chairman for International Management Assistants, a voluntary management assistant networking organization in over 25 countries that promotes learning and self-development as well as global networking with like-minded assistants.

Sue has also been involved in raising money for children's charities by participating in sponsored walks on the Great Wall of China, the Inca Trail in Peru, Mount Etna and the Grand Canyon amongst others. Sue is the proud mother of Samantha and Sara and is now the proud and doting grandmother of Bella, Theo and Sophie.

How to contact the author: I would be delighted to hear from you and I am happy to travel anywhere in the world to facilitate workshops and speak at conferences or to create bespoke online webinars. You can contact me for one-to-one coaching in the UK and telephone coaching or video coaching around the world. My email address is **sue@suefrance.com** and you can also contact me via my website at **www.suefrance.com** or via LinkedIn: **http://uk.linkedin.com/in/suefrance**, Facebook: **https://www.facebook.com/SueFranceTraining** or you can follow me on **Twitter @suefrance**.

ACKNOWLEDGEMENTS

I would like to acknowledge my two wonderful and loving daughters for their unconditional support and love: Sara Reading and Samantha Lewis who support and encourage me in everything I do.

I would like to give a huge thank you to every one of you who have bought this book, and *The Definitive Personal Assistant & Secretarial Handbook*.

I would also like to thank all those who have hired me to speak at conferences and workshops around the world. I have thoroughly enjoyed meeting everyone and having the opportunity to work in so many different cultures and with so many different personalities. The interaction of all assistants has been amazing and also useful as I continually learn and grow with the knowledge I gain from you.

I would also like to thank and show my appreciation to the following organizations and people for their help with input into this book:

My publisher Kogan Page and in particular my editor – Ryan Norman – who has been a tremendous help with advice and helping me to achieve my goals and my deadlines.

Laura Schwartz for taking time out of her busy schedule to read this book and write the Foreword for which I am very grateful.

Belbin.com for allowing me to reproduce Belbin® team roles. For more information on Belbin® please see their website: **www.belbin.com**.

Professor Steve Peters for granting permission for me to reproduce the Commitment Screen from his book *The Chimp Paradox*.

Viktor Cessan for granting permission to reproduce his EPIQ Feedback Model.

Kevin Eikenberry co-author of *The Long-Distance Leader* for granting permission for me to reproduce his leadership model The Three O Model.

The World Administrators Alliance for granting permission to include the Global Skills Matrix and in particular Helen Monument who is the WA-Alliance Chair.

Introduction

I have written this second edition to reflect the changing world of work. We have been working in the VUCA (Volatile, Uncertain, Complex, Ambiguous) world for many years now and continue to do so. VUCA was coined by the US military and the term was adopted by the corporate world. The VUCA world means that we all need to be visionary, understanding ourselves and others as well as our environment, gain clarity and be agile. We all need to be self motivating, self reliant, resilient, emotionally intelligent as well as extremely collaborative. Remote working practices are more common and the leadership role needs to change to reflect this.

I have included new information from my continual learning and increased wisdom from research and as I continue to teach thousands of assistants around the world in person and online. As my fascination continues with neuroscience and because of the encouraging feedback from my first book and my workshops which both contain neuroscience tips and advice, I have updated this book with wisdom from neuroscience so you can work with maximum effectiveness. For more in-depth advice from neuroscience and to understand how to think and behave in a more productive way, I encourage you to buy *The Definitive Personal Assistant & Secretarial Handbook*, 3rd edition.

As a leader, or someone who wants to instil leadership qualities into their everyday lives, you will find this book your most knowledgeable and motivating friend; it will act as a reference book full of insights, tips, tools, advice and earned wisdom for you to dip into and out of when looking for inspiration, support and answers. You will find insights and top tips learned from years of experience, research and from my personal learning.

This book builds on learning from the best-selling book *The Definitive Personal Assistant & Secretarial Handbook*, 3rd edition, published in August 2015. The two books complement each other and can be bought as a set to be used as your friend, advisor and motivator enabling you to be the most effective and efficient assistant and leader, helping you to progress in your career. This book assumes that you are already proficient in communicating and building relationships as well as in technical areas and computer programs such as Word, Excel, Outlook/calendar, contact databases and

PowerPoint, and are aware of all new technology and the plethora of useful apps.

Throughout this book the term 'assistant' will be used to encompass various roles, titles and levels for whom this book is relevant, such as personal assistant, executive assistant, business partner, secretary, management assistant, office manager, team leader and so on.

I have also used the term 'leader' as we are all true leaders whether we have the title or lead an actual team of assistants or not. We all lead ourselves, our bosses and our colleagues at some point to some degree every day.

It is also written for those who already lead teams or aspire to lead teams, giving you all the knowledge you need to be an effective and inspiring team leader. It is also extremely useful for anyone who is simply a team member and Chapter 4 in particular defines what a 'team' is and what a leader's role is within it. It will explain about team dynamics and the five stages of team development including the importance of creating a Team Charter using the example of 'Developing an internal assistant network'. I have also described ground rules for effective teamwork that can be included in the Team Charter.

Chapter 7 will explain how you can communicate with different personality and behavioural styles using techniques such as Transactional Analysis, my own behavioural profiling Flock Personality Styles and Belbin® team roles. This chapter has insights and tips to enable excellent communication and to help avoid conflict and promote healthy teamwork.

Chapter 1 is about 'The leadership challenge' and it explains the styles that leaders can use and the strengths, skills and behaviours required to be effective leaders. There are tips on how to motivate yourself and others, how to empower and delegate, and how to make decisions both on an individual basis and within groups.

You will find out exactly what thinking strategically is and how you can develop your strategic thinking to help you, your boss, your team and your organization. This book will particularly help those who have people reporting to them and explains why vision and values are so important.

The following chapters are peppered with tools and techniques based on neuroscience and neuro-linguistic programming and they are about the skills you need to motivate, negotiate, influence and persuade, as well as offering practical tips on managing and leading people and projects. The book will enable you to manage change for yourself and help others through change as well as increase your brain power, resilience and emotional intelligence.

It has a chapter on managing the performance of yourself and others that explains the processes and procedures for recruiting, from attracting people to managing their performance. It helps you to define or analyse the role of a 'professional assistant' and learn what the characteristics, attitudes, skills and behaviours are. You can also download a resource from my website that details a sample job description and person specification that you can use to help you when recruiting, or simply check your own skills, abilities, behaviours and attitude against.

There are tips on making onboarding worthwhile and memorable using a structured onboarding programme so that you can help new recruits feel a part of the organization from the start. It will explain how to create a 'Standard operating procedures' binder to help everyone with the knowledge they need to do their jobs effectively, and also gives advice on best practice in coaching and mentoring others.

The book discusses the evolution of performance management and how to give and receive effective feedback.

With the help of this book your skills will increase, your output will excel, your career will flourish, relationships will succeed and communication skills will be exceptional, which all enable the bottom line of the company to increase. You will develop the ability to lead yourself and your team, think strategically, check your values and be an example to others.

For most chapters there will be a bonus reference to extra resources for you to be able to download from my website www.suefrance.com on *The Definitive Executive Assistant & Managerial Handbook* 2nd edition resources page. All you need to do is enter your email for each resource.

The book can be used as part of a training programme or when working towards professional qualifications.

I would love to hear from you and to hear your comments about my book(s). I am available for one-to-one coaching, delivering workshops, seminars, webinars and as a motivational speaker at conferences worldwide. I am always delighted to meet new people and I love travelling so please contact me at **sue@suefrance.com**. You can also connect with me on LinkedIn, Facebook and Twitter – I look forward to hearing from you.

Sue France

To download the free resources mentioned throughout the book please go to **www.suefrance.com**; and enter your email address.

The leadership challenge 01

This chapter is designed to rethink leadership in this Volatile, Uncertain, Complex and Ambiguous (VUCA) world we live in. Leaders are having to learn new skill sets including leading remotely. We are all leaders whether we have the title not, as we need to lead ourselves, our bosses and our colleagues at some point and to some degree and on most days. I will explain the styles that leaders can use, and the strengths, skills and behaviours required to be effective leaders. You will learn how leaders think, what they do and how they do it. There are tips on how to involve colleagues so as to keep them motivated, how to empower and delegate, and how to make decisions both on an individual basis and within groups.

You will find out exactly what thinking strategically is and how you can develop your strategic thinking to help you, your boss and your organization. This chapter will particularly help those who have people reporting to them, and explain why vision and values are so important.

Who or what is a leader?

Rethinking leadership

Leadership is about effectively leading people through prosperous as well as challenging times, eg change, crisis and uncertainty. It's also very much about relationships and coaching, mentoring and leading by example. Leaders must, however, prioritize their people if they want to get the best from them. You must have an honest understanding of who you are, what you know and what you can do. Emotional intelligence, flexibility, vulnerability and showing appreciation are non-negotiable skill sets. Also, note that it is the followers, not the leader or someone else, who determine whether the leader is successful. If the followers do not trust their leader or if they lack confidence in him or her, then they will be uninspired and unlikely to be influenced by that person. To be successful you have to convince your followers that you are worthy of being followed.

Definitions of leadership

> The leaders who get the most out of their people are the leaders who care most about their people.
>
> Simon Sine)

> The greatest leader is not necessarily the one who does the greatest things.
> He/she is the one that gets the people to do the greatest things.
>
> Ronald Reagan

Leadership is about motivating people towards achieving a common goal via social influence rather than hierarchy or seniority so anyone with the right skill set can be a leader.

Leadership is about how you think as that is what produces your behaviour so your mindset matters. Your mindset is the frame in which you see the world at any particular moment, for example having a growth mindset where you believe you can learn a skill and can change as opposed to a fixed mindset where you think you are either good at something or you are not.

The Three O Model of Leadership

With remote working (working from anywhere), flexible working and working from home being more common, Kevin Eikenberry, the co-author of *The Long-Distance Leader*, created a leadership model called The Three O Model.

The Three O Model of Leadership outlines three areas of focus – 'Outcomes', 'Others' and 'Ourselves' – that all leaders must recognize and use to reach maximum success. The model encourages you to clarify and prioritize your thoughts and actions in a complex world.

Outcomes

Focusing on Outcomes (goals, mission, vision, objectives and success) can be harder for leaders leading from afar, due to isolation, lack of cues and potentially less repetition of messages. You lead people with a purpose of achieving a desired outcome by communicating creatively and as often as possible to keep all team members engaged, in sync and focused on the goals and objectives of the team and organization.

Others

All leaders need to focus on Others because their role is to aid, support and guide Others to reach our Outcomes. Focusing on Others builds trust, relationships and teams which enables influencing and engagement and success. When you focus on Others' needs you get better results.

Ourselves

No one can lead in a sustainable, successful way without being a servant to Others and Outcomes. What you believe and how you behave is critical to your success. Its important to be authentic, be able to prioritize, influence and continually learn and improve.

Servant leadership

Servant leadership is the ideal leadership strategy for today's world in order to achieve excellent relationships and great results. As a servant leader you serve your team by focusing on the needs of each team member empathetically to understand how you can help them succeed especially with remote workers. Servant leaders have a skill set of actively listening to colleagues to seek their opinions, consciously developing and encouraging colleagues. They have the mindset to collaborate and work alongside their team members to create high performing organizations. This is generally the mindset of successful assistants.

Professor John Kotter of Harvard University established that leaders engage in activities that fall into three categories:

- setting direction – providing a team with a vision, mission and a strong direction of how to get there;
- aligning the team so that they may believe in the mission and follow the strategies;
- motivating and inspiring team members (ie to put meaning into their efforts and helping them understand their purpose).

Everyone can demonstrate 'leadership'. You don't have to have a title to be a leader; you simply have to believe in yourself that you are the true leader you are. Twitter, Facebook, the internet and the breakdown of traditional hierarchical models have all contributed to changes in leadership. Progressive organizations need 'bottom-up' leadership fuelled by initiatives, new ideas and empowerment.

Leadership skills

You will find valuable information on leadership skills in other chapters in this book. *The Personal Assistant & Secretarial Handbook*, 3rd edition, also contains much information that leaders require such as how to set SMARTER goals, including a form that you can download from my website www.suefrance.com to structure your SMARTER goal setting and a downloadable personal development plan, as all leaders need to continually develop, keep up to date and know where they are heading.

All team members, including leaders, have to be able to communicate clearly and concisely and in particular to lay out the vision, mission, goals and strategy of the team, department and organization in order for everyone to understand what the aims and objectives are. Clear communication will prevent misunderstanding, frustration and confusion and it will encourage motivation and a proactive attitude for everyone to aim in the same direction. A useful tool to help in this regard is the Team Charter suggested in Chapter 4, 'Leading effective office based and virtual teams to success'.

Effective communication occurs only if the receiver understands the exact information and meaning that the sender intended to transmit. Many of the problems that occur in organizations are due to misunderstanding that is probably caused by miscommunication as it leads to confusion and ultimately failure. It is the chain of understanding, between all team members, of what is being said and what is meant that makes a cohesive and collaborative team that produces successful results.

Communication is key and as such it will be dealt with in Chapter 7.

First understand yourself and then understand others

Understand your own beliefs and values. Seek responsibility and take responsibility for your actions. Search for ways to guide individuals and ultimately your organization to success. If and when things go wrong, do not blame others. Analyse the situation, take corrective action and move on to the next challenge. Also see Chapter 3 on 'Developing emotional intelligence'.

In order to learn about yourself, what your values are and how your experiences have shaped who you are today, you should complete Resource 1 – the 'Life timeline' exercise. This can be downloaded from www.suefrance.com on the resources page for this book. Answer the questions on Resource 1 and realize what matters to you the most. How do you deal with the tough times and how have your past experiences helped you grow your resilience? Gain insights to your own personality and understand how you deal with your emotions and the emotions of others. Also be aware of your values and be aware that values can change through the journey of life which is why keeping in touch with your values is a lifelong exercise.

Leadership styles

Once you understand yourself, then you need to understand your team and how to interact with them. Successful leaders should be flexible and adapt their style of leadership and approach to their team members' needs for task guidance and psychological support, via the following four styles of leadership (based on Situation Leadership Styles by P Hersey):

- Direct: High need for task guidance
              Low need for support
              The leader defines the roles of the individual or group and provides the what, how, when, and where to do the task.

- Coach: High need for task guidance
              High need for support
              The leader is still providing the direction; he or she is now using two-way communication and providing the support that will allow the individual or group being influenced to buy into the process.

- Support: Low need for task guidance
              High need for support
              Shared decision making about aspects of how the task is accomplished; the leader is providing less task behaviour while maintaining high relationship behaviour.

- Delegate: Low need for task guidance
              Low need for support

The leader is still involved in decisions, but the process and responsibility has been passed to the individual or group; the leader stays involved to monitor progress.

Another leadership model is by John Adair called Action Centred Leadership. It focuses on the group you are leading and their needs. Your job as leader is to meet their needs:

Task need: Getting the job done – they need clarity and a sense of purpose.

Team need: Building and maintaining the team with a shared sense of purpose and a shared culture by setting and maintaining standards.

Individual need: Developing the individuals in the team, knowing and valuing them, ensuring working conditions are fair and providing them with recognition, status and opportunities to develop in a way that will build confidence and keep them motivated.

These three needs overlap, and meeting any one of them will have a positive effect on one or both of the others.

Adair says to meet the team's three needs, there are eight functions you must carry out and these will improve your leadership. These functions can be learned, practised, observed and refined. They are:

- **Defining the task:** Set out a clear goal and objectives for your team. Ensure they understand what they are supposed to do.

- **Planning:** Work with your team to put together a creative plan that breaks the task into stages and lays out clear roles for team members.

- **Briefing:** Use your plan to build a shared understanding among your team. Communicate clearly, simply and in vivid terms. Use this opportunity to address individuals' questions and concerns.

- **Controlling:** Get the most from the assets and resources available, including the team. Gradually build self-reliance so the team members can control their own work.

- **Evaluating:** Constantly review performance and give timely good and constructive feedback to the team and individuals against the objectives set. It will be motivating and improve performance.

- **Motivating:** For example, demonstrate your own positive motivation, recognize and celebrate achievement, build relationships, empower others, enable learning and create a fair and inspiring environment. (See more on motivation in Chapter 2.)

- **Organizing:** Set up systems and processes to help your team work efficiently.
- **Setting an example:** Decide on what message you want to give your team then live it. Set standards and demonstrate your integrity. Know your own values and ethics.

Leading in the VUCA world

A VUCA world where change is rapid and unpredictable can be dangerously disruptive.

Volatile:	We now live in a globally connected society with a plethora of social media and technology, where change can be fast-paced, constant and unpredictable. It feels uncontrollable with the rate of rapid and unpredictable change. Challenges are unexpected and of unknown duration.
Uncertain:	It is difficult to prepare for a future that is unpredictable. Economic recessions, politics, wars, pandemics all add to the uncertainty.
Complex:	Different cultures, time zones, diversity all add to the confusion and chaos we feel.
Ambiguous:	We lack clarity because it is hard to understand the root cause with misunderstanding, miscommunication, mixed messages, different perceptions of each other.

How to counteract and lead in the VUCA world with VUCA:

Visionary and values:	Counter 'Volatility' by acknowledging and understanding where we are presently and using that to create a compelling innovation-led vision using your values and the organization's values. Visionary leadership is about passion and purpose and building a picture of a much bolder and ambitious future. Choose the right mindset (eg a positive, resilient, creative or growth mindset) and communicate clearly as this will give a coherent focus and help you to react quickly to change.

Understand and unlimited:	Meet 'Uncertainty' by understanding the situation and projecting a purpose-driven vision with open, honest and clear goals. Help people believe that they can contribute to the creation and delivery of the goals and vision with unlimited pertinacity. When you understand, you are better able to anticipate threats and take advantage of new opportunities. Look and listen, get a fresh perspective, reframe for the positive. For example: 'FEAR' – 'Feeling Excited And Ready'.
Creative and collaborative:	Respond to 'Complexity' by using strategic creativity to find order in chaos and unlock barriers in order to find new ways to solve complex problems. Challenge the status quo and look at different perspectives in collaboration with others. Be curious, ask questions, stop seeking permanent solutions and develop expertise.
Agile and authentic:	Bring adaptability and a genuine, honest, positive and believable leadership approach that enables people to trust in the vision and strategy. Be authentic and vulnerable – sharing emotions and mistakes helps us improve our self-awareness and accountability as well as developing our growth mindset. It also shows others that we are human, builds trust and empathy, and helps build relationships allowing us to work together more. Understand cause and effect and learn from mistakes. Be adaptable especially during uncertain times so learn new skills and embrace creativity.

Vision

> *'Vision is a destination – a fixed point to which we focus all effort. Strategy is a route – an adaptable path to get us where we want to go.'*
>
> SIMON SINEK

Creating a vision is the first step in a goal setting or planning process. It is also part of the solution to counteract the volatile world we live in. While mission statements guide day-to-day operations, visions provide a sense of direction for the future.

If you view the VUCA world we live in as an exciting challenge, you can turn it into an opportunity to improve your leadership and management skills. You can help make your boss and team members more effective.

You may even help influence and build the vision of the organization as well as live it.

A vision statement helps to provide inspiration to employees. A good vision statement should have ambition, be easy to remember, forward thinking, short, simple, specific and meaningful to your organization and leave nothing to interpretation.

> Captain Sir Tom Moore at the age of 100 inspired and led people to visualize that 'Tomorrow will be a good day.' So counteract the Volatile, Uncertain, Complex and Ambiguous world by Visualizing a better future with passion and purpose, making it clear for everyone to be able to Understand. Be Creative and Collaborative to solve complex problems with Authenticity and an Agile mindset.

> ## Vision examples
>
> *'Create economic opportunity for every member of the global workforce.'*
> LINKEDIN
>
> *'Create the most compelling car company of the 21st century by driving the world's transition to electric vehicles.'*
> TESLA INC

Values

Your values are the beliefs and principles that you believe are important in the way you live and work to achieve your goals and objectives. You feel satisfied and contented when the things you do and the way you behave match your values. You will also feel stressed and possibly have internal conflict, if your behaviour does not match your values. For example, one of my values is family and how important they are to me. However, there was a time in my career when I had two young children and I was over-zealous with my work, and I chose to ignore this value and was a workaholic, staying late almost every evening and even taking my children into work at weekends. When I realized what I was doing I put in place some boundaries for myself and set the expectations of others and I felt much happier within myself when I started to live my core value of family.

I also realized that my boss's value at the time was family so I made sure he attended family occasions and was there for his children by keeping in contact with his wife and making sure I understood his home commitments and keeping his calendar free to leave on time when required. You should know and understand your boss's values and align your values with them and your organization.

You will realize your values when you complete Resource 1: Life time-line. However, be aware that values can change during our life's journey depending on what is important to us at that particular time of our life. It is why it is important to keep in touch with your values as a lifelong exercise.

Your leadership values play an important part in how you make decisions and what actions you take and how you behave. Having a strong set of values as a leader helps build trust and respect amongst your team which in turn enables you to influence and encourage high performance and excellence.

Examples of values:

- Family
- Integrity
- Authenticity
- Honesty
- Passion
- Pertinacity
- Resilience
- Accountability
- Empathy
- Agility
- Reliability
- Loyalty
- Continuous improvement
- Making a difference

A company can become well known for its values when the entire work-force, at all levels, live and breathe the principles. For example if a company has the values of honesty and integrity to be used every day in everything its members do, these can be seen by everyone in the fact that they keep promises, have personal accountability and respect each other as well as the clients/ customers. When every leader and employee in the company knows, understands and follows the values of the organization then it will be successful.

As a leader, it's up to you to know these rules and codes of conduct, disseminate them, follow them yourself and make sure you enforce them. Good leaders follow their personal values as well as organizational values by understanding what standards of behaviour are really important to them and their organization.

Once you understand or even help to create your team's or organization's core values, you can begin to create the right environment for your team and your organization. Leading by example is the best way to do this. It is what you do, not what you say, that demonstrates to your team what you care about. So, if your company values honesty above all else, then make sure you demonstrate that by being honest with everyone around you. If your company values honest and open feedback, then make sure you allow your team to communicate openly.

You have to establish and make known the consequences for team members who don't follow corporate values. For example, if you allow someone to come in late continuously without prior arrangement, that won't set a good example for the rest of the team and it could cause upset and conflict amongst team members. You have to be seen as being fair and treating everyone the same. You should also set up some kind of reward system for team members who consistently act according to the company values as this also acts as an incentive.

Reputation

Concentrate on how others may perceive you, and develop the right image and appropriate behaviours so that others want to follow you.

Be a good role model

You should be the type of person that other people look up to and would aspire to have as their 'distant' mentor (see Chapter 6 on 'Coaching').

Lead by example

Make sure you 'walk the talk'. Have you ever been disgruntled by someone coming in late or arriving back at work after lunch 15 minutes later than allowed? If you think about it – you have also been late sometimes (for very good reasons I'm sure). Have you ever criticized someone for being on social media in work time and found yourself doing the same? Do you have the mentality of 'Do as I say, not as I do?' No matter what the situation is, to see people saying one thing and then doing another always feels like betrayal. If you can remember a time when this happened to you, you can probably remember a sense of disappointment and a feeling of being let down.

If you are a leader, then you know that you have a responsibility to your team. They look to you for guidance and strength; that's part of what being a leader is. And a big part of your responsibility is to lead them with your own actions.

When you lead by example, you create a picture of what is possible and you make it easy for others to follow you. People believe that if you can do something, then so can they.

Leading a team of your peers is a definite challenge. It can put all of your leadership skills to the test: from setting goals to involving team members in decision making to creating a climate of openness and honesty. If you remember to put your team's needs first, and if you work hard to protect their interests, you'll prove to them that you're committed to and passionate about their success. When you demonstrate that you believe in the value of their work, and when you're willing to work through any obstacles you encounter, your team will respect your integrity and pertinacity – and they'll want to work hard with you, and for you, to achieve results.

Employee involvement

Employee involvement is creating an environment in which people have an impact on decisions and actions that affect their jobs. It is a management and leadership philosophy about how people are most enabled to contribute to continuous improvement and the ongoing success of their organization. In times of crisis, such as the 2020/21 pandemic, great leaders grasp the opportunity of rethinking and reshaping leadership and employee involvement as the traditional ways of thinking and leading are disrupted and called into question. In this section we will discuss empowerment, delegation and decision making.

> To me, leadership is not about necessarily being the loudest in the room, but instead being the bridge, or the thing that is missing in the discussion and trying to build a consensus from there.
>
> Jacinda Ardern, New Zealand Prime Minister

Empowerment

Due to the pandemic of 2020/21, remote working, working from any-where (holiday homes, regular home) was enforced abruptly on most organizations who normally worked out of an office. The trend of remote working continues by many.

Empowerment is key to leading remote and office workers. Empowering remote workers means giving them the ability to create their own work schedule around the home life and manage their own time. This allows them to become decision makers and leaders of their own destiny. Truly empowered employees have the trust of their boss to be creative in their thinking and managing their time and priorities autonomously.

However, creating clear expectations with deadlines is crucial for remote workers to understand what is expected of them. It is also key to encourage the remote workforce to set clear work/home boundaries. (See more on remote working in Chapter 4.)

Empowerment is a great motivator and people are more inclined to work hard for leaders who empower them to accomplish great things. Being empowered means that you are trusted, and when people feel trusted they want to take on more responsibility and they work harder.

> Remember that we choose to follow leaders based on the way the leaders make us feel. Therefore we're more likely to follow people who make us feel strong, powerful, valued, etc. Remote associates are no different. You just have to concentrate on ensuring that your remote people feel included, supported and part of a team.
>
> Steve Coats

When leading your peers, be creative with reward and recognition and give praise wherever it's due due – public is even better.

Working in teams can be satisfying and productive when team members work well together. Without sufficient direction, teams may focus on the wrong objectives, fail to use important resources, be torn apart with avoid-able infighting, and may fail, with sometimes dire consequences for the organization.

Experience has proved that we should involve people as much as possible in all aspects of work decisions and planning, which encourages their buy-in and cooperation. This involvement increases ownership and commitment, retains your best employees, and fosters an environment in which people choose to be motivated and contributing. It is also important for team building.

To get employees involved in decision making and continuous improvement activities you can include such methods as managing a project team, suggestion systems, taskforce teams and continuous improvement meetings.

Empowering others is an integral part of getting things done efficiently, however uncomfortable you may feel about delegating. Once you get used to delegating and your confidence builds, you can use proactive delegation as an empowerment tool. Plan to delegate larger projects and more decisions. Where appropriate, include your team in delegation decisions. Allow people to have a say in what tasks they want to take on. This increases their motivation, empowers them and reinforces their value to the overall team.

The art of delegation

Virtual assistants mostly have always worked remotely and other assistants may work from home or the office or have a hybrid arrangement. However you work, the skill of delegating correctly is paramount, not only from the point of of view of the person delegating but also from the person being delegated too.

As assistants we sometime have to teach our bosses on perfecting their delegation skills so that no time or effort is wasted. Common reactions when thinking about delegation are when you hear your inner voice saying:

- 'I know it will be right if I do it myself.'
- 'They will resent being asked, and think that I should do the work myself.'
- 'It's a boring job, so I will "lead by example" and do it myself.'
- 'It will be quicker if I do it myself.'

However, the belief that you can do it better and faster with fewer mistakes leads to a lack of leadership skills and a vicious cycle of too little time and too much to do. Team members may feel disgruntled because you are keeping all the work to yourself and it may lead to inefficient and ineffective use of time and even to a lot of unnecessary stress.

If you feel that when you delegate there is a risk of not having the job done properly, then you need to make sure you are delegating effectively. Successful delegation takes time and energy to help team members succeed, develop and meet your expectations. Delegating will help build the employee's self-confidence and people who feel successful usually are successful.

Match the communication tool to the task and choose the appropriate project management application

Know when to use instant messaging versus email, phone call, virtual call or a face-to-face meeting. Be prepared to navigate different preferences as team members of all ages prefer different communication channels.

You can use project management tools such as Basecamp, Teamwork, Trello, Podio, Asana, OneNote, Evernote, Monday.com, Wrike etc where you can upload emails, documents and other files so everyone can access them when they need to. The project management tools also help you to keep to budget, track time, allow file sharing and team dashboards. You may have to use one stipulated by your organization or you may want to do some research and introduce one that suits your needs. It could be a simple shared spreadsheet but whatever it is make sure you all know where it is and how to work with it.

If it is a new project then call, email and chat as much as you can early in the project to make sure that everyone knows what they should do and give full information or ask for more information.

Effective delegation is also about choosing the right person to delegate to, knowing what is already on their to-do list so you do not overwhelm them and setting realistic deadlines. You also need to be approachable should they need to come back to you for any reason. You need to give honest feedback throughout the project and when it is completed. Give praise where it is due and thank them and also provide development training if required.

Ultimately, it's about learning to trust that the work will get done, correctly and on time and to ensure this happens here are some tips to help you.

Tips for effective delegation

- Clarify your expectations. Tell the person to whom you are delegating what you need accomplished and why it's important. When he or she knows the desired results, it's much easier to see the 'big picture' and work accordingly. If possible, connect the task to organizational goals.

- Clearly identify constraints and boundaries. Where are the lines of authority, responsibility and accountability? Should the person wait to be told what to do? Ask what to do? Recommend what should be done, and then act? Act, and then report results immediately? Or initiate action, and then report back periodically?

- Understand that you can delegate some responsibility, but you are ultimately accountable.

- Provide adequate support and be available to answer questions. Ensure the project's success through ongoing communication and monitoring as well as provision of resources and credit.

- Focus on results. Concern yourself with what is accomplished, rather than detailing how the work should be done. Your way is not necessarily the only or even the best way! Allow the person to control his or her own methods and processes. This facilitates success and trust.

- Avoid 'upward delegation'. If there is a problem, don't allow the person to shift responsibility for the task back to you; ask for recommended solutions, and don't simply provide an answer.

- Build motivation and commitment. Discuss how success will impact financial rewards, future opportunities, informal recognition and other desirable consequences. Provide recognition where deserved.

- Establish and maintain control. Discuss timelines and deadlines; agree on a schedule of checkpoints at which you'll review project progress; make adjustments as necessary and take time to review all submitted work.

- If you can't delegate a whole task, make sure people understand the overall purpose of the project or task as they are more likely to contribute most effectively when they are aware of the 'big picture'.

- Make sure they understand exactly what you want them to do. Give clear and full instructions and don't assume that they know something. Ask questions to make sure they understand, and ask them to paraphrase back.

- Let them know it is okay to keep on asking you questions rather than spend an hour or two getting it wrong.

- Ask for periodic updates and feedback to make sure your instructions were understood. Identify the key points of the project or dates when you want feedback about progress. You need assurance that the delegated task or project is on track and if for any reason people cannot meet the deadline then assure them it's okay as long as they let you know in good time before the deadline so that you can do something about it.

- If you have a vision/picture of what a successful outcome or output will look like, then share it.

- Identify the measurements or the outcome you will use to determine that the project was successfully completed.

- Thank and possibly reward them for their successful completion of the task or project you delegated.

- Talk openly about consequences of missing deadlines and expectations and explain to them that you expect them to try and think of solutions to problems they encounter, instead of simply asking for more instructions.

- Understand that delegating requires enough time and support from you so that everyone can be successful. You know that delegation is a key part of empowerment, and your team is stronger because of it.

- Delegate larger projects to teams of people, giving them appropriate responsibility and clearly defining their authority for decision making.

Delegation is a time management strategy that you must practise. You can't do everything – so decide what you must do yourself and what you can delegate to others. When you learn to delegate effectively, you'll be rewarded with more time and a more empowered and satisfied staff. That's a win–win!

The most appropriate time to delegate

To determine when delegation is most appropriate ask yourself the following questions:

- Is there someone else who has (or can be given) the necessary information or expertise to complete the task? Essentially, is this a task that someone else can do, or is it critical that you do it yourself?

- Does the task provide an opportunity to grow and develop another person's skills?

- Is this a task that will recur, in a similar form, in the future?

- Do you have enough time to delegate the job effectively? Time must be available for adequate training, for questions and answers, for opportunities to check progress, and for rework if that is necessary.

- Is this a task that you should delegate? Tasks critical for long-term success (for example, recruiting the right people for your team) genuinely do need your attention.

- How much time is there available to do the job?

- Is there time to redo the job if it's not done properly the first time?

- What are the consequences of not completing the job on time?

- How important is it that the results are of the highest possible quality?

- Is an 'adequate' result good enough?

- How much would failure impact other things?

When you first start to delegate to someone, you may notice that he or she takes longer than you do to complete tasks. This is because you are an expert in the field and the person you have delegated to is still learning. Be patient; if you have chosen the right person to delegate to, and you are delegating correctly, you will find that he or she quickly becomes competent and reliable.

Decision making

Decision making is an essential leadership skill. If you can learn how to make timely, well-considered decisions, then you can lead your team to well-deserved success. (Problem solving is related to decision making and you can find information on problem solving in *The Definitive Personal Assistant & Secretarial Handbook* 3rd edition, including a downloadable form for a problem solving technique.)

While many of the decisions we make on a daily basis are quite simple with little consequence, some are difficult and could have huge consequences. These decisions may involve assimilating a huge amount of information, exploring many different ideas and drawing on many strands of experience.

The neuroscience of decision making

Decision making has become a focus for cognitive neuroscience and can be seen as the link between memory of the past and future actions. The human brain is extremely powerful but it does have its limitations. We all have cognitive biases which come from our subconscious mind and affect our decision making. We find it much easier to notice biases in other people but not within ourselves but once we are aware, we can learn to mitigate them.

Cognitive biases are mental shortcuts and are designed to help us survive as our brains still work the same way they did when we lived in caves, and their priority is to keep us safe. We receive so much information at all times but we are not capable of processing all of the information so our brains delete, distort and generalize information. We also have mental shortcuts in order to help us make quick decisions.

- **Some biases are related to memory.** The way you remember an event may be biased for a number of reasons and can lead to biased thinking in decision making, eg the more success you have had in applying certain knowledge and decisions, the harder it is to imagine an alternative decision.

- **Other cognitive biases might be related to problems with attention.** Our brains quickly use up energy and therefore have limited resources, such as when paying attention. We are therefore selective as to what we pay attention to.

Cognitive biases hinder our decision making so we need to be aware of them, challenge them and improve our decision making. Your first step is to spot the biases and understand what they are. Here are a few sentences that should alert you to possible bias.

'That's the way we have always done it.'
'I know what they want.'
'I feel more comfortable with people like me.'

Here are some examples of cognitive biases but there are many more:

Self-serving bias:	Favouring decisions that enhance self-esteem. Tending to ascribe success to own abilities but failure to external factors.
Gender bias:	The tendency to prefer one gender over another.
Confirmation bias:	The inclination to draw conclusions about a situation or person based on your personal desires, beliefs and prejudices rather than on unbiased merit.
Conformity bias:	The tendency that people have to act in a similar way to those around them, changing what they believe in, or their values, in order to be included in a group.
Attribution bias:	The phenomenon of trying to make sense of a person's actions based on prior knowledge or engagement with them.
Age, name, beauty, height bias:	Basing judgement around one particular characteristic such as someone's age, their name, their physical attractiveness or size, and making assumptions about what they can or can't do based on that characteristic.
Contrast effect:	Assessing two or more similar elements, such as common content across different résumés, and comparing them with one another, rather than looking at each based on their own merits.
Halo effect:	The tendency of placing someone on a pedestal after learning something very impressive about them.

Horns effect: Viewing a person negatively once you learn something unpleasant or unattractive about them.

Similarity bias: Whether you are in the 'in-group' or 'out group'. We look for people who are like us and believe they are better than others ('in-other' group). We recommend people for jobs who are similar to us. (Be careful: this goes against diversity.) They may have a similar background, have gone to the same university, come from the same area, same religious beliefs, similar interests, similar career track etc

Loss aversion bias: Sticking to a decision made rather than taking risks due to fear of losing what you have gained so far. We attach more value to something once we have made an emotional investment in it.

Distance bias: This is extremely important in remote working. It is the tendency to favour people who are closer to us in time and space. This could result in remote workers feeling isolated and disengaged. So, things happening in the near past we give more weight to. If we work in an office we are in closer proximity, but working from home creates distance between us. Therefore we need to increase time communicating with remote workers, to form teams based on skill rather than location.

Strategies to mitigate bias:

1 Do not fall in love with your solutions!
2 Get feedback from others.
3 Know your triggers.
4 Slow down decision-making process and ask more questions.
5 As you realize it is occurring or has just happened pause and...

 • Ask yourself 'Why am I making this decision?'
 • Deliberately ask others for their opinions and truly consider them.
 • Imagine you are deciding for someone else.
 • What if the opposite of this bias were true at this point?

Prevention measures to mitigate future behaviours are 'if–then...' plans. If situation X occurs then I will perform behaviour Y. Think about possible biases you may have before a meeting or event and make 'if–then...', plans. For example:

> **If**   I am relying heavily on my own experience
>
> **then**   I will actively seek the perspectives of other people

Overcoming cognitive biases is about challenging your instincts, cultivating more rational thinking and having the assertiveness to speak up.

The consequences of the right or wrong decision may be profound for our reputation, for the team and for the organization; therefore it is crucial that we have a framework to get it right.

The seven key steps to decision making are:

1 Define correctly the real decision to be made.

It is easy to leave out important information that we require in order to make a fully informed decision because we start to filter things out and make assumptions based on our previous experience and our own personal values. To identify the true issues that the decision must address, the key questions to ask yourself are: Why am I making this decision – is the objective clear? What has led to the situation that now demands a decision and what does it really require? What will the consequences be of making this decision? What will the consequences be of not making a decision?

Understand the real drivers of the need to make the decision and try and think of some initial options.

2 Understand the context in which the decision needs to be made.

Each situation is unique. It is critical to do an analysis of the situation. Ask yourself what has been done previously in similar situations and what has worked? Who are the people involved? What are the key critical success factors? Who will be impacted by the decision? Who needs to be involved in the decision and in what way?

To enable you to analyse the risks, you must strike a balance between the risk of the decision and the amount of information you have. Remember knowledge is power and you must have the right level of information to make an informed decision. Always err on the side of caution as usually what you know is a lot less than what you think you know!

3 Identify the options.

It is often the case that a major difficulty is the lack of options, especially when the options don't address the needs. This could be the result of a lack of creativity or inadequate analysis that has not identified the real situation and what might be done to address the issues. You could get creative and brainstorm the options with your team and think of as many 'out of the box' options as you can – if you don't dream it, it can never happen! Get input from others outside of the situation and develop your ideas. Don't think 'this can't be done'; think 'how can this be done?'

4 **Evaluate the consequences of each option.**

Decision making is about how to take reasonable risks. You now need to look at the different options and assess these risks. Reasonableness is subjective and will differ with each person. You have to find the most acceptable set of consequences, given your current context and desired goals. You should also consider: What will be my level of regret if I do this and what will it be if I don't? When evaluating, you have to consider deductive or inductive analytical tools. Deduction is when there is a logical flow of reasoning that leads to a 'therefore' conclusion. Induction presents a group of facts or ideas from which a conclusion can be inferred, and they are probably open to several different interpretations. You should also check out the benefits of the options.

The assessment of the consequences of your decision is about which option will produce the optimum result, in relation to the context and your objectives, of making your decision. It involves understanding the very real consequence of your decision.

5 **Prioritize the options and choose one.**

Most people find taking a decision difficult if not impossible and will try to avoid or defer commitment. This arises from self-doubt or an unwillingness to be held responsible. Often an organization's culture encourages and reinforces such behaviour by employees and will determine the general tendency for people to take responsibility for decisions. If you have decided on more than one option then you have to prioritize them.

Tip

In order to make a good decision, once you have made a decision – make it a 'Draft' decision. If you sign off a decision then that is a sign to your brain to not think about it any more as our brain likes to conserve its energy. If in your mind it is a 'draft' then subconsciously your mind will continue to analyse, evaluate and work on it for you, even whilst driving, having a shower, going for a run, or whilst you are asleep, which is why people say 'Let me sleep on it and I'll get back to you tomorrow.' The next day you may find you have had another thought on it. If you haven't then you know you are making the right decision. So work with how the brain works and slow that decision-making process down and you will make better decisions.

Having analysed, brainstormed and assessed your options, you should now have a list of possible ways forward. You need to commit to a decision, own it and ensure that you can justify the why and the how of your decision. Do you know what the consequences of each option are and is your reason decisive and convincing?

6 Review the decision taken.

The frequency and depth of the review will depend on the magnitude of the decision. There are three types of review: 'periodic', such as annual reviews, committee meetings; 'emergency ad hoc reviews', where something has changed or new information has emerged which warrants this, eg a disaster recovery meeting; and 'sequential reviews' where other decisions are based on the outcome of previous decisions.

7 Take action to effect the decision.

Once a decision has been made it must be implemented. Where stakeholders have not been involved in the decision-making process you will need to get the buy-in to the decision after it has been made. Handle this extremely carefully or implementation can go wrong. Wherever possible those involved with implementing the decision should be involved with making it.

Thinking strategically

You may need to think strategically about the area you are responsible for and involved in, for example when managing projects. You may work for an executive who has the responsibility for organizational strategic thinking. Showing that you understand and helping wherever you can goes a long way to being a strategic thinker and leader. You can help executives by making sure they have the time and resources to think strategically – demonstrate your business acumen and show them your keenness to understand. If you understand what strategy is and can think in this way, then you will help the people around you to be more strategic and it will make you a better assistant, leader and team member.

Three different levels of strategy

- **Corporate strategy:** concerned with the overall purpose of the business to meet stakeholder expectations. This is a crucial level since it is heavily influenced by investors in the business and acts to guide strategic decision making throughout the business. Corporate strategy is often stated clearly in a 'mission statement'.

- **Business unit strategy**: concerned more with how a business competes successfully in a particular market. It concerns strategic decisions about choice of products, meeting needs of customers, gaining advantage over competitors, exploiting or creating new opportunities etc.

- **Operational strategy**: concerned with how each part of the business is organized to deliver the corporate and business-unit-level strategic direction. Operational strategy therefore focuses on issues of resources, processes, people etc.

To think strategically, you need to understand:

- What direction is your organization going in? What are the aims and goals to be obtained? Where is the business trying to get to in the long term? What is the vision and mission of the organization? What are its growth, size and profitability goals?

- What are the current strategies – planned or implied? Which markets should your organization compete in? Which geographical areas should it compete in?

- How can your organization gain an advantage and perform better than the competition in those markets? What kind of activities are involved in such markets? What is happening in the industry, with your competitors and in general? What external, environmental factors affect the business's ability to compete?

- What resources – skills, assets, finance, relationships, technical competence, facilities etc – are required in order to be able to compete effectively? What products and services will we offer? What technologies will we employ? What capabilities will we require? What will we make, what will we buy, and what will we acquire (through alliance)?

- What are the values and expectations of the stakeholders (ie those who have power in and around the business)?

Strategic analysis tools

There are several strategic analysis tools to help you analyse the strength of an organization's position and understand the important external factors that may influence that position. The process of strategic analysis can be assisted by the following tools:

- **PESTLE strategic investigation**: a technique for understanding the 'environment' in which a business operates. See Chapter 8 on 'Managing projects' and events for a full explanation of how to conduct a PESTLE analysis.

- **SWOT analysis**: a useful summary technique for summarizing the key issues arising from an assessment of a business's 'internal' position and 'external' environmental influences. What are the strengths, weaknesses, opportunities and threats?

- **Scenario planning**: a technique that builds various plausible views of possible futures for a business.

- **Market segmentation**: a technique that seeks to identify similarities and differences between groups of customers or users.

- **Directional policy matrix**: a technique that summarizes the competitive strength of a business's operations in specific markets.

- **Competitor analysis**: a wide range of techniques and analysis that seek to summarize a business's overall competitive position.

- **Critical success factor analysis**: a technique to identify those areas in which a business must outperform the competition in order to succeed.

- **Five forces analysis**: a technique for identifying the forces that affect the level of competition in an industry.

Tips to think strategically are:

- **Anticipate**
  Have 'peripheral vision'; think 'out of the box' and not just aim straight for the goal. To anticipate well:
    - look for game-changing information at the periphery of your industry;
    - search beyond the current boundaries of your business;
    - build wide external networks to help you scan the horizon better.

- **Interpretation**
  Make sure there is no ambiguity, take time to understand, validate what is true and discard assumptions. Analyse the different information from the different sources and:
    - seek patterns in multiple sources of data;
    - encourage others to do the same;
    - question assumptions and test theories simultaneously.

- **Align**

  A strategic leader must encourage open dialogue, build trust and engage key stakeholders, especially when views differ. You need to:

  - understand what drives other people's agendas, including hidden agendas;
  - bring tough issues to the surface, even when it's uncomfortable;
  - assess risk tolerance and follow through to build the necessary support.

- **Learn**

  Success and failure are valuable sources of learning. You need to:

  - encourage and demonstrate honest, thorough debriefs to extract lessons to learn;
  - shift course quickly if you realize you are off track;
  - celebrate both success and (well-intentioned) failures that provide insight.

- **Strategic choice and implementation**

  This process involves understanding stakeholder expectations, and identifying, evaluating and selecting strategic options; then the task is to put them into action.

Critical thinking

Critical thinking skills are repeatedly referenced as sought after skills for the future workforce. Critical thinking is thinking on a higher level and will help enormously when thinking strategically, negotiating or when influencing and persuading and these skills are not easily replaced by artificial intelligence.

Effective assistants align their thinking with the boss and the organization.

Questioning is the key to critical thinkers and you need to question everything. Through questions you get to explore the deep layers of meaning and reasoning that may otherwise go unnoticed.

To master this skill you must ask the question of a critical thinker:

- What's happening? Gather the basic information and begin to think of questions.
- Why is it important? Ask yourself why it is significant and whether or not you agree.

- What don't you see? What are you missing and is it important?
- What else is there? What other ideas exist?
- What if ...? Are there other possibilities?
- What biases are there in the thinking and how can you mitigate them?
- Is there hypocrisy and manipulation?
- Challenge current beliefs and mindsets – including your own!
- Reframe problems – the ability to see a problem in a different way is crucial. Reframing encourages you to shift your focus from the symptom to the root cause.

Summary

'Leadership and learning are indispensable to each other.'

JOHN F KENNEDY

Now that you know you too are a leader in your own right, practise the skills of a VUCA leader – be visionary and know and use your values, understand what is happening and be unlimiting in your resources and think with pertinacity, give clear communication in a collaborative way and be agile and adaptable in this unpredictable world where change is constant. Remember to make a vision for yourself and your team, think strategically including using your critical thinking skills, check your values and set the right examples. Explore new ideas, be fair and treat everyone with equality but as individuals and understand what is a threat or reward to each one of them. You should take the opportunity to develop every day through interacting with others, learning from mistakes, reflection, self-study and formal learning.

You can achieve so much more by involving others, making the right decisions (mitigating biases) and delegating effectively. Remember to choose the right tasks to delegate, identify the right people to delegate to, and delegate in the right way.

Look at your strengths and build on them, look at your weaknesses and improve them, look at yourself and be proud!

How to motivate yourself and your teams

02

'*You don't have to be great to start, but you have to start to be great.*'

ZIG ZIGLAR

Action leads to motivation – not the other way round!

Motivation can be defined as internal and external factors affecting the reason or reasons anyone has for behaving in a particular way and the general desire or willingness to do something. Have you ever procrastinated because a project felt too painful to start? You are not alone – the area in the brain that lights up when you look at a daunting job is the same area as if you have been slapped – it is like feeling physical pain. The good news is that the second you start that project, the pain goes away! So don't wait to feel motivated – just take action and motivation will follow.

Motivation needs to be combined with dedication, accountability and pertinacity.

As motivation is driven by your subconscious mind which is driven by emotion, just because you may not 'feel' like doing something should not stop you. Therefore if motivation is combined with: dedication to act and achieve your desired outcome; being accountable for delivering the right work, on time and to the best of your ability; as well as pertinacity to never give up, then as soon as you take action to start that job, your feeling will change to enthusiasm to get the job done and even excitement.

If you wait for motivation first, you may never get started. Instead, you need to use your dedication to take action no matter how you feel and then motivation follows. Start small if you have to and build momentum as

Figure 2.1   Sue France's Motivation Model

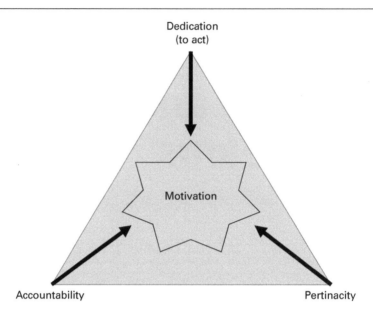

motivation and inspiration will follow as soon as you start. Therefore schedule time for your priority list, making sure you schedule the difficult tasks in the morning after a good night's sleep when your brain is fresh and has full capacity energy. The brain uses 20 per cent of the energy intake and this is soon used up. You can concentrate well for 25 minutes at a time and then you will need to take a brain break. The break can be a three-minute mindfulness exercise to reboot your brain, or a walk around the block, or make a drink. Moving and getting away from your screen will help reboot your brain. Also the day after a two-day break is a good time to schedule difficult tasks.

This chapter will include insights from neuroscience and covers motivational theories by Professor Steve Peters (author of *The Chimp Paradox*) – the Commitment Screen; Tony Robbins – the Six Human Needs theory; Maslow's Hierarchy of Needs which I have updated with an important change to include information from neuroscience, as Maslow wrote this theory in 1943 and we have learned a lot about the brain since then; and Daniel Pink's Autonomy, Mastery and Purpose. It will explain how to look out for the signs of demotivation and it will help you to understand how you can motivate yourself and others, especially if working remotely. It also includes tips on how to motivate your boss.

The heart of job satisfaction is in your attitude and expectations; it's more about how you approach your job than the actual duties you perform.

Understanding your own and other people's motives and reasons for doing something is the key to becoming a good employee, team player and leader. We need to understand how to create an environment where people are motivated – including ourselves.

In order to lead and motivate you need to be able to:

- understand and communicate the vision and mission of what the business stands for and where it is heading;
- demonstrate your values and priorities and the values of the organization;
- know what you as an individual intend to do, in order to realize that vision and reflect those values;
- learn what individual employees can do to realize that vision and reflect those values for themselves.

(See more on vision, mission and values in Chapter 1, 'The Leadership challenge'.)

'A leader shapes and shares a vision which gives point to the work of others.'

CHARLES HANDY

Motivational theories

The Commitment Screen

Figure 2.2   The Commitment Screen

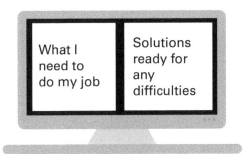

SOURCE Steve Peters, *The Chimp Paradox*

Steve Peters explained in his book *The Chimp Paradox* that commitment comes from the conscious mind and is not based on emotions. Commitment means following a plan even if you don't feel like it.

> When you decide to do something, remind yourself that it is commitment not motivation that matters.
>
> Professor Steve Peters

In order to assess your commitment you can use the Commitment Screen. The first aspect (screen) is working out what you will need to do the job. The second aspect (screen) is preparing solutions to overcome any obstacles and difficulties that may occur and which will stop you from succeeding. This relates to my setting SMARTER goals on page 53, and making sure you have thought about any obstacles that might get in the way of achieving your goals so that you are prepared and ready to work around them if and when they happen.

First screen

What you need for the job can be broken down into three types:

- Essential

  This is split into the conscious and subconscious needs. So for the conscious needs it would be what practical and logical things you require and for the subconscious needs it would be what feelings and emotions you need. For example if you are thinking about giving an online presentation to your peers, the conscious mind would want to know what essential equipment you require, such as a reliable computer, a good wifi or ethernet connection, the appropriate timing and the logistics. The subconscious mind would want to know whether you are confident in your content and excited about giving the presentation.

- Significant

  These will have an influence on the outcome and must be considered. Taking the online presentation example, you will need to think about back up computer or memory stick for your presentation, correct lighting and audio equipment in a quiet space, especially if working from home. All these will improve your chances of success.

- Desirable

  These are the things that may or may not help but will make things more comfortable. With the online presentation you may want someone to prepare and bring your lunch or drinks in the break.

The above answers to whatever your job is, will be different for different people – so this is personal to you but it may be helpful to consult a peer or friend and see if, from their perspective, you have covered everything.

Not working out potential problems before you start sets you up to fail. You need to work out what you have to overcome to be successful in your plans both in practical and emotional terms.

Second screen

What are the challenges you might face? These are broken down into three types:

- Hurdles

  These are the things there is no getting around, you can't move them, you have to jump them! There are often difficult and challenging things in what you have to do but you have to work out what they are and what coping strategies can you put in place. Poor coping strategies include ignoring, running away or fighting them.

  Taking the online presentation as an example, a hurdle may be that you are worried and frightened about giving a presentation so you need to practise, practise, practise and know your content 100 per cent. You can learn breathing techniques before you start the presentation to calm your mind and prepare you.

- Barriers

  These are things you can get around with good planning. Barriers can be removed unlike hurdles. For example dealing with something that you don't have the experience or expertise to do can often be delegated to someone who has the capabilities.

  Taking the online presentation example, you may wish to use a colleague who has the expertise to set up breakout rooms, watch the chat and question and answer panel and feed those back to you whilst you concentrate on giving your presentation.

- Pitfalls

  These are areas that could easily be your downfall if you are not looking out for them. An example would be entering a difficult conversation without any preparation.

  Taking the online presentation example it could be letting yourself become emotionally and physically exhausted before recognizing you need a break and giving the presentation feeling exhausted.

Six Human Needs theory by Tony Robbins

This theory is based on the belief that all humans have the same six human needs (drivers) and all are universal; everyone is – or can be – motivated by their desire to fulfil them. Our behaviour is an attempt to meet these six needs. If we don't satisfy them productively then we will satisfy them unproductively. It is a useful way to look at people's behaviours and a good framework for leaders to use to add more depth to their leadership style. Remember you are a leader of yourself and your boss even if you don't actually lead a team.

You may want to consider these needs when thinking about developing your team members or leading your boss and ask the question: 'What need or needs do my team/boss have that will enable them to fulfil their job roles effectively?'

The six needs

Deep at the core of our thoughts, feelings and behaviours lie six basic needs that we are driven to fill.

1 Certainty/comfort

We want to feel in control and know what is coming next so we can feel secure. We want assurance that we can avoid pain and stress, and gain pleasure. It affects how much risk we are willing to take. Of course there is no absolute certainty, but even having certainties such as the car will start all helps with the feeling of certainty and having less stress. As does the certainty that bosses will check in regularly, the certainty that people will get back on time to answer queries and the certainty that we will have a job. When we get total and too much certainty we can get bored and then we have a second human need.

2 Variety

At the same time as we want certainty, we also crave variety. We all like surprises but only the surprises we want, not the surprises we don't want! Paradoxically, there needs to be enough uncertainty to provide spice and adventure in our lives. Maybe we could do things in a different order, meet new people and grasp opportunities. If variety is your core need, you will not be afraid of taking risks and you run the risk of not being able to commit to a job or a relationship.

3 Significance

We want to feel special, unique, different and valued. Deep down, we all want to be important. We want our lives to have meaning and significance. We want to look back on our lives and know we made a difference. Some people seek significance in a destructive way by bad behaviour and wanting to stand out, which can upset other people around them. They may continually be late for work or make a spectacle of themselves. We need to influence them by helping to change their mindset. One way could be to get them involved in a project or helping them to become an expert in an area where they can feel valued and significant and stand out in a good way.

4 Connection/love

Connection with other human beings is one of the most important needs we have. We want to feel part of a group or team. We want to be cared for and cared about. It's the essence of teamwork. It's what we crave when we work with others. Some people may be solitary but they still have a need for a connection in some way – maybe with church or the community. See more on how important connectivity is under Malsow's Hierarchy of Needs below.

5 Growth

We should all aim to have a growth mindset which means you know you can continually develop and improve. We all have neuroplasticity of our brains which means we are able to learn and change until the day we die. We should all believe in lifelong learning and strive to increase our skill set which helps make us feel satisfied and fulfilled.

6 Contribution

The desire to contribute something of value – a sense of service and focusing on helping and supporting others and making the world a better place than we found it – is in all of us. Take that need away, and you lose all motivation. Human beings get excited to contribute once they have the chance to experience it and not just talk about it.

Evaluate the six human needs to better understand your personal motivations and examine which ones seem the most significant to you. Then, look at what you do to fulfil the needs of your boss and other team members. It will likely make a difference in what you do and how you do it. People may want to meet the same needs (for example, significance) but different people will do it differently.

It is possible to meet any or all of these six needs by changing:

- your perception (belief or appreciation of...);
- or your procedure (vehicles or approach to...).

See Table 2.1 for examples of how a leader can meet the six human needs of a team.

Table 2.1 Examples of how a leader can meet the six human needs of a team

Certainty	Write a Team Charter together with the team (see Chapter 4, 'Leading effective office based and virtual teams to success') that sets out expectations of the team and each other.
Variety	Make sure everyone gets a chance to work on different projects and/or with different people. Maybe job-shadow for a day. Vary the tasks they do throughout the day.
Significance	Each team member brings unique skills to the team – make sure these are known, appreciated and rewarded. Use their skills to help them shine. An important skill for a leader to develop is being able to appreciate team members aloud in front of the rest of the group. A simple thank you goes a long way.
Connection	Icebreaker activities can be conducted at the beginning of meetings. Make sure the team members have time to get to know one another by organizing team meetings and social events such as team lunches including virtual social events for people who work remotely. Team-building events would be excellent, especially ones where they get to know one another's values and beliefs.
Growth	You can help a team grow by creating opportunities for quality discussion and knowledge sharing. Make available learning and development tools and techniques, whether through virtual learning, face-to-face learning, being a coach or coaching others etc.
Contribution	Help groups connect with the overall purpose of the team. Create a mission statement so they know where they are heading and how they can help each other to get there. It helps if individuals see a connection between their own work and the success of the team and organization.

Maslow's Hierarchy of Needs (updated to fit with the findings of neuroscience)

Maslow's theory of motivation states that people have five main needs and you must meet the needs in the following order of importance: physiological, safety, social, self-esteem and finally self-actualization. People are motivated by things that help them meet these needs. What motivates people will therefore differ depending on what need they are trying to fulfil.

The first stage of Maslow's needs is '*physiological*': these are basic needs and they are the requirements for human survival: that is, the need to eat, drink, work and sleep.

Many believe that the only reason we work is to earn money. Some people may be motivated by money and the opportunity to work overtime in order to pay bills or to save for their next holiday or car. There is no question that money, or what it buys (food, housing etc), is a prime motivator; however, money alone does not create the sense of fulfilment and accomplishment that many seek.

The second need is '*safety*': once the physical needs are satisfied, your safety needs take precedence and influence your behaviour. Safety includes the need for shelter, personal and financial security, health and well-being, including a safety net against accidents and illness and the certainty that you feel of keeping your job.

The third stage of Maslow's Hierarchy of Needs is '*social*' and involves feelings of 'belonging to' and friendship: for example belonging to an organization, group or team. We all need to feel a sense of belonging and acceptance. In the absence of these, many people can feel lonely.

The fourth stage comprises '*self-esteem*' needs: the need to feel good about yourself and to be recognized and praised for your achievements with a feeling of respect for yourself and from others. Self-esteem concerns your feelings of confidence, self-worth and the desire to feel accepted and valued and how you feel you compare to your peers. It also includes your competence and self-confidence. Deprivation of these elements can lead to an inferiority complex, weakness and helplessness.

The fifth need is '*self-actualization*': the need for personal fulfilment, mastery and recognition and realization of how you have grown and developed. The rewards you get and feel for doing a job well done. This need is the summit of Maslow's Hierarchy of Needs and unlike lower level needs, this need may never be fully satisfied as there are always new opportunities to continue to grow and continual self-development should be your aim.

However, I would like to update Maslow's Hierarchy of Needs as neuroscience and how the brain works is continually bringing new evidence to light. Maslow does not give enough credence to the role of social connection. None of the needs on the hierarchy can be met without social connection. Connection is as important as Maslow's first level of basic needs of eating, sleeping etc. Without social connection there would be no survival. For example, how would a baby grow without a parent/carer to take care of it?

Our reliance on each other grows and collaboration becomes more prevalent as society grows more complex and interconnected. Belongingness is the driving force of human behaviour. This has been witnessed by the increase of mental illness during the pandemic through forced isolation.

Matthew Lieberman, one of the founders of social cognitive neuroscience, stated:

> Being socially connected is our brain's lifelong passion. Our predisposition to
> be social may explain our need to interact through social media and gossip, as
> well as why people are interested in watching others' social interactions on soap
> operas and reality television.

In his book *Social*, Lieberman described a study of 60,000 leaders which found that less than 5 percent excel at both achieving important results and building social relationships. 'Not many people effectively combine the two,' Lieberman said.

Leaders would benefit from understanding people's social motivations as feeling liked and respected in the workplace activates the brain's reward system in the same way that financial compensation does and social rewards might be at least as effective as money in motivating employees. We know that one of the top reasons for leaving an organization is because of bad working relationships. We should not be surprised at nor resist the rapid adoption of tools and apps that enable one of our most basic survival instincts: connection.

The theory of extrinsic and intrinsic motivation

(Based on Carl Jung's psychology of the conscious mind as described in his book *Psychological Types*.)

Extrinsic motivation

Extrinsic motivation is when you are motivated by external factors that are given or controlled by others, for example by salary or by praise. Our jobs are usually based on extrinsic motivation, although there will be some intrinsic motivation involved if you enjoy aspects of what you do.

You may need an extrinsic motivator for doing your filing. This is something you may find boring but the extrinsic motivator could be the fact that you know if it does not get done, then your boss or you may not be able to find something quickly, thus wasting Time. Also, your boss may get irritated if it is not where it should be when he or she wants it. In order to avoid the boss's wrath, you make sure it is done on time. External motivators, such as cash and bonuses, over time lose their effectiveness as motivators and are seen as entitlements. Use extrinsic rewards to motivate (such as praise, tangible awards, travel awards and social recognition) to distinguish exceptional involvement with the job and commitment to the company.

Intrinsic motivation

Intrinsic motivation is when you are motivated by internal factors to meet your own personal needs. Most hobbies and leisure activities are based on intrinsic motivation. We do them because we enjoy them, not because we have to.

Even if we do a job we enjoy, problems can crop up where we need to do something that we don't inherently like – such as filing, speaking with staff about performance issues, completing reports and so on. We have to do undesirable tasks as part of our job, so we have to find a way to motivate ourselves to complete them. That's where self-motivation is necessary.

To maximize intrinsic motivators, people must perceive they have the skills and a supportive environment that fosters creativity and responsibility.

Is your company providing the necessary training, education, tools and resources for an employee to be effective? Is leadership providing a controlling environment (strict dress codes, static office hours, micro management, etc.) that diminishes internal motivation? Or is management providing a more flexible and open workplace where innovation is nurtured? To motivate yourself, you must examine and understand your needs, so that you know what you find valuable and rewarding. Then, by changing your environment and perspective, you can find the intrinsic and extrinsic motivation to complete those undesirable tasks. So, rather than relying on others to make a task more rewarding, you make it more rewarding yourself.

If you want to be more intrinsically motivated, you need activities that are moderately challenging – that stretch you but you feel you can do well, which will give you satisfaction.

Intrinsic motivational theory: Autonomy, Mastery and Purpose by Daniel H Pink (2009)

Daniel Pink (speaker and author of *Drive: The surprising truth about what motivates us*) developed the motivational theory of Autonomy, Mastery and Purpose, and this epitomizes the very real concept of intrinsic motivation within all of us.

Autonomy, mastery and purpose may seem pretty much common sense, but many managers forget how internal the drive to motivation may be. Pink's ideas may well identify why external motivators don't work effectively all the time.

Autonomy

Our default setting, says Pink, is to be autonomous and self-directed. Most management today conspires to change this setting from intrinsic to extrinsic motivation. To encourage intrinsic motivation, autonomy is the first requirement.

People need autonomy over task (what they do), time (when they do it), team (who they do it with) and technique (how they do it).

Mastery

While external motivation techniques require compliance, Pink says that real motivation requires engagement. Only engagement can produce mastery, becoming better at something that matters. Mastery isn't just the ability to do things well; it revolves around being able to carry out optimal experiences where the challenges we face help us to grow and stretch our capabilities.

Smart organizations supplement day-to-day tasks with stretching tasks, not too hard but not too easy. There are three elements to this drive to mastery:

It is a 'mindset' – it requires the capacity to see the abilities you possess as infinitely improvable.

It is a 'stretch' –　it demands effort.

It's 'progressive' – it's impossible to fully realize, which makes it frustrating, challenging and attractive, all at the same time.

Purpose

Human beings seek purpose – a cause greater and more attractive than just themselves – and businesses realize this. Purpose-maximization is taking its place alongside profit-maximization, expressing itself in three ways:

- goals that use profit to reach purpose;
- words that emphasize more than self-interest;
- policies that allow people to match their work with their passion.

These three ideas may well explain why many businesses can't get the most out of their people. They rely too heavily on the extrinsic forces to drive their staff, but people will always work with greater energy at something they themselves have decided to do.

In summary, people get motivated and engaged if they feel they are in command of their own destiny in their roles, particularly while at the same time learning expertise and contributing creatively. So Pink's ideas add value to the motivation debate and allow us to see what is really driving people's performance.

Motivational theories, some of which I have covered above, help you to understand better what motivates and demotivates you, your boss and your team, and knowing this will help you to achieve your personal and professional goals. It is important for you to identify what motivates you and share it with your boss. If you are a leader then ask your team to identify what motivates them and make sure you discuss this with them.

The threat (demotivation) and reward (motivation) system in the brain

Our brain constantly scans the environment as it makes predictions in order to keep us safe. Our brain has an aversion to uncertainty, dislikes ambiguity and is looking for how we can avoid threats (demotivation) and encounter rewards (motivation). We actually look for threats much more than we look for rewards.

Understanding how the brain's 'threat and reward system' works helps us to motivate ourselves and others and also helps us realize how to prevent demotivation.

When the brain perceives a threat, cortisol is released which is a stress hormone that also suppresses the immune system. Under threat, adrenalin is also released which increases blood flow to muscles ready to fight or flight and maybe your mouth goes dry, your palms go sweaty and your heart rate increases.

It is important to become familiar with potential psychological and social threats so you need to learn to spot threats early. Become sensitive to them so that you're less likely to unintentionally create threats that demotivate yourself and others.

Minimizing threat and maximizing reward

- Because the brain dislikes uncertainty it values being in control and therefore likes autonomy and treats it as a reward (motivation). Stress occurs when the brain perceives a threat and feels demotivation if the threat is outside of our control whether it is perceived or real.

   Therefore to motivate people and give their brain a sense of reward give them autonomy over projects and schedule, allow them to prioritize and encourage and support them in making their own decisions.

- Social connectivity is extremely important to humans and threat can occur in the brain if someone is left out of an email they think they should have been included in, if they have not been invited to a meeting (virtual or face-to-face), or if they feel you are ignoring them when they talk to you (that includes virtual meetings so make sure you look into the camera when speaking to someone, especially if you are talking about a sensitive matter). Make sure they have the feeling of reward and being motivated by being inclusive, transparent and when working remotely contact them more than you would in the office, as you are not able to have those incidental meetings you get working in an office together. Make them feel a part of the team.

- Social acceptance and status can either motivate (reward feeling) or demotivate (threat feeling). So you can motivate someone by publicly praising them. Or have a public notice board reward system that changes each month, perhaps showing the employee of the month with a flattering photo of them. If you publicly humiliate and criticize someone negatively you will demotivate them immediately.

- Fairness and equality can create a reward or a threat feeling in the brain. However, treating everyone equally is not always fair. For example, you could ask two people to give a presentation to the leadership group; one person may find this motivating and rewarding, thinking it will help with raising their profile and possibly furthering their; whereas another person may find it threatening and just want to run away. Therefore you need to treat people as individuals and get to know them on a personal level in order to better understand what they find rewarding (motivating) and threatening (demotivating). Equal treatment isn't necessarily fair treatment.

Signs of demotivation

People who don't take responsibility for their work or actions are likely to have a negative impact on their team. Look for apathy, finger-pointing, missed deadlines or phrases like 'It's not my fault' to spot team members who are avoiding accountability.

To help people take more responsibility for their work, provide them with the skills and resources to actually do their job. Then set up an environment that makes it easy for them to change, and help them take responsibility for their decisions and actions.

You can do this by:

- ensuring adequate resources are available;
- communicating roles, responsibilities and objectives;
- re-engaging people;
- helping them take control;
- avoiding micromanagement;
- giving praise.

You can recognize when people are demotivated by observing, empathizing, understanding and simply keeping an awareness of what is going on around you.

Notice any changes in attitude or quality of work; there may be a lack of concentration or careless or incomplete work. Your workforce could be lacking in motivation if you have a high turnover, low productivity, a poor workplace atmosphere and a lot of employee grievances.

A lack of motivation can also be recognized by noticing whether there is an increase in absence from work, increased sickness, arriving late into work or a lack of enthusiasm, and if people appear frustrated and possibly are not communicating well, if at all.

What are demotivators in the workplace?

In addition to needs not being met, as explained in the motivational theories above, here are some additional demotivators:

- change that introduces uncertainty, including stress and anxiety, in those affected by and those implementing the change;
- being under-resourced;
- listening to others who complain or try to avoid work and are not reprimanded, while you are working hard;
- being given too much work just as you are about to leave for a holiday;
- being patronized or talked down to by colleagues;
- inequality of pay.

Remember that demotivation is contagious and can have a knock-on effect. I am sure you can think of more things that demotivate you but all of the above and more should be taken into consideration when you may be affecting others. Let's move on to understanding motivation more and what you need to do to help yourself and others, including your boss, with practical suggestions to help you be more proactive and motivated.

How to motivate yourself and others

Keeping yourself and your team motivated is a challenge and is crucial to the success of the organization. Unfortunately some people use fear to try to achieve results. This only works for a while and ultimately damages credibility. Motivating others is more about using incentives to influence people to motivate themselves.

When it comes to staying motivated, we are all different and therefore need different incentives. Some like a boot-camp style personal trainer to push them hard; others want an encouraging and supportive friend. For some, working first thing in the morning is perfect; others are night owls.

When you feel it is difficult to motivate yourself, think about what you are good at and what you have achieved. Neuroscientists have identified that gratitude, when regularly foused upon, is most likely to propel your mind and body into an upward spiral. It is more difficult to think of what you are grateful for when you are demotivated, upset or distressed but this is exactly the time you need to do it. If you make a habit of thinking of three things you are grateful for as soon as you wake up in the morning, it will set you up for the day. As your attitude is contagious you will also motivate others around you. This builds confidence, which helps you motivate yourself. Above all remember to take action first and motivation will follow.

Below are some example questions to help you motivate yourself and I am sure you can think of more. When you are motivated yourself you can then motivate others.

- My proudest moment has been when...
- The most difficult thing I ever accomplished was...
- Something I am good at is...
- The greatest thing I have ever achieved is...
- I have helped others by...
- The best decision I ever made was...
- Something I have learned to do recently is...
- If I want to I can...
- The most successful project I ever organized was...
- What happened when I motivated someone else to success was...

To help build up team morale, there are tried and tested ways to keep yourself and your team motivated. Find out what works for you and write it down on Table 2.2 (page 58).

Vision board motivation

Vision boards work because your brain has neuroplasticity which means you can train your brain and rewire it for success. Visualization is one of the most powerful ways to do this.

How to motivate remote workers

1 Frequent communication and check-ins

2 Agree on the communication tools to use and when to use them

3 Establish clear goals and expectations

4 Respect different time zones

5 Understand their boundaries

6 Offer training and development

7 Recognize efforts made

8 Provide tips and training to help remote employees manage their time

9 Ensure they have a work–life balance

10 Offer mentorship and coaching

11 Make sure they take time for themselves every day – walk, a proper lunch time away from the computer

12 Encourage them to establish a routine but at the same time allow some flexibility for home chores and children

13 Allow them autonomy over their schedule – understand if they prefer to take two hours off in the day and work in the evening instead

14 Help with equipment to be ergonomically correct

15 Find out which work energizes them

16 Organize social virtual meetings as well as the occasional face-to-face social events when appropriate

17 Provide regular feedback

18 Have instant messaging open some of the day so you can simply 'chat' or ask and answer questions

19 Provide ongoing support

How to motivate your boss

Bosses and leaders need to be motivated too. If you can do this, it will in turn motivate you and you will both feel energized and engaged – a win–win situation for you both.

Motivate your boss to delegate more to you, allowing him or her to free up time for other things. Your boss may not be aware that you are ready to assume more responsibilities and that you wish to take on new challenges, so be proactive; offer your help reminding them that you are there to support them. Don't wait to be asked to do it – take the initiative and take work from them, producing good work and showing them that you can do it builds trust so they will delegate more. You may be able to think of better ways to do the work and suggest solutions and ideas to make improvements. As they trust you more, ask for more challenging tasks that also motivate you to develop. Here are some practical things you can do:

- Compliment your boss when they do something they are proud of or have just made a successful presentation, or succeeded in winning a new client etc. Let them know how good they are – they need praise just as much as everyone else.

- Show your appreciation and thank them if they have explained something really well to you, have passed on an interesting project for you to complete or have entrusted you with some confidential work. Talk to your boss and make sure you both understand and agree on priorities, based on what it will take to get the job done.

- Show that you care about your work, your colleagues and the organization, and of course about your boss. Find ways of working smarter and your boss will be thrilled that you can get more things done in less time, creating a better work–life balance. Remember to encourage and motivate your boss to balance work and life as well, as this will promote health and probably better personal relationships for them.

- Value your boss's time; make sure people arrive at meetings on time by reminding the attendees. Make sure you remind your boss when to leave for a meeting so they are there in good time with all documents and papers required. Choose the right time to speak to them by observing their body language and listening to them. Keep time thieves away from them so they keep motivated and on target.

- Keep a positive attitude, be enthusiastic and remember to smile – it's contagious and when they smile back it changes your brain chemistry, making you feel good. Smiling is an underused business tool. No one wants to be around negative people – look on the bright side of things and look for solutions. If you want a positive relationship with your boss, be positive yourself.

- Show respect for your boss and make sure you show that you recognize their role of authority and adhere to their requests as much as possible. Be prepared to forgive them for any outbursts etc, and let them know that you don't take things personally and that you understand the pressures they are under.

- Prove you can keep confidences and are discreet. By building trust you can motivate them to have you as their confidant and sounding board, knowing you will listen to them and keep it to yourself allows them to bounce ideas off you and also get things off their chest.

Motivational listening

Motivational listening is simply the act of motivating a person to action by listening to what they say. Here are a few tips to help you become an effective 'motivational listener':

Silence yourself

The simplest, most important technique for being a great active listener is not to interrupt or say what you think people are about to say by finishing off their sentences for them. Let the other person say what they need to say and give them time to think in the pauses. Do not feel that because there is a pause you need to fill the gap. Some people just need time to gather their thoughts and carry on. Of course you should still give off all the signs of listening and say things like 'yes I understand' or 'do carry on I'm all ears' or 'hmmm' etc. Remember too to use your body language and appropriate facial expressions, to nod your head as well as keeping eye contact (not staring!) and all the active listening skills you know. Sometimes people just want to 'let off steam' and then clear their heads and get to deeper feelings. If you jump in on the first sentence or two, you are cutting them off before you can understand what they really want to talk about.

Pay attention

Make sure you are focused on the other person and not looking over their shoulder to see who is walking through the door or looking out of the window. When you are working remotely make sure you look at the camera rather than the screen then it will look like you are looking at them directly. People need to know you are paying real attention to them or they will stop talking. When someone is talking, you must really pay attention. Think about what they are telling you and if there is something important for you to remember, then repeat that sentence over in your head to put it in your long-term memory instead of keeping it in your short-term memory; ask if it is okay for you to make notes if it is appropriate. Remember you should always have your pad and pen with you at all times, or you can use the technology available such as the facilities and apps on your phone or tablet. Don't let your mind wander, and push away random thoughts that pop up in your head. Also, resist the urge to immediately come up with a solution but wait for the right moment and continue to listen to what they have to say. If you pay close attention, you may find another solution may arise that you can impart at the right time and in the right way.

Try to understand

One of Stephen Covey's habits in *The Seven Habits of Highly Effective People* is to 'seek first to understand, then to be understood'. This advice is so helpful and is worth remembering. It is not only about what is being said but it is also about what is being meant! These two things can be entirely different from each other, or at least the way you perceive the situation and what is being said could be different from what the speaker is trying to say. Before you start jumping into solutions and 'here's what I would do' advice, make a real effort to understand the other person's needs, wants and motivation. Remember that everyone is unique and different from anyone else; we all have different needs and motivators. Two people can be in the exact same situation and have the same problem but need very different solutions. By understanding first, you can determine the best way to help them.

Give advice from the other person's perspective (if appropriate)

Once you have listened, paid attention and really understood the other person, including what they mean as well as the words they use, then you can offer advice. Your advice should reflect the fact that you have empathized with them by putting yourself in their position and it should be from their perspective, not yours. They may have come up with some solutions and not be sure what path to take, or only have half solutions, but base your solutions on those. You should be objective, look at it from their point of view and give them the benefit of your advice now that you understand their desires, needs and long-term goals. Offer the advice knowing what their strengths and weaknesses are, and think about their particular situation and the constraints they have. Once you get to know people you can give customized feedback when you have thought about what is going to work for them in their particular situation.

Assessing yourself and your own motivators

Using Table 2.2 (page 58), consider whether your motivators are being met both on and off the job, and how well your own job matches your motivational profile. Then list suggestions of how, where and when you can satisfy these motivators.

Achievement

Do you regularly review what you have achieved and set 'SMARTER' goals for yourself?

SMARTER goal setting is an important method of:

- deciding what is important for you to achieve in your work life;
- separating what is important for you from what is irrelevant;
- motivating yourself to achievement;
- building your self-confidence based on measured achievement of goals.

Guidelines for setting SMARTER goals

- Write them down and in the present tense and positively.
- Define them precisely.
- Prioritize multiple goals.
- Split larger goals into smaller achievable chunks of goals.
- Keep them manageable: not too hard, but not too easy.
- Write down why you want to achieve your goals – what will achieving your goal do for you emotionally, financially and spiritually?
- Think about who can support you.
- You can share your goals with your boss. You should align some of your goals with your boss and your organization.
- Visualize your goals as if you have achieved them – what do you hear, feel and see once they are achieved? Trigger your imagination and creativity, write out a clear description of your ideal end result and be clear about the goal but be flexible about the process. Visualize achieving it over and over.
- Imagine yourself 90 years old and sat in your rocking chair – think about what you might wish you had done, seen, learned. What would you have regretted not doing?
- When you set goals look for the possible obstacles and think about how you can overcome them, then when you hit the obstacle you can keep being tenacious and determined to achieve them.

When writing 'SMARTER' goals the following should be taken into consideration:

Specific and Stretched goals

The goal should be Specific to make it easier to recognize and achieve a goal, for example, 'Check the stationery cupboard every day just before going back to my desk after lunch, make sure it's tidy and order anything that is low in supplies on a timely basis.' Writing 'Ensure stationery supplies are available' is not sufficient.

Create Stretched goals to develop your capabilities. For example: check you are getting value for money, and possibly change suppliers and negotiate to buy different brands. When we 'stretch' ourselves we rise to the challenge and increase our motivation which in turn gives us confidence in our abilities when we succeed. Success breeds success and we feel exhilarated when we achieve more than we realized we could.

Measurable/Meaningful/Motivating

A goal has to be Measured to know that you have achieved it. It has to be Meaningful and Motivating in order to satisfy the need to know why it should be done. In the stationery cupboard example, it would be that everyone finds the area tidy at all times and that there are always plenty of supplies of whatever they need and know that you are saving costs without compromising the quality.

Achievable/Acceptable/Agreed/Accountable

The goal has to be **Achievable** as well as **Acceptable** to you and you should be involved in setting the goal which may need to be broken down into smaller goals and accomplished step by step. It may be necessary to **Agree** it with your boss depending on what it affects and if there is a budget involved. You should take responsibility and be held **Accountable** for reaching the goal by the set deadline. Decide how many goals it is realistic for you to be working on at any one time.

Realistic/Relevant/Results-oriented/Responsible

The goal has to be **Realistic** as well as **Relevant** to your role, your aims, your objectives and your aspirations. You need to be **Responsible** for creating, aligning, maintaining focus and achieving your goals. The aim is to achieve **Results** and in the stationery cupboard example, it means you will always have sufficient supplies to meet demand and in the most cost effective way.

Time frame

You need to specify the **Time frame** for a goal. For example in the stationery cupboard example, when will you check the area and how often – would it be every day (realistically) or every other day? Would it be first thing in the morning, after lunch or at the end of the day? You need to specify when you need to negotiate for new supplies and put in your orders to replenish stock to ensure everything is available whenever they are required. Set a realistic timescale with stated dates by which the goal is to be accomplished. For some goals you will also require a time on that date.

Evaluate/Extend/Enthusiastic

All goals should be monitored and **Evaluated** on an ongoing basis. Be flexible because we live in an ever-changing world – if you are too rigid about your goals you can end up missing out on opportunities. Due to changes you may need to **Extend** and change your goals and always remain **Enthusiastic** about achieving them – never give up!

Revise/Reward

After evaluating the goal, it may be necessary to **Revise** and change it to keep it appropriate. Once the goal has been achieved then **Reward** yourself, even if it is patting yourself on your own back, treat yourself to a new outfit, have a lunch out in a nice restaurant or whatever it is that you prefer as a reward.

You can find information on setting SMARTER goals in *The Definitive Personal Assistant & Secretarial Handbook* including a downloadable goal setting form.

Achievement-oriented people like challenging tasks, clear goals and specific measures of success. They set their own goals and work collaboratively with their executives. They want to be recognized for their accomplishments and like working for an executive who appreciates their abilities. Opportunities for ongoing skill development and possibly career development are important to them. They also look for ways of continually developing themselves, whether it is by searching out feedback, reading, sharing knowledge, networking, coaching and teaching others etc...

Interaction with others

Most of us, and especially those in the professional administrative roles, are people oriented and like, want and need to continually communicate, build relationships and keep updated. We enjoy frequent and friendly interaction with others and like to communicate face-to-face, over the phone, by email, text or via social media, especially when we have busy executives to take care of. We value relationships with colleagues, enjoy learning about other people and may extend co-worker relationships into friendships. I still have friends among people I used to be an executive assistant to 30 years ago!

Creativity

People motivated by creativity tend to value jobs that involve varied duties and opportunities to be innovative. They like to be creative and to have some autonomy over what they produce, and don't like being restrained. They may like to write blogs and articles and 'think outside the box'. They get bored with repetition and like finding new ways to do familiar tasks, and enjoy brainstorming sessions. Usually, they would rather be the one to get a project started than the one to handle all the implementation details. They work best for an executive who is open to new ways of doing things, one who recognizes the value of their ideas and encourages them to be creative.

Leadership

People can be motivated by being empowered and may run community groups or chair assistant-networking meetings. They like to manage projects with full autonomy. They enjoy making decisions and directing the activities of others. They find power interesting, and may find ways to seek out interaction with higher-level executives and possibly volunteer to take minutes at board meetings so they know what is going on in their organization. They understand the vision, mission and values of the organization and department they work in. Promotional opportunities are important to them, and they want to be sure that their title, salary and perks appropriately match their position level. They prefer an executive who provides a lot of autonomy.

Support

Some people are largely motivated by the opportunity to help and nurture others or make the world a better place. They are good team players and like to help keep a conflict-free workspace. They need to feel that their activities and efforts ultimately have a positive impact on people and like to be appreciated and thanked for what they do. They are often attracted to helping professions, causes, charities or volunteer groups. They like to work with people who share their values and beliefs.

Problem solving

Tackling complex and challenging problems is a motivating factor for some people. They like the challenge and the feeling of satisfaction when they solve a problem. They can get bored with work that is too easy and seek out mental stimulation. They often enjoy providing advice and assistance to help others deal with both simple and complicated issues. Being seen as the expert in a particular field is rewarding for them, as they like to be recognized for their knowledge and expertise. They enjoy working for executives who appreciate their ability and who ask for help with solving problems. They are not likely to take a problem to an executive or anyone else without first thinking of a possible solution that they can offer.

Work–life balance

Having an excellent work–life balance means having time for your family and yourself as well as your career. You treasure and enjoy the amount of free time that you have to use as you choose and this helps to motivate you. You can re-energize yourself when away from the office so that you recharge your batteries and are ready to face whatever work throws at you. If you are a leader then lead by example and leave work on time, see your children in their school play, go to social events in the evening, take proper lunchtimes and encourage others to do the same. With working from home, flexible working, hybrid working, remote working from anywhere being more common place, these arrangements all lead to an energized, motivated and happy workforce. Are you motivated by your work–life balance?

Look again at Table 2.2, and enter your ideas in terms of the categories described above, and then consider how you fit in. If your job and your profile are similar, then you should be highly motivated at work. If your job provides some factors but not others, you may have to meet those needs outside work, for example in your home life or by doing charitable work, writing articles/blogs, joining in with LinkedIn discussion groups or Twitter chat etc. You could also satisfy your motivators by being a member of a voluntary networking organization such as International Management Assistants (IMA), IAAP, AAPNZ, OSAP and the many other networking associations that you can find in each country around the world.

Table 2.2   Motivating assessment table

Motivating factors	Importance to you (scale of 1–5)	Present in your job (scale of 1–5)	Present in other areas of your life – write where	List suggestions of where, when and how you can satisfy these motivators and write SMARTER goals
Achievement				
Interaction with others				
Creativity				
Leadership				
Service				
Problem solving				
Work–life balance				

Summary

It is human nature to have days where you are not as motivated as you would like; however, if you continue to surround yourself with positive and motivational people, those days will be minimized. It's important to have motivation in your life as it gives you energy to continue striving for your goals and a good feeling.

Motivation needs to be constantly worked upon and invested in. If you want to succeed and you want your team to succeed, motivate yourself, your team and your boss by using all the above tips and by leading by example.

The benefits of motivation are that there will be more fun and laughter in the air (which is motivating itself), and higher retention of staff and therefore less stress on trying to cover positions that are being recruited for. There will be higher levels of quality productivity with the increased use of innovation and creativity and therefore better results. A motivated workforce will gain an exemplary positive reputation among its members, potential employees, suppliers, customers and clients.

Developing emotional intelligence

03

Emotional intelligence (EI) is the ability to perceive, manage (by understanding what your emotions are telling you) and regulate your own emotions for the best outcome in different situations and to be able to understand the emotions of others. Using your emotional intelligence means you can make informed decisions about what matters to you most, you can empathize with others, communicate effectively, build strong relationships, overcome challenges, defuse conflict and relieve stress. The skill of emotional intelligence can be learned and developed and is critical to have for personal and professional success.

Exercising our emotional intelligence makes a difference to how we think, speak, behave and our ability to influence ourselves and others. This chapter will give you some neuro-linguistic programming tools and techniques, as well as tips and advice from neuroscience.

> This chapter is applicable to each and every assistant, and remember when I refer to a leader – that means you! You don't need to have the title of 'leader' to be a leader. We all lead ourselves, our bosses and the people around us.

Why emotional intelligence is important

You need to use your emotional intelligence in order to be a good leader, team member and to help others lead. Your mood dictates your pace, enthusiasm and interactions with others. Emotions drive your behaviour, health, sense of fulfilment, motivation and your ability to make effective decisions. When feeling overwhelmed or defeated, a simple task seems harder and it is clear that emotions and feelings affect performance. Being emotionally intelligent gives you the ability to handle interpersonal problems well; remember that people don't leave organizations, they leave colleagues!

Leadership and emotional intelligence

Leaders who have high emotional intelligence are better able to create psychological safety amongst employees. Psychological safety is a fundamental requirement for employees to feel comfortable asking questions, asking for help, taking risks, making suggestions and challenging the status quo without fear of rejection, being made to feel incompetent, embarrassed or any type of negative consequences. Importantly people should feel confident that they can admit to mistakes without fearing punishment, and then share their learning so others do not make the same mistakes. Organizations that promote psychological safety are more likely to have employees who are confident, adapt to change well, are curious, creative and are better able to take advantage of diversity.

Leaders need to role model the mindset and behaviours in order to create the right climate for building psychological safety amongst teams. The mindset for leaders and all team members is one of being supportive, positive, trusting, curious, supportive of risk taking, valuing each other's contributions, caring about each other and using your emotions intelligently! Leaders should also be consultative by seeking out opinions which are different from their own so that their team members' views, thoughts, ideas are taken into consideration and acted upon where appropriate.

Emotional intelligence and psychological safety are very important for team success, especially when working remotely, as we all have cognitive biases, which are our brain's way of making shortcuts to save energy. One is 'distance bias' which means you may not be thought about as much when you are not working physically closely together.

Once psychological safety is in place you can then go on to challenge, delegate and empower your teams to learn, improve and innovate for successful outcomes.

As an assistant, whether you are leading a team of peers or subordinates, managing a project, or working for one or more bosses, it is your role to display leadership, encourage individual emotional intelligence and promote everyone in your organization to cultivate psychological safety for all because it is the difference between whether behaviour is driven by fear or confidence. It will affect how happy the employees are, how good the profits are and how successful the organization is. This emphasizes the need for high emotional intelligence to be an effective leader.

Definitions of emotional intelligence:

- The ability to recognize that we have emotions, are able to name them and control them enough to enable us to choose how to behave.

- Emotional intelligence is the ability to understand and manage both your own emotions, and those of the people around you. People with a high degree of emotional intelligence usually know what they are feeling, what this means, and how their emotions can affect other people.

- Emotional intelligence is the principles and values that dictate the thoughts and feelings behind our reactions, which guide our response patterns in different situations.

Developing emotional intelligence in leaders

'People are persuaded by reason, but moved by emotion; the leader must both persuade them and move them.'

RICHARD M NIXON

Leaders often claim: 'Our people are our greatest asset' and therefore they recognize the value of having an engaged workforce. Understanding, developing and using EI enables leaders to have meaningful and effective relationships. It enables them to recognize and appreciate how decisions will affect people and how emotions influence everything we do. Leaders who are emotionally competent are able to recognize these different emotional patterns in themselves and others, and to direct them in appropriate ways.

Goldman, author of *Emotional Intelligence* (1995), claims that emotional intelligence is not new; Aristotle mentioned the importance of emotion in human interaction back in Ancient Greece:

> *As Aristotle put it, 'Those who have the unique skill to be angry with the right person, to the right degree, at the right time, for the right purpose, and the right way' will have the edge in all aspects of life.*

Those 'leaders' who lead without emotional intelligence might not be aware of the negative or demotivating effect that their style of leadership has on the people they are leading. Their level of emotional intelligence is often made apparent in the way they communicate with people.

We have long been taught that emotions should be felt and expressed in carefully controlled ways and then in certain environments and at certain times. This is especially true when at work, particularly when managing others. It is that our biggest mistakes and regrets are when we have had an emotional outburst.

R Caruso and Peter Salovey argue the emotion centres of the brain are not relegated to a secondary place in our thinking and reasoning but instead are an integral part of what it means to think, reason and to be intelligent. They show that emotion is not just important but absolutely necessary for us to make good decisions, take action to solve problems, cope with change and succeed. The authors detail a practical four-part hierarchy of emotional skills:

- identifying emotions;
- using emotions to facilitate thinking;
- understanding emotions;
- managing them and showing how we can measure, learn and develop each skill and employ them in an integrated way to solve our most difficult work-related problems.

There are four emotional skills that all the other emotions can be built around:

- **Identifying/perceiving emotions**
  Be able to read people and recognize how you and those around you are feeling. We must be aware and be able to accurately identify and recognize the emotions of others and be able to convey and express our emotions to others in order to communicate effectively.

  The initial, most basic, area has to do with the non-verbal reception and expression of emotion. Facial expressions such as happiness, sadness, anger and fear are universally recognizable in human beings. The capacity to accurately perceive emotions in the face or voice of others provides a crucial starting point for more advanced understanding of emotions.

- **Using emotions to facilitate thought**
  Get in the mood – how we feel influences how we think and what we think about. Emotions direct our attention to important events; they get

us ready for certain actions and they help guide our thought processes as we solve problems. We let our emotions influence how we think and use them to facilitate thought – the ability to generate emotion and then reason with this emotion.

Whatever we respond to emotionally is something that grabs our attention. We should learn to direct our emotional energy and thinking towards more important matters.

- **Understanding emotions**

We need to find out what emotions mean for everyone and how we can predict how others are feeling and will behave. Emotions are not random events as they have underlying causes. We need to be able to understand complex emotions and emotional 'chains': the way emotions transition from one stage to another.

Emotions convey information: happiness usually indicates a desire to join with other people; anger indicates a desire to attack or harm others; fear indicates a desire to escape, and so forth. Each emotion conveys its own pattern of possible messages, and actions associated with those messages. A message of anger, for example, may mean that the individual feels unfairly treated. The anger, in turn, might be associated with specific sets of possible actions: peacemaking, attacking, retribution and revenge-seeking, or withdrawal to seek calmness. Understanding emotional messages and the actions associated with them is one important aspect of this area of skill.

- **Managing emotions**

Manage emotions with feeling and empathy – as emotions contain information and influence thinking, we need to incorporate them intelligently into our reasoning, problem solving, judging and behaving. This requires us to stay open to emotions – whether they are welcome or not – to choose strategies that include the wisdom of our feelings. Managing emotions focuses on how to integrate logic and emotion for effective decision making.

Each of the above four abilities can be isolated from the others, and at the same time each builds on the others.

Emotional intelligence has a part to play when assessing a person's potential for leadership. This is because emotions influence everything we do in the workplace. Managed correctly, they can lead to enhanced team spirit and increased output. However, emotions can also have the opposite effect on a workforce.

One of the biggest challenges for leaders is gaining or having the respect of the people who follow them. For a leader there are always challenges and hurdles to overcome. To meet these challenges, you have to be aware of your own emotions and the emotions of others. It has been suggested that observing the way people interact with their team members and other colleagues, on an emotional level, will give some indication of how they might act in a leadership role. This creates the opportunity to identify any development needed to boost skills and attributes, to increase their effectiveness as leaders and to help them learn how to modify their reactions to difficult and challenging situations.

Employees are looking more and more for a good work–life balance and for meaning in their work as well as remote working. To motivate and develop people in today's fast-paced and challenging work environment requires a leadership approach that recognizes and appreciates how decisions will affect people.

Leaders who use the concepts of emotional intelligence can therefore have a strong impact. By understanding how and why people react emotionally to different situations in the workplace, you can implement change more effectively as you will be more responsive to the needs and expectations of the people you are leading. Leaders with a high degree of EI will have complete trust in their staff, always speak kindly, listen to their team, are easy to talk to and make careful, informed decisions.

According to Goleman (author of *Emotional Intelligence*, 1995) there are five main elements of emotional intelligence:

- **Self-awareness**: knowing your emotions.
- **Self-regulation**: managing your emotions.
- **Motivation**: motivating yourself.
- **Empathy**: recognizing and understanding other people's emotions.
- **Social skills**: managing relationships (ie managing the emotions of others).

Goleman states that the more that you manage each of these areas, the higher your emotional intelligence will be.

Self-awareness

If you are self-aware, you always know how you feel. And you know how your emotions, and your actions, can affect the people around you. Being self-aware means having a clear picture of your strengths and weaknesses, and it also means having humility.

To improve your self-awareness you could keep a diary and spend a few minutes a day completing it – writing down your thoughts in order to move you to a higher degree of self-awareness. At any time that you experience anger you have to slow down to examine why. Remember, you can choose how you react to any given situation, no matter what it is.

Self-regulation

People who regulate themselves effectively rarely verbally attack others, make rushed or emotional decisions, stereotype people, or compromise their values. EI is about staying in control of your emotions.

To improve your ability to self-regulate:

- **Know your values:** Do you have a clear idea of where you absolutely will not compromise? Do you know what values are most important to you? Spend some time examining your 'code of ethics'. If you know what's most important to you, then you probably won't have to think twice when you face a moral or ethical decision – you'll make the right choice.

- **Hold yourself accountable:** If you tend to blame others when something goes wrong – stop. Make a commitment to admit to your mistakes and face the consequences, whatever they are. You will quickly earn the respect of those around you.

- **Practise being calm:** The next time you are in a challenging situation, be very aware of how you act. Do you relieve your stress by shouting at someone else? Practise rhythmic breathing exercises such as box breathing – breathe in through you nose for the count of 4, hold it for 4, breathe out through your mouth for the count of 4 and hold it for 4 and repeat to calm yourself. Also, try to write down all of the negative things you want to say, and then rip the list up and throw it away. Expressing these emotions on paper (and not showing them to anyone!) is better than speaking them aloud. It also helps you challenge your reactions to make sure you are being fair!

Motivation

Self-motivated people consistently work toward their goals and they have extremely high standards for the quality of their work. (Please also read

Chapter 2 on 'How to motivate yourself and your teams'.) Motivated people are usually optimistic no matter what they face. Adopting this mindset might take practice, but it is well worth the effort. Every time you face a challenge, or even a failure, try to find at least one good thing about the situation. It might be something small, like a new contact, or something with long-term effects, like an important lesson learned. But there's almost always something positive – you just have to look for it.

Empathy

For leaders, having empathy is critical to managing their boss, a successful team or organization. Leaders with empathy have the ability to put themselves in someone else's situation. They help develop the people on their teams, challenge others who are acting unfairly, give constructive feedback, and listen to those who need it. If you want to earn the respect and loyalty of your team, then show them you care by being empathetic.

To improve empathy:

- **Put yourself in someone else's position**: It's easy to support your own point of view but take the time to look at situations from other people's perspectives.

- **Pay attention to body language** (yours and theirs): You know you have rapport when you are matching and mirroring each other. Also be aware others will read your body language and make very quick assumptions, so be aware of what is going on.

- **Respond to feelings**: Someone may ask you if you can help them out with some work, which means you have to stay late again. If it is really important to them you will be able to hear it in their voice and by their body language, so respond to the way they sound and appear. If you say you can't help on this occasion and you hear the disappointment in their voice, then try and find someone who can help, or arrange to go in early the morning to help. Read their body language, facial expressions, listen to the language they use and respond accordingly.

Social skills

Leaders who do well in this element of emotional intelligence are great communicators. They're just as open to hearing bad news as good, and they're experts at getting their team to follow and support them and be excited about a new project.

Leaders who have good social skills are usually also good at managing change and resolving conflicts diplomatically. They're rarely satisfied with leaving things as they are, but they're also not willing to make everyone else do the work. They set the example with their own behaviour.

Thanks to the many challenges and opportunities that arise when working with others, leaders must have a solid understanding of how their emotions and actions affect the people around them. The better a leader relates to and works with others, the more successful s/he will be.

Take the time to work on self-awareness, self-regulation, motivation, empathy and social skills. Working on these will help you excel in the future!

By developing our emotional intelligence in the above five areas, we can become more productive and successful at what we do, and help others to be more productive and successful too. The process and outcomes of emotional intelligence development also contain many elements known to reduce stress for individuals and organizations, by decreasing conflict, improving relationships and understanding, and increasing stability, continuity and harmony.

NLP and emotional intelligence

Emotional intelligence embraces and draws from numerous other branches of behavioural, emotional and communications theories, such as neuro-linguistic programming (NLP) and Transactional Analysis.

NLP takes this a stage further, enabling us to learn from emotions at the unconscious level.

I will first describe the basics of NLP and the NLP communication model to help you better understand the NLP models.

The origin of NLP

Neuro-linguistic programming was created in the early 1970s by Richard Bandler, a computer scientist and Gestalt therapist, and Dr John Grinder, a linguist and therapist. Bandler and Grinder invented a process known as 'modelling' that enabled them to study three of the world's greatest therapists: Dr Milton Erickson, father of modern hypnotherapy; Fritz Perls, creator of Gestalt therapy; and Virginia Satir, the mother of modern-day family therapy. They wanted to know what made these therapists effective and to train others in their methods.

NLP consists of a set of powerful techniques for rapid and effective behavioural modification, some of which I have talked about in other chapters and some are outlined here. The operational philosophy to guide the use of NLP comes under four operational principles:

1 Know what outcome you want to achieve.

2 Have sufficient sensory acuity (clear understanding) to know if you are moving towards or away from your outcome.

3 Have sufficient flexibility of behaviour so that you can vary your responses until you get your outcome.

4 Take action now.

Understanding and using NLP, including being able to read body language, will help you develop your emotional intelligence, which means you will be better equipped to build rapport and develop relationships, as well as prevent conflict and misunderstanding.

NLP communication model

This model helps us to construct our reality – understanding what is going on in our world both physically and emotionally.

We are inundated with information through our five senses, and we code, order and give meaning to our experience in words, sounds, pictures, feelings, tastes and smells (our reality).

The brain can only deal with around four things at any one time so when we take in millions of pieces of information through our senses we filter the incoming information.

In order to reduce the overwhelming amount of information we receive and to be sane, we reduce and change the input of experience in three ways:

- **Deletion**: we leave out much of the input and choose unconsciously what we want to hear and retain.

- **Distortion**: we change the input to make it fit our model of the world through the filters of our perception, what we want to believe.

- **Generalization**: we create categories or classes from single examples, by chunking, or our brain simply fills in the blanks (rightly or wrongly).

To communicate verbally, we repeat the process of deletion, distortion and generalization by:

- deleting or selecting information to put into words; or

- distorting by giving a simplified version that generally distorts the meaning; or

- generalizing by minimizing all the exceptions that would make conversation very lengthy.

We also filter the information through our values, beliefs, decisions we have made in the past, our memories and experiences as well as whether we mainly process our world through visual, auditory, kinaesthetic (feelings based) or auditory digital (logic and our internal chatter).

Knowing these facts should make you realize just how easy it is for us to miscommunicate with each other, misunderstand each other and get mixed up with what is being said and what is actually being meant!

Emotionally intelligent NLP tools and techniques

Your brain creates the thoughts and emotions you have so you need to take responsibility for them.

Self-awareness

Beliefs

(You will find information and an example on limiting beliefs and empowering beliefs in Chapter 10, 'Change, resilience and brain power'.)

Well-formed outcome

A well-formed outcome is an essential application of NLP as it is the ability to create and maintain an outcome that meets certain well-formed conditions.

Follow the process below and you will experience an improvement in your ability to reach your goals.

How to develop a well-formed outcome

1 What do I want?

Ask this question about the context you are considering. State what you want in positive terms: what do you want, and what do you want it to do? Where do you want it? When do you want it? You should strongly resist ever thinking what you DON'T want and always aim for what you

DO want. What you think about is what you attract, what you focus on is what you get!

2 Is it achievable?

Is it possible for a human being to achieve the outcome? If it has been done by someone, then in theory it can be done by you, too. If you are the first, find out if it is possible.

3 Is achieving this outcome within my control?

Can you, personally, do, authorize or arrange the outcome? Anything outside your control is not 'well formed'. For example, asking your employer for time off is not well formed; the time off will only become well formed if it is granted.

4 What will I accept as evidence that I have achieved my outcome?

Is the outcome measurable? What evidence will you accept that lets you know when you have the outcome? Ensure that your evidence criteria are described in sensory based terms (ie that which you can see, hear and/or touch that proves to you and/or third parties that you have done what you set out to do).

5 Are the costs and consequences of obtaining this outcome acceptable?

Ensure that the outcome is worth the time, outlay and effort involved in achieving it, and that the impact on third parties or the environment is accounted for.

6 Do I have all the resources I need to achieve my outcome?

Do you have or can you obtain all the resources, both tangible and intangible, that you need to achieve your outcome? Resources include knowledge, beliefs, objects, premises, people, money, time.

7 If I could have it now, would I take it?

Are all costs and consequences of achieving your outcome (including the time involved) acceptable to you and anyone else affected by it? Consider the costs, consequences, environmental and third party impact of having the outcome.

Alternatively you can download Appendix 5 for setting SMARTER goals from www.suefrance.com, on the resources page for *The Definitive Personal Assistant & Secretarial Handbook* 3rd edition

Self-regulation

Break the state

Slow your thoughts down, listen to how you talk to yourself, challenge it and think what evidence do you have to justify your thoughts and feelings or simply let it go. Actively and consciously choose to think a different thought.

Cause and effect

We have a choice to live in either 'cause' or 'effect'; although you may think things are inevitable, you need to realize that you DO have a choice in everything you do. Do you usually live at cause or at effect? (Consider the symptoms shown in Table 3.1.)

In NLP terms, cause and effect are linguistic patterns that clarify where two or more events are related in a way that one impacts on the other. The difference between cause and effect is one of responsibility/accountability versus one of blame (self) limiting beliefs and lack of choice.

Table 3.1 Cause and effect

At cause signals	At effect signals
You feel comfortable in your environment	You feel stressed in a particular environment
You can naturally say what you like	Others dictate what you say and when you say things
You act with a level of competence and abilities	You are panicking and questioning your abilities
You feel at ease, energetic and vibrant	You have low energy and feel overwhelmed
You are at ease to be yourself	You doubt whether you are good enough
You take difficulties and setbacks in your stride	You cannot say 'No' and try your best to please
Your choices are based on what you want	You do what you should do, not what you want to do

Understanding the causes and effects of various emotions is an important element of emotional intelligence.

It is the rare individual who always lives his or her life 'at cause'; however far too many of us live a large portion of our lives 'at effect' – responding to the whims, desires or emotional states of others. Being 'at cause' means that you are decisive in creating what you want in life and take responsibility for what you have achieved or will achieve. You see the world as a place of opportunity and you move towards achieving what you desire. If things are not unfolding as you would like, you take action and explore other possibilities. Above all, you know you have choice in what you do and how you react to people and events.

If you are 'at effect' you may blame others or circumstances for your bad moods or for what you have not achieved or for your life in general. You may feel powerless or depend on others in order for you to feel good about yourself or about life – 'If only my boss, my colleagues... understood me and helped me achieve my goals or did what I wanted, then life would be great.' If you wait and hope for things to be different or for others to provide, then you are 'at effect' or a victim of circumstances. Believing that someone else is responsible or making them responsible for your happiness or your different moods is very limiting and gives this person some mystical power over you, which can cause you a great deal of anguish.

The internal dialogues that we go through often reveal the limiting beliefs that we hold as hard facts opening up outdated judgements and prejudices, distortions and generalizations or even other people's opinions. Listening to your own internal dialogues can help you to find the 'oughts', 'buts' and 'can'ts' that limit your own freedom of choice.

Here are a few examples:

- I am bored.
  How exactly are you boring yourself?

- Change is impossible.
  How is changing impossible?
  From what into what?
  Why is change impossible?

- I ought to do this.
  What would happen if you didn't?
  What would happen if you did?

- I just can't do this.
  What is stopping you?
  Why can't you do this?
  If you could do this, what would it look like?

- He doesn't like me.
  How do I know this exactly?
  What exactly does he not like about me?

- It is impossible to decide.
  How am I finding it impossible to decide?
  Why am I experiencing it as impossible to decide?
  What is preventing me from making a decision?

I try to live my life at cause as much as possible but it's not feasible all the time; however, at the 'effect' times I remember an NLP presupposition: 'There is no failure only feedback.' Then I endeavour to start living at cause again as I can now quickly identify when I am at effect and rectify it. Try it for yourself – there is nothing stopping you!

Remember you have control over what happens to you and you can learn to lead yourself!

Anchoring

An anchor is a trigger or stimulus that retrieves a desired emotional state. Anchors are automatically formed when we make repetitive actions and have associated feelings with that action. A great example of an anchor is when you hear a certain piece of music that brings back a particular emotion or feeling associated with something that you were doing when that music was playing. For example, when I was teaching in the Middle East an expat who worked there for a very demanding boss and had a difficult job used to play Christmas songs in her car on the way home, whatever the time of year, and sing along for an hour until she got home which completely changed her mood from feeling stressed to feeling content and happy just like she did at Christmas.

Marketing companies are creating anchors for us all the time to make us want their products. Anchoring is such a powerful tool because with it, you can recall any particular emotional state you desire. You could purposefully create an anchor for creativity, motivation or confidence etc.

To create an anchor, you need to create it at the highest intensity state of a feeling by creating an anchor trigger at the time the emotion or feeling is growing and becomes intense. The anchor trigger could be something like pressing your thumb and forefinger together or pressing you right forefinger into your left palm, or touching your earlobe or tucking your thumb inside your clenched fist etc – make it unique and what feels good for you.

For example, if you want to create the feeling of confidence, then remember a time when you really felt confident, remember what you heard, saw, felt, realize what your body language is doing and really get your brain back into that time as if you were there and as the feeling of confidence is growing and intensifies to its highest level then do your anchor trigger to anchor that feeling so you can bring the feeling of confidence back whenever you want. The more times you set the trigger when you have a required intense emotion, the better the emotion will become associated with the action and the better it will stick and be effective.

So the next time you need confidence to give a presentation, to ask for a rise, to get out of your comfort zone and are feeling inadequate or lacking confidence, then you can activate your trigger, break that emotional state and feel confident to be able to do whatever you want to do.

Empathy

Sensory acuity

Sensory acuity is the ability to be acutely aware about the detail of the person in front of you, including body language, facial expressions, voice, tone and their emotions.

Notice what you notice, keep your eyes and ears open and be aware of what is going on around you. Notice and match their language and body language, use your ability to put yourself in another person's situation from their point of view and validate their feelings but never minimize their feelings. Empathy does not mean you have to agree with their views; it means you have to understand/feel what they experience from their viewpoint.

Offer support and understanding. Use tentative exploratory language:

'I imagine that could make you feel ...'

'I suppose that situation could make you think ...'

Say 'Yes, and ...' instead of 'Yes, but ...'' to help validate their feelings.
Before you take actions, realize how your actions may affect others by putting yourself in their shoes. If you have to take the action and you know it is going to be difficult, how can you soften the blow and help others deal with it?

Social skills

Pacing and leading

The applications of this technique are many and varied. It is a good influencing tool. It can be used when people are upset, angry or defensive, or when you want to change someone's opinion at a meeting.

It builds rapport and relationships and shows you where rapport may be missing. When the quality of rapport is good it is possible to encourage an individual to follow the movements and thinking that you are using. Pacing and leading involves matching the other person's body language, and you can match breathing too (pacing) until you have gained a sufficient level of rapport and slowly start to change what you are doing, so the individual will follow you (leading). In this way you can lead your partner into different body postures naturally. Once you are in rapport, which is demonstrated by them following your lead, then your social skills increase and you are better able to build relationships, influence and persuade.

Emotional learning and transformation: reframing technique

EI has become an essential technique to understand in the business world. It is useful to be able to reframe your own thoughts and also help others to reframe their thoughts if you find yourself with a problem or 'faulty thinking'. Reframing is the process of making a shift in the nature of a problem. It is the process of changing a negative statement into a positive one by changing the 'frame' or reference used to interpret the experience (ie saying it in a different way and therefore thinking about it from a different angle). For example, you could reframe feeling angry into an opportunity of feeling motivated or energized. If all meaning is context dependent, and if you change the context or content, then you will change the meaning. All content can be reframed simply by changing the structure, the process or the context. The basis of reframing it is to separate the intention from behaviour and the consequence.

Almost all behaviours are useful or appropriate in some context. Interrupting a speaker by standing up and offering your view in the middle of a lecture may be judged as inappropriate. To do this same behaviour at the end of the presentation in order to provide a different perspective may be welcomed by all present.

A context reframe is useful for statements such as 'I am too pushy' or 'I wish I did not focus on what could go wrong.' In this type of situation, people have assumed that this type of behaviour has no value. Your job is to discover when it is of value by asking yourself the question: 'When or where would this behaviour be useful or viewed as a resource?' A possible reframe might be: 'Isn't that a great skill to have when you need to get things done or to avoid potential problems?' Once you become more resourceful, you can then assist them to discover behaviours that may be more appropriate in other situations.

If a person is involved in an undesirable experience, think of a new context, a different situation, in which the person will respond differently to the same behaviour or meaning. Ask, 'When else would this behaviour be effective?' Or, 'Where would this be an appropriate response?'

Example

'He is so pedantic in meetings; he slows us up' (not good)
'Yes and doesn't he make an excellent finance manager, spending the budget carefully.' (good)

If a person is involved in an undesirable experience, think of another meaning for the same behaviour that will change their response. Ask yourself, 'What else could this behaviour mean?' or internally think of an opposite frame or a different meaning. 'What is it that this person hasn't noticed (in this context) that will bring about a different meaning and change their response (behaviour)?'

Content/meaning reframe

The content or meaning of a situation is determined by what you choose to focus on. An electrical power failure can be viewed as disruptive, a major disaster given all you have to get done. Or it can be viewed as an opportunity to spend some intimate time with your spouse or to have fun with your children finding innovative ways to manage the situation.

A content reframe is useful for statements such as: 'I get annoyed when my boss stands behind me while I am working.' Notice how the person has taken the situation and given it a specific meaning – which may or may not be true – and in so doing limits their resourcefulness and possible courses of action. To reframe this situation, there is an NLP presupposition that says: 'Every behaviour has a positive intention' and therefore ask questions such as:

- What other meaning could the boss's behaviour have? Or for what purpose does he or she do it? A possible reframe might be: 'Is it possible they want to help and do not know how to offer their assistance in any other way?'

- What is the positive value in this behaviour? The positive value could be related to the boss's behaviour (as above) or it could be related to the speaker's behaviour. A possible reframe might be: 'Isn't it great that you know your boundaries and are not prepared to allow someone to violate them?'

Examples

'My boss just leaves me to get on with it; he never pays me any attention.' (not good)
Can be reframed as: 'He must really trust you and rely on you to do a good job. I wish my boss was like that.' (good)

'This organization is always sending you on courses. You never have time to get anything done.' (not good)
Can be reframed as: 'Wow! What wonderful development opportunities there are! Do you think I can get a job there?' (good)

Steps towards better performance using emotional intelligence

Here are a few suggestions to improve your and your team's performance:

Emotional hijacking by the amygdala in the limbic system

As part of our survival instinct we need to respond to perceived or real 'threats' instantly. When under threat our amygdala flares up to get us ready to either fight, flight, freeze or flock (go to friends for help). We are not looking for the sabre tooth tiger today but just your boss calling your name and asking you to go and see them immediately is enough for your amygdala to go on high alert! When your amygdala goes on high alert then your executive thinking, rational brain – your prefrontal cortex – shuts down.

Traits of the limbic system's emotional ways of thinking:

- Jumps to conclusions quickly and looks for evidence it is right!
- Thinks in black and white – tends to think of one possibility.
- Catastrophizes and gets things out of perspective.
- Irrational – unfounded reasoning – even silly.
- Judgemental – judges others quickly.

The best way to prevent an amygdala hijack is to increase your emotional intelligence. When you feel you are having an amygdala hijack then tell yourself to 'STOP' and take a few rhythmic breaths – give yourself some space to think before you respond and do not react immediately. Notice your emotion and reflect on it and **label** it correctly. There are many words to describe different emotions and if you google emotions you can find lists of them or you can google the 'Feeling wheel' or the 'Wheel of emotions' to help you understand, describe and articulate your actual emotion and the way you are feeling and even the intensity of it. You can look for the words that really resonate with you at the time. For example if you are feeling scared – are you actually feeling bewildered, insignificant, foolish, embarrassed, insecure etc?

Also to help calm you down and give you space to think, you can add a verb as the verb helps to objectify it. For example if you are feeling angry, say to yourself 'I **notice** I am feeling worried', 'I **perceive** I am feeling angry' or 'I **observe** that I am feeling frustrated'. This will begin to open up your rational part of the brain (prefrontal cortex) and give it time to make informed decisions. What can you influence and control? Is it real or perceived? You can choose to treat it as a threat or a challenge to overcome and think creatively as well as what experiences can you draw from the past to help? The 'Feeling wheel' or the 'Wheel of emotions' also has the opposite emotions on the opposite side so you can determine where you are on the wheel and where you want to be.

Remember: Thoughts are information – not directives or instructions!

Also remember: you always have choice!

'STOP'

S pace: pause for a few seconds

T ake a few rhythmic breaths

O bserve: What am I thinking?

- Is this fact or opinion?
- What am I reacting to?
- See the bigger picture. Put it into perspective

P roceed: What's the best thing to do for me, for others, for the situation?

Be emotionally attractive

Focus on being emotionally attractive. Cultivate the ability to manage your own emotions and to influence those of others in a manner that drives the success of teams and organizations. Try and create a positive emotional tone in the organization and engage and inspire people. You should possess the three core qualities of mindfulness, hope and compassion.

Look for good in others

One of the main objectives of a leader is to make sure others are aware of the greatness that lies in them. Be known in your organization as someone who is always on the lookout for what is right with people. It promotes goodwill and is good for business.

Be pleasant and cooperative

If all team members throughout the organization had these qualities wouldn't life be wonderful? If you are one of the team members who may not have it right yet, then you are halfway there simply by reading this chapter. Work on it and it will get you far. If you are a team leader then EI is imperative; it is almost impossible to have executive presence without it. For example sharing ideas and short cuts, helping each other out, coaching and mentoring each other – it all helps. This is another example of how moods and emotions affect productivity. Take responsibility for your actions and apologize when needed in order to build relationships and people are more likely to forgive and forget than if you avoid them or act defensive.

Model meeting behaviour

Take an honest look at your behaviour in meetings. Do you set a positive tone from the start? Or is it about however you are feeling at the time? Control your emotions and aim for a calm, relaxed mood, and a consistent, positive approach.

Emotionally intelligent thoughts

Think about a time when you felt really angry, upset or sad. Remember what you saw, heard, felt. Are there any smells or tastes associated with the memory? Really get those feelings in your head of how you felt at that time, hear what you heard, feel what you felt when you were really really angry, upset or sad. Once you feel the emotions rising up inside you, I now want you to calm yourself down, bring yourself back into this peaceful and happy time where the world is good and pleasant. Now, know that it was in the past and it is not now worth your time and energy focusing on it – let it go and keep practising letting it go until it becomes a subconscious habit. Bring forward good, happy, pleasant thoughts and feelings. I always think of my grandchildren Bella, Theo and Sophie when I want to change my mood and be in a happy moment where I can't help but smile. Find out what it is for you that makes you feel happy. Calm yourself down and bring your mind back to a peaceful world where everything is good. You have now started on your road to becoming an expert in becoming emotionally intelligent.

Now think of this example: You are at work and a colleague (who has been hankering after your job for a few months now) has noticed that you have made a couple of errors in a document that is lying on your desk and starts to point them out loudly as your boss walks out of their office. The natural internal response would of course be to get angry with this colleague, especially as they have their own agenda in mind (ie working for your boss). It is at this point that you have to remember how to bring your temper down to a calm, peaceful place and, without showing your anger to the person, calmly point out with a genuine smile, that you had already noticed the errors as soon as you had printed it as you always check your work before handing it over; thank your colleague for pointing it out and say you appreciate it. It is easy for tempers to fly, especially if you are busy and you feel people are interfering for no good reason and you can feel your blood starting to boil. It can take all your effort to keep control but this is what emotional intelligence is about – keeping in control, choosing our response rationally.

Every time you experience an emotion ask yourself:

What is my emotion telling me?
Is this emotion serving me well?

Summary

All emotions are normal and natural, it's not about what we experience, it's about how we recognize, name and manage them!

Understanding emotional intelligence enables us to increase our ability to control our own emotions and understand and support the emotions of others. This skill results in increased cooperation and a healthy work environment. Practise using the tools and techniques so they become second nature and a subconscious habit; they will help you become 'emotionally attractive' and in full control of your emotions. Remember to have emotionally intelligent thoughts, notice what you notice, and live at cause and not effect. You now have the edge to have confidence by anchoring, boost your career and home life and are also equipped to help those around you.

Use your emotional intelligence to improve communications and relationships, have better empathy skills, act with integrity, gain respect from others, manage change more confidently and have a more peaceful existence whilst feeling healthier and happier. Understand how you can help others use EI and help to reduce their stress levels.

Leading effective office based and virtual teams to success

04

This chapter will define what a 'team' is and what a leader's role is within a team. It will explain team dynamics and the five stages of team development, including the importance of creating a Team Charter using the example of 'Developing an internal assistant network'. With the kind permission of Belbin® Associates, Belbin® team roles are explained so you can read the descriptions and determine what your preferred behavioural style is, together with each style's strengths. This will enable you to form well-balanced and productive teams. It also describes what each team role's allowable weakness and non-allowable weakness are so that you can be aware of how you can reduce your weaknesses where possible. I have also laid out ground rules for effective teamwork that can be included in the Team Charter.

This chapter also addresses best practice for virtual and remote working and how to effectively stay connected with your team.

Definition of a team

A team is two or more people working together inter-dependently, who have the same purpose and goals and work towards achieving a shared objective. They have the complementary skills necessary to carry out that purpose successfully together.

We all work in teams, whether we are working with one boss or more and alongside our colleagues and whether in the same office or virtually. You may lead a team, a committee or task force, organize an event with a team, lead a project management team or be part of one, or coordinate a group of people to achieve a common goal. This chapter is about giving you the tools and techniques to be a powerful team member and lead effective teams, including your boss(es), for a successful outcome.

Assistants are the fount of all knowledge, the technical expert, the strategic counsel, the problem solver, the resource investigator, all of which is helped by having networks both internal and external to the organization. Your networks are invaluable to your success, to prevent reinventing the wheel and to share knowledge and have outstanding support for each other. You may lead an assistant networking team within your company, and if you haven't got one yet then I suggest you think about organizing one and becoming its team leader. Assistant networks are an invaluable source of support, resources, training, self development and keeping connected as they can be conducted online, in person or a hyrbid. There is a section below on how to develop an internal assistant network.

We are all guilty of not taking breaks when we should and rarely get an opportunity for training sessions or networking with colleagues. One thing that I have found that successfully remedies this, is to organize a network for likeminded people (assistants and office managers). Continuous communication can do wonders for staff morale and at the same time build relationships with your colleagues, share knowledge and solve problems.

Catherine Thomas, PA for the Director of
Shared Services Partnership, NHS Wales

Team-leader role

All the best teams, whether virtual or office based, need good and thoughtful direction. As a team leader, it's your role to help your team to work together to get the best results and help the business run smoothly. You should play a vital role in creating and maintaining a high performance. With teams where they may be working in the office, hybrid working or fully virtual, the team leader's role is to make sure their teams collaborate and communicate effectively. Cloud computing and collaboration software has enabled teams to build relationships, co-work on projects, chat, hold meetings, train, hold conferences etc and are designed to facilitate group work. There are three types of collaborative tools: communication, conferencing and coordination.

Communication software enables teams to easily talk to each other even when working from different locations. Instant messaging apps such as G-chat, WhatsApp and Slack are examples of communication tools.

Conferencing software such as Zoom, Google Meet and Microsoft Teams have two core functions:

1 Allow two or more people to communicate via video.

2 It enables groups to share their screens and simultaneously access apps and documents.

Co-ordination technology has both teamwork and task work functions which allow teams to manage projects and schedules efficiently. Examples include Trello, Monday and Asana as well as a range of e-calendars.

Your duties will vary depending on the type and size of the organization/ team and who and how many you are leading. Your workload may involve managing processes, managing change, delegating tasks, monitoring the team's performance and motivating them, organizing and chairing online and face-to-face meetings, giving presentations, organizing training and development, negotiating contracts, implementing plans and handling complaints. It may involve working with budgets, stock ordering and taking part in special events. You may have to deal with team disputes and handle conflict management. You could also have wider duties like human resource matters such as dealing with sickness absence, return to work interviews, interviewing and selection, performance management, onboarding of new staff, acting as coach and mentor, reporting to senior level management and more.

As a team leader you need to understand what motivates the people who work with you – please see Chapter 2 on 'How to motivate yourself and your teams'.

Team dynamics

Successful team members can improve team dynamics by:

- forming teams in which members complement each other's strengths and weaknesses;

- understanding yourself: work style, communication preferences and team interaction preferences;
- understanding people's personality and behavioural styles: both internal and external to your organization;
- looking for ways to emphasize similarities and capitalize on differences between you and the people you work with.

Potential problems when working in teams

- It takes longer to make decisions with more people involved.
- There are more people and therefore more possibilities for disagreements.
- There may be personality conflicts.
- Miscommunication can happen.
- Individuals have conflicting goals or priorities and their own agenda.
- There may be insufficient sharing of information.
- Inappropriate/unproductive or boring meetings are common.
- The leader makes most of the decisions.
- Lack of trust can arise.

As we are human, we will inevitably come across disagreements, miscommunication and difficult people and you can read more about how to deal with this in *The Definitive Personal Assistant & Secretarial Handbook* 3rd edition in the chapter on dealing with difficult people and managing conflict.

Benefits of working in teams

- Higher-quality decisions come from better ideas and higher-quality information.
- There is more creativity and innovation in solving problems.
- Productivity increases due to division of responsibilities.
- Job satisfaction is enhanced by team member interaction and greater accomplishments.
- There are social benefits. The team can provide a sense of community and camaraderie.

- It encourages networking. Team members can get to know their colleagues better.
- Team members gain visibility by showcasing their skills and talents for senior executives monitoring the team's progress.

The benefits of working in teams can be summarized as 'synergy' – the whole is greater than the sum of the parts. As a team, we can do much better work than when working individually and accomplish more with better results. Working in effective teams can have its problems but these are far out-weighed by the benefits.

Characteristics of effective teams

The acronym T E A M W O R K summarizes the effective characteristics of working in teams:

TRUST:	Trust is the foundation of teamwork. Effective teams cultivate and maintain trust among members. Team members have faith in each other to honour their commitments, maintain confidence, support one another and generally behave in a consistent and predictably acceptable fashion.
EFFORT:	Teamwork requires hard work and energy to communicate and coordinate among members.
ATTITUDE:	Teamwork requires a facilitative/helping mindset. This means that team members are flexible in providing leadership at certain times and supporting team decisions at others. Team members see themselves as belonging to a team rather than as individuals who operate autonomously. They are committed to goals above and beyond their personal goals.
MOTIVATION:	Team members are motivated to collaborate rather than compete with one another.
WIN–WIN:	Team members strive to reach win–win solutions that satisfy all team members.
OPEN COMMUNICATION:	Team members communicate openly and honestly with one another. Communication refers to the style and extent of interaction – among members and

between members and those outside the team. It also refers to the way that members handle conflict, decision making and day-to-day interactions.

RESPECT: Team members respect and value the differences among members, including diverse views, expertise and backgrounds.

KNOWLEDGE: Team members share knowledge and avoid reinventing the wheel.

Stages of team development

Psychologist Bruce Tuckman (1965) described the path to high performance that most teams go through as 'Forming, Storming, Norming and Performing'. Later, he added a fifth stage that he called 'Adjourning' although I prefer to call it 'Mourning' as it is the way I feel once I have worked well with a team and have bonded to such an extent I don't want to break the team up.

Reading Chapter 7, 'How to communicate with different personality and behavioural styles', will help in understanding people's behaviours and actions during team-development stages. The five stages of team development that help groups transform into successful high-performing teams are described in detail below:

Stage 1: Forming

If you can select your team or team members going forward, think about the various areas of skills and knowledge that you need as well as behavioural styles and in particular Belbin® team roles (see below). At the very least you should have individual face-to-face meetings with every member of the team to find out their wants and needs, and what they hope the team will achieve, and also to find out what experience, knowledge and skills they can bring and how they prefer to work.

When teams first get together they initially go through a 'Forming' stage in which members are on their best behaviour and are positive, cordial and polite. Beneath their calm and professional exterior, however, they are sizing each other up and forming opinions (rightly or wrongly). They have unclear objectives and they avoid conflict. This stage is usually fairly short and may only last for one or two meetings at which people are introduced to one another and start to get to know and understand each other. At this stage there may be discussions about how the team will work, which can be frustrating for some members who simply want to get on with the team task. Some team members experience anxiety, try to get a feel for the situation, test to see what behaviour is appropriate or inappropriate, and check to see how much help or assistance can be provided by the leader or boss. Others are simply excited about working in the team and what it may involve.

As team leader, you have an important role to play in managing first impressions so as to make sure the team has the best possible chance of success. It is often how the leader behaves that dictates the chances of success. At this stage, you have a dominant role and make most of the decisions whilst other members' roles and responsibilities are less clear. Listen patiently to concerns, emphasize that the team is needed and be prepared to answer lots of questions about the team's purpose, objectives and external relationships.

Stage 2: Storming

Reality sets in and your team moves into a 'Storming' phase. It is important to realize that this will be followed by a normal phase of team development. As team members become more comfortable, they feel free to express differences of opinion. Your authority may be challenged as others claim their position, their roles are clarified and the ways of working start to be defined. Members compete with each other for power and are more willing to confront things they disagree with. As leader, you must be aware that some members may feel overwhelmed by how much there is to do or are uncomfortable with the approach being used. You should work at understanding people rather than judging them. Some may react by questioning how worthwhile the goal of the team is and by resisting taking on tasks. This is the stage when many teams fail, and even those that stick with the task may feel that they are on an emotional roller coaster as they try to focus on the job in hand without the support of and established processes or relationships with their colleagues.

It is important to note that at this stage the leader may be perceived as under-performing, unable to keep control and less dynamic than the team first thought s/he was. You may therefore find yourself challenged by the group. Although it can feel like a looming disaster, it is actually a sign of progress because a group with no disagreement will inevitably fail. It is important to remember that constructive conflict can improve decision making, it allows greater diversity and innovation and it avoids 'group think'. So as long as you know that this stage will be coming, you can anticipate it and give answers to questions that you think they may ask before they even ask them, proactively lead from the front and deal with situations as they arise.

Please note that not all teams will go through this process, but many will. It is important therefore to mention that as there usually is a 'Storming' phase in some form, you have to make sure that team members do not use knowledge of the 'Storming' stage as an excuse to behave inappropriately!

Stage 3: Norming

Gradually, the team moves into a 'Norming' stage, as a hierarchy is established. Team members come to respect your authority as a leader, and others show leadership in specific areas. There will be greater team cohesion and a willingness to actively listen to each other without confrontation. Now that the team members know each other better, they may be socializing together, and they are able to ask each other for help and provide constructive criticism. The team develops a stronger commitment to the team goal, and you start to see good progress towards it. There is often a prolonged overlap between Storming and Norming behaviour. As new tasks come up, the team may lapse back into typical Storming stage behaviour, but this eventually dies out and there is more of a sharing of ideas and the level of trust increases. This process is helped by the pressure to produce results. If you get new members of the team joining at this stage, be aware that they may challenge what is in place and a step back to Storming may occur.

Allow roles within the team to evolve naturally: each member of the team needs to play his or her role for the whole team to be effective. Take advantage of each person's unique strengths and avoid unreasonable exposure to individual weaknesses. Look for ways to bring out the best in those who may lack skills or experience. Motivate by being a positive force, even in negative situations.

Stage 4: Performing

When the team reaches the 'Performing' stage, hard work leads directly to progress towards the shared vision of their goal, supported by the structures and processes that have been set up. Members will now be working together productively and accomplishing team goals. To stay motivated, they need to feel that their task is meaningful and that they have the resources to succeed. They will be equally focused on the task and people and have a common purpose. Morale will be high and they will be motivated to share accountability and cooperate fully with each other. There will be an air of supportive group decision making.

As leader, you are able to delegate much of the work and can concentrate on developing team members. Being part of the team at this stage feels 'easy' compared with earlier on.

Project teams exist only for a fixed period, and even permanent teams may be disbanded through organizational restructuring. As team leader, your concern is both for the team's goal and the team members. Look at what works well and continue to do those practices. Continually develop the team and look at what you can do to keep on improving performance.

The only certain thing in life is change. At some point teams will change, members will leave and new members will join and successful groups will keep the momentum going with a leader who can effectively guide them through change.

A leader should encourage suggestions from the team and build a sense of joy and fun for the team, perhaps incorporating social activities, stress busters and outings to build team cohesiveness and celebrate successes.

Stage 5: Mourning (also referred to as Adjourning and Transitioning)

The 'Mourning' stage is important in reaching both team goals and personal conclusions.

Some teams are ongoing while others finish their project or task and move on. The break-up of the team can be hard for members who like routine or who have developed close working relationships with other team members, particularly if their future roles or even jobs look uncertain. For project-based teams, the last stage involves dissolution of the team, which can be difficult for team members who are loyal to the team and want it to carry on. It is important to reflect on performance and evaluate it, possibly writing a report for others to learn from. Celebrate achievements and allow time for personal goodbyes.

As a team leader, make sure that you leave plenty of time to coach team members through each stage. Therefore you need to identify which stage your team is at from the descriptions above. So once your team has 'Formed' you need to consider what you can do to effectively move your team towards the Performing stage. You will need to schedule regular reviews of where your team is and keep adjusting your behaviour and leadership approach to suit the stage your team has reached and make sure you are doing the right thing at the right time. It may be that your team is a project team with a start and an end so consider how to celebrate its success.

Creating a Team Charter using 'Developing an internal assistant network' as an example

Team Charters help your team in the 'Forming' stage of developing a team and helps to make sure that everyone is focused on the right things from the start. Drawing up a Team Charter can also be useful if a team is in trouble and people need to regain their view of the 'big picture'.

Team Charters are documents that define the purpose of the team, how it will work, and what the expected outcomes are. It will make sure that all involved are clear about the direction in which they are heading.

The precise format of a Team Charter can vary in each situation and from team to team. However, much of the value of the Charter comes from thinking through and agreeing the various elements. Time taken agreeing a Team Charter will be well worth it as the team progresses.

Planning the Charter will help to speed the processes of Forming, Storming and Norming so that the team can effectively perform sooner.

The following are suggestions for inclusion in a Team Charter:

- context;
- mission;
- goals and objectives;
- roles and responsibilities;
- authority and boundaries;
- resources and support;
- operations;
- seven ground rules for effective teamwork;
- negotiation and agreement.

Context

This is the introduction to the charter. It sets out why the team was formed, the problem it's trying to solve (such as collaborating on best practice, staying connected even when working virtually, developing relationships and asking for and giving help), how this problem fits in with the broader objectives of the organization, and the consequences of the problem going unchecked.

- What problem is being addressed?
- What result or delivery is expected?
- Why is this important?

Example context when setting up an internal networking team of assistants:

The team has been formed to increase cooperation, collaboration and cohesion between assistants who work within the organization, no matter in which department or whom they work for or whether working virtually. The historic lack of cooperation between assistants has meant that they have reinvented the wheel on many occasions, have lacked support, wasted time and prevented productivity and has sometimes caused stress and missed deadlines. This has cost the organization money and sometimes has meant recruiting new people. The network team including the Team Charter helps to give team members a sense of belonging to a supportive team. It is also an extremely useful tool for new starters to get to know everyone, know who they contact for help and who are the experts in different areas and feel they belong to the team immediately.

Mission

The mission and objectives are at the heart of the Charter. By defining a mission, the team knows what it has to achieve. Without a clear mission, individuals can too easily pursue their own agendas independently of, and sometimes irrespective of the overall goal.

For example: Sharon Severn, PA at Rolls-Royce plc, worked with her team and together they developed the following mission statement for their team to work towards:

The mission of this team is to work cohesively, sharing knowledge, advice, tools and techniques to improve meeting deadlines and producing excellent work. We will work closely as a team in order to exceed expectations of our boss(es), internal and external clients/customers.

Goals and objectives

The next stage is to take the mission and turn it into measurable goals and objectives. These are the critical targets and milestones that will keep the team on track.

Example goals for 'Developing an internal assistant network':

- *To interview all assistants to find out what they would like from the Team Charter and what ground rules they would like to be included by (date).*

- *To survey all executives to find out what they would like to be included in the Team Charter for their assistants to be able to help each other by (date).*

- *To present first draft proposals by (date).*

- *To hold a face-to-face meeting with all assistants to agree on the Team Charter by (date).*

Example goals for inclusion in the Team Charter:

- To meeting once a month from 12:30 to 13:30

- To hold lunch and learn sessions

- To hold an annual away day conference to include presentations from the leadership group and outside sources

- To foster an atmosphere of collaboration, camaraderie, and working together towards the mission

- To have at least one social event every quarter as there is no better way to get to know people, build relationships and start to work together even more effectively

Roles and responsibilities

Teams are most effective when they have members with the skills and experience needed to do the job. Team members can bring experience and approaches from a range of different backgrounds. Look to your mission and objectives to determine who is needed on the team to make sure its goals can be accomplished.

All members need to know their role or assignment on the team and what they are responsible for doing. In particular, they need to know how their work will contribute to the overall work of the team. Roles need to remain flexible so that team members do not think 'that's not my job!' when others need help and roles can be rotated. Some work will be shared by all, but not everyone can do everything, and so members need roles because they need to know what they can expect from each other. Without clarity, no one will be able to feel a valuable and valued member of the team.

You may want to include catering, facilities, graphic reproduction, audio visual and IT personnel within your network if you think their presence on your internal networking team will enhance your working abilities and productivity, or may at least want to invite them to some of your regular meetings so you can all understand each other and know what is required of each other.

Once you know who should be on the team, you need to look at what each person will do to support the team in its mission. The best way to go about this is to list each team member and define the roles and responsibilities of each. This will help you:

- match team members to roles;
- spot gaps in skills and abilities that are necessary for the team to reach its goals;
- decide who will be the team leader and who will chair the meetings and should this be on a rotation basis;
- decide who is the liaison spokesperson between the team and the other stakeholders (ie a 'champion');
- determine who is responsible for what duties and outcomes.

Example:

The team will be made up of all assistants in the organization plus a 'champion' from the senior executive team, a member of the facilities department, catering department, information technology, graphics department and the audio-visual department.

You may also want to appoint specialist roles using the expertise and experience of certain assistants to whom others can go for help: for example, an expert on Excel, PowerPoint or social media or bilingual speakers etc.

Example of role description for team leader:

[Name of leader] will take the role of Team Leader in which she/he will be responsible for:

- *ensuring this Team Charter is followed and kept up to date;*

- *managing the day-to-day operations of the team and the team's deliverables;*
- *managing people conflict;*
- *providing support and assistance to individual team members;*
- *ensuring updates for the company intranet are implemented.*

Authority and empowerment

With the roles defined, you now need to look at what team members can and can't do to achieve the mission. For example, in what capacity are team members allowed to use social media and for how long? What is within the team's remit and what actions require approval? How should team members resolve any conflicts between their day jobs and the team mission?

Resources and support available

This section lists the resources available to the team to accomplish its goals. Whether lunch will be provided for face-to-face team meetings, budgets, time allocated for meetings and for carrying out 'expert' roles, equipment and people. In conjunction with the performance assessments, changes to the resources required should be monitored regularly.

As well as this, it should detail the training and coaching support available to the team.

Operations

This section outlines how the team will operate on a day-to-day basis. This can be as detailed or as minimal as appropriate.

Example: Team meetings

- *The first team meeting will be on 28 February... at 2.00 pm.*
- *The team will meet every month during lunchtime, 12.30 pm to 13.30 pm, and lunch will be included.*
- *Every other month will be a lunch-and-learn session with a different trainer – topics to be discussed and decided by the whole team. This will last 1 hour.*
- *Each member is expected to update the team on any new findings or suggestions that can help the team work better together.*

- *If a member is unable to attend, a notification must be sent to the team leader and someone else designated to report on the status and communicate further expectations.*
- *A summary of each meeting will be prepared by the 'minute-taker' and posted on the intranet two days later.*

Seven ground rules for effective teamwork

The following guidelines will help you set fair and reasonable team rules and you should customize the ground rules to fit the needs and mission of your team:

- **Respect**: Make it clear that team members should remain polite, attentive and respectful at all times, with unconditional respect for everyone.
- **Admit to mistakes and learn from them**: Team members should not lay blame on anyone else. If they make a mistake they should admit to it and learn from it. This will help to create a supportive, non-threatening environment that's conducive to effective relationships and teamwork.
- **Be productive at all times**: As the team leader, make it clear to everyone that they must be on time for work in the morning and back from lunch. They should try and keep procrastination to the minimum and keep on track with the goals, aims and mission of the team. No team member should shirk their responsibilities and all should be accountable.
- **Actively listen to each other**: The team should listen to each other, not only to their words but also to their body language and congruence. Understand what is meant and not just what is said.
- **Confidentiality**: Team members should be confidential at all times and avoid gossiping, helping to keep office politics to a minimum.
- **Make everyone feel equal and included**: No one should feel alienated and everyone should feel the support and friendship of each other. Team members should be able to freely interact, understand and respect each other's differences and debate ideas with openness. Everyone's contribution should be taken into consideration and appreciated. If you have a team lunch meeting remember to invite everyone.
- **Deal with conflict**: Conflict should be dealt with by nipping it in the bud and not by waiting for it to escalate. Be open and honest, act like 'adult to adult', look for win–win solutions and clear the air, making way for a productive working environment.

Negotiation and agreement/sign off

A good Team Charter emerges naturally through a process of negotiation. The team and other stakeholders establish the context and mission. Objectives, composition, roles, boundaries and resources ideally emerge through negotiation between the champion, the team leader, the team and other stakeholders.

Five keys to success when creating a Team Charter:

- Discuss within the team and with the team leader to make sure that the mission and Team Charter is credible.

- Have assertive negotiation with the 'Champion' and the team leader to ensure that the mission is achievable, and that sufficient resources and budget (if appropriate) are available.

- Ensure discussion amongst all members and stakeholders to make sure the team has the relevant support in terms of development, feedback and training.

- All members and stakeholders need to approve the Team Charter and sign it off. This helps everyone to commit fully to the mission, objectives, principles, roles and responsibilities and then hold each other accountable.

- Continually evaluate, enhance, improve and develop the Team Charter with change of procedures, rules and processes.

Belbin® team roles

Importance of team balance

The management writer Jim Collins talks about team building in terms of 'getting the right people on the bus'. Collins argues that while it is the leader's role to decide where the bus is going and how it's going to get there, there's little point in setting out until the right people are on the bus, in the right seats.

When a team is being formed, it is advisable to employ a variety of team styles to ensure a balanced team profile. Successful sports teams make sure that the right person is playing the correct position. In a football team, for example, not having enough forwards who can score the goals will make it very hard for that team to win. The same principle applies in a work team.

Too many of one behavioural style will create gaps in other areas of the team.

The ideal team will have a balance of all the team styles that make up a winning team. However, in the real world most teams do not have a complete set of roles. It is important to recognize where the gaps are and try to ensure someone fulfils the role.

Most people have a number of 'preferred team roles' or behaviours they frequently and naturally display. We also have 'manageable roles', or secondary roles that might not be the most natural course of behaviour for us, but that we can assume if required and that we might wish to cultivate. We can take these roles when there is a gap in the team or where there may only be four or five in a team and so members need to double up on their behavioural styles in order for the team to be the most effective it can be.

We also have least preferred roles, those we should not assume since we'll be playing against type. In this instance, the effort is likely to be great, and the outcome poor. If work requires team roles other than our own, it is a much better bet to find and work with others who possess roles complementary to our own. The Belbin® philosophy is about celebrating and making the most of individual differences. By identifying our team roles, we can ensure that we use our strengths to advantage and that we manage our weaknesses as best we can. Sometimes, this means being aware of the pitfalls and making an effort to avoid them.

Belbin® team roles explained (with the kind permission of BELBIN® www.belbin.com)

In the 1970s, Dr Meredith Belbin and his research team at Henley Management College set about observing teams, with a view to finding out where and how these differences come about. They wanted to control the dynamics of teams to discover if and how problems could be pre-empted and avoided.

Dr Meredith Belbin has defined nine team roles:

Action-oriented roles: Shaper, Implementer, Completer-Finisher.
People-oriented roles: Coordinator, Teamworker, Resource Investigator.
Thinking-oriented roles: Plant, Monitor-Evaluator, Specialist.

As well as the strength or contribution that each role provides, each 'team role' was also found to have an 'allowable weakness' that is the flipside of the behavioural characteristics. This is allowable in the team because of the strength that goes with it.

Shaper (SH)

Characteristics: Shapers are highly motivated people with a lot of nervous energy and a great need for achievement. They are honest, straightforward and open with others. Usually they are aggressive extroverts and possess strong drive and are challenging, dynamic and thrive on pressure. SHs like to challenge others and their concern is to win. They like to lead and to push others into action. If obstacles arise, they will find a way round. Headstrong and assertive, they tend to show strong emotional response to any form of disappointment or frustration. They make sure the team is achieving goals.

SHs are thick skinned and argumentative and may lack interpersonal understanding. This is the most competitive team role.

Function: SHs generally make good managers because they get things moving, generate action and thrive under pressure. They are excellent at sparking life into a team and are very useful in groups where political complications are apt to slow things down.

Allowable weakness: Prone to frustration and irritation. Could risk becoming aggressive and bad-humoured in their attempts to get things done. Offend people's feelings.

Disallowable weakness: Inability to recover a situation with good humour or apology.

Implementer (IMP)

Characteristics: Implementers have practical common sense and a good deal of self-control and discipline.

They favour hard work and tackle problems in a systematic fashion. On a wider front the IMP is typically a person whose loyalty and interest lie with the company/team/boss and who is less concerned with the pursuit of self-interest. IMPs may lack spontaneity and show signs of rigidity. They are reliable and efficient and can turn ideas into practical actions. They organize systems and ensure everyone follows the laid out procedures.

Function: IMPs are useful to an organization because of their reliability and capacity for application. They succeed because they are efficient and because they have a sense of what is feasible and relevant.

Allowable weakness: Adherence to the orthodox and proven. Somewhat inflexible. Slow to respond to new possibilities.

Disallowable weakness: Obstructing change – might be slow to relinquish their plans in favour of positive changes.

Completer-Finisher (CF)

Characteristics: Completer-Finishers have a great capacity for follow-through and attention to detail.

They are conscientious, search out errors and omissions, and polish and perfect whatever they are working on.

They try to raise standards in all they do and promote excellence. They are unlikely to start anything that they cannot finish. They are motivated by internal anxiety, yet outwardly they may appear unruffled. Typically, they are introverted and require little in the way of external stimulus or incentive. CFs can be intolerant of those with a casual disposition. They are not often keen on delegating, preferring to tackle all tasks themselves.

Function: CFs are invaluable where tasks demand close concentration and a high degree of accuracy. They foster a sense of urgency within a team and are good at meeting schedules. In management they excel by the high standard to which they aspire and by their concern for precision, attention to detail and follow-through.

Allowable weakness: Perfectionism. Inclined to worry unduly. They can split hairs on trivial issues.

Disallowable weakness: They can allow perfectionism to turn into obsessive behaviour, becoming over protective of the boundaries of their job area.

Coordinator (CO)

Characteristics: The distinguishing feature of Coordinators is their ability to clarify goals, promote decision making and encourage others to work towards shared goals. They establish an air of authority over the team with a mature approach as they are trusting, confident and they delegate readily. In interpersonal relations they are quick to spot individual talents and to use them in the pursuit of team objectives. COs have a broad and worldly outlook and generally command respect. They bring others into discussions when they have things to contribute and hold the group together. They give praise and encourage others.

Function: COs are well placed when put in charge of a team of people with diverse skills and personal characteristics. They perform better in dealing with colleagues of near or equal rank than in directing junior subordinates. Their motto might well be 'consultation with control' and they usually believe in tackling problems calmly. In some teams COs are inclined to clash with Shapers due to their contrasting management styles.

Allowable weakness: Inclination to be lazy if someone else can be found to do the work. Can be seen as manipulative. Can offload personal work. Might over-delegate, leaving themselves little work to do.

Disallowable weakness: Taking credit for the effort of the team.

Teamworker (TW)

Characteristics: Teamworkers are the most supportive members of a team. They are cooperative, perceptive, diplomatic, sociable and concerned about others. They have a great capacity for flexibility and adapting to different situations and people. They are good listeners and are generally popular members of a team. They promote a good team atmosphere by reacting to the needs of others. They support members of the team when necessary. They become brokers in times of argument and defuse any hostility. They operate with sensitivity.

Function: The role of the TW is to prevent interpersonal problems arising within a team and thus allow all team members to contribute effectively. Not liking friction, they will go to great lengths to avoid it. It is not uncommon for TWs to become senior managers, especially if Shapers dominate divisional management positions. This creates a climate in which the diplomatic and perceptive skills of a TW become real assets, particularly under a managerial regime where conflicts are liable to arise or to be artificially suppressed. TW managers are seen as a threat to no one and are therefore the most accepted and favoured people to serve under. TWs have a lubricating effect on teams. Morale is improved and people seem to cooperate better when they are around.

Allowable weakness: Indecision on crucial issues and might become indecisive when unpopular decisions need to be made.

Disallowable weakness: Avoid situations that may entail pressure.

Resource Investigator (RI)

Characteristics: Resource Investigators are often enthusiastic, quick-off-the-mark extroverts. They are good at communicating with people both inside and outside the company. They are natural negotiators and are adept at exploring new opportunities and developing contacts. Although not a great source of original ideas, the RI is effective when it comes to picking up other people's ideas and developing them, so they would develop the ideas of the 'Plant'. As the name suggests, they are skilled at finding out what is available and what can be done. They usually receive a warm reception from others because of their own outgoing nature.

RIs have relaxed personalities with a strong inquisitive sense and a readiness to see the possibilities in anything new. However, unless they remain stimulated by others, their enthusiasm rapidly fades.

Function: RIs are good at exploring and reporting back on ideas, developments or resources outside the team. They are the best people to set up external contacts and to carry out any subsequent negotiations. They also have an ability to think on their feet and to probe others for information.

Allowable weakness: Loss of enthusiasm once initial excitement has passed. Talk too much so others cannot get enough air time.

Disallowable weakness: Letting clients down by neglecting to follow up.

Plant (PL)

Characteristics: Plants are innovators and inventors and can be highly creative. They can create an original piece of work and invent a new way of tackling the issues in hand. They provide the seeds and ideas from which major developments spring. Usually they prefer to operate by themselves at some distance from other members of the team, using their imagination and often working in an unorthodox manner. They tend to be introverted and react strongly to criticism and praise. Their ideas may often be radical and may lack practical constraint.

They are independent, clever and original and may be weak in communicating with other people on a different wave length.

Function: The main function of a plant is to generate new proposals, ideas and suggestions, and to solve complex problems and work out solutions. Plants are often needed in the initial stages of a project or when a project is failing to progress. Too many plants in one team may be counterproductive as they tend to spend their time reinforcing their own ideas and engaging each other in combat.

Evaluate your own ideas. Look at things from a different angle.

Allowable weakness: Could be unorthodox or forgetful and neglect practical matters. Ignore incidentals. Too preoccupied to communicate effectively.

Disallowable weakness: Claim ownership of ideas when cooperation would yield better results.

Monitor-Evaluator (ME)

Characteristics: Monitor-Evaluators are serious-minded, cautious individuals with a built-in immunity from being overenthusiastic. They are slow in making decisions, preferring to think things over. Usually they have a high critical-thinking ability. They have a capacity for shrewd judgements that take all factors into consideration. A good ME is seldom wrong. They are strategic and perceptive and see all options. They judge accurately and provide a balanced opinion on all ideas and options. They can dampen the positive approach of the team.

Function: MEs are best suited to analysing problems and evaluating ideas and suggestions. They are very good at weighing up the pros and cons of options. To many outsiders the ME may appear as dry, boring or even over-critical. Some people are surprised that they become managers. Nevertheless, many MEs occupy strategic posts and thrive in high-level appointments. In some jobs, success or failure hinges on a relatively small number of crunch decisions. This is ideal territory for an ME; for the person who is never wrong is the one who scores in the end.

Allowable weakness: Scepticism with logic (ie somebody who doubts something is true).

Disallowable weakness: Cynicism without logic (ie somebody who believes that others' actions are insincere). Could be overly critical and slow moving.

Specialist (SP)

Characteristics: Specialists are dedicated individuals who pride themselves on acquiring technical skills and specialized knowledge. Their priorities centre on maintaining professional standards and on furthering and defending their own field. While they show great pride in their own subject, they usually lack interest in other areas. Eventually the SP becomes the expert by sheer commitment. There are few people who have either the single-mindedness or the aptitude to become a first-class SP. They cultivate a sense of professionalism and encourage fellow team members to trust their knowledge. They need to keep their expertise and skills up to date. They provide knowledge and skills in rare supply.

Function: SPs have an indispensable part to play in some teams, for they provide the rare skills upon which the organization's service or product is based. As managers, they command support because they know more about their subject than anyone else and can usually be called upon to make decisions based on in-depth experience.

Allowable weakness: Acquiring knowledge for its own sake. May have a tendency to focus narrowly on their own subject of choice.

Disallowable weakness: Ignoring factors outside own area of competence.

By identifying our own 'team role', we can ensure that we use our strengths to advantage and that we manage our weaknesses the best we can. Sometimes, this means being aware of the pitfalls and making an effort to avoid them.

A person's overall strongest roles are the ones most appreciated by other people. When you know your strongest team role, you should develop and play the role with enthusiasm because this is where you are likely to raise your profile. However you should remember to play down the allowable weakness of that role and also to try and eliminate the non-allowable weakness.

One way of arranging the nine task/preferences is as follows: two functions are concerned with leadership and setting direction (Shaper and Coordinator); two are concerned with establishing and extending ideas and external contacts (Plant and Resource Investigator); three are concerned with aspects of the detail and quality of the internal working of the team and its performance and products (Completer-Finisher, Monitor-Evaluator and Teamworker); one is concerned with getting that work out into the world once it is under way (Implementer), and one has a focus on the Specialist contribution of professional knowledge etc.

To achieve the best balance in a team there should be:

- one Coordinator or Shaper (not both) as leader;
- chairperson;
- a Monitor-Evaluator to maintain honesty and clarity;
- one or more 'Plants' to stimulate ideas;

- one or more Implementers, Teamworkers, Resource Investigator and Completer-Finishers to make things happen.

How Belbin® and the 'Flock Personality Model' behavioural styles work together in the stages of team development

Belbin®'s team roles can be mapped against my 'Flock Personality Model'. Read Chapter 7 on 'How to communicate with different personality and behavioural styles'.

In the 'Forming' stage, the type of behaviours shown by those needing to act, who like a challenge and are not afraid of taking risks (for example the 'Passionate Parrot' and Belbin®'s 'Plant') may jump into action enjoying the excitement and novelty of exploring something new. There are others who need specific information, full details and time to plan schedules ('Orderly Owl' – Belbin®'s 'Completer-Finisher'), may not be able to do anything straight away and are more likely to wait for the information they need to take matters forward.

The 'Storming' stage will last for a longer or shorter time depending on personalities and behavioural styles within the team and also of course on whether the people involved have the knowledge and willingness to use the information in this chapter! The 'Diplomatic Doves' and Teamworkers will be trying to get everyone working alongside each other and helping each other making sure everyone is included.

The 'Norming' phase is when deadlines are looming and a sense of urgency is created for action to be taken. The need for action is the key as it unfreezes those held in place by a 'need to know before acting' ('The Eager Eagle' and Belbin®'s 'Monitor-Evaluator').

It's during the 'Norming' stage that productivity starts to rise and the teams start to perform well together. The Performing stage is when the team's focus will be entirely on how best to work and share knowledge together to achieve the best possible results. Individual and team profiles should be shared so that everyone understands how everyone fits into the team and which of your strengths come into play and when.

Remote and virtual team working best practice

With the plethora of technology available and cloud computing, work can be done anywhere and effective virtual teamwork is paramount to a successful organization. Since Covid-19, there is a lot more flexibility in working patterns, whether it's a combination of office and remote working or even being fully remote. Companies have realized that they don't need to pay for premises as the work still gets done without office overheads.

For some, working from home will be a welcome opportunity that offers flexibility and cost saving, but for others it can be challenging due to circumstances at home and whether they are able to remain focused and motivated when isolated. Ensuring a successful remote working experience for your team needs thoughtful and efficient management.

Virtual and remote teams may be across the globe in different countries and different timezones, or may be people who work from home full or part-time and part-time in the office (hybrid working), working from anywhere (preferably with wifi availability), satellite offices (nearer to their home), shared co-working spaces and coffee shops etc.

You may be a part of a team or lead teams that are virtual/remote and/or office based or are working virtually yourself.

A virtual team has at least two things in common:

- Two or more people work together to achieve common goals.
- At least one of the team members works in a different location and possibly in a different time zone.

There is no doubt that technology has made and continues to make a vital impact on our societies, careers, health, and networking. Technology can improve our lifestyles, relationships, ability to attend online training and growing professional connections. New technologies are constantly being launched while others are improving daily.

Advantages of virtual working:

- There is no commute to the office so you have more time for home life or you can take advantage of flexible working to work around your home life, you also save on the cost of commuting.
- Assistants can effectively support their executives remotely when communicating often.
- The technology is available and works well and improves all the time – home broadband can be as fast as that at the office.
- Productivity can increase, due to fewer interruptions, as long as home life has been organized to suit working from home.
- There is a favourable impact on the climate with lower pollution in the air and carbon footprint.

- Research shows that virtual teams who use video conferencing (with camera on) as opposed to audio or written, are almost as effective as face-to-face communication as you can see non-verbal language and it allows immediate feedback.
- It is easy to record a meeting.

Practical considerations for virtual meetings

- Technical connection
  Having an excellent wifi connection is important when working virtually or you can connect via ethernet cable to ensure that your connection does not go down or is intermittent in important meetings.
    - Safety:
    - Have a documented 'work from home' security policy.
    - Ensure comprehensive antivirus and internet security is installed and working.
    - Unplug cameras when not using and cover camera lenses on laptops.
    - Make sure all passwords are strong and secure.

- Cameras on
  Research shows that virtual teams, who use video conferencing with cameras on as opposed to audio or written, are almost as effective as face-to-face communication, as you can see body language, facial expressions, gestures and posture and it allows immediate feedback. When you can see people, it brings a different atmosphere of inclusivity. It also means you will pay more attention and not be distracted by emails and mobiles etc as you are being watched and you don't want to appear rude.

  The camera should be placed so that the angle is flattering, you must be able to look directly into your camera lens or look slightly up to it. Psychologically people don't like being talked down to and we don't like looking up people's noses, so raise the camera/laptop. Have your head and shoulders comfortably positioned in the centre of the screen.

- Distance bias
  As humans we all have cognitive biases and one that is prominent in virtual working is 'distance bias' which means when you are out of sight you are out of mind. It is the tendency to favour people who are closer to us in time and space. You may get forgotten for certain meetings or events or you may not be kept informed, or even contacted for a social chat, and

you can start to feel isolated and unappreciated. Therefore you need to increase your visibility and keep your profile raised.

Tips for keeping your profile raised:

- Volunteer to be a part of project groups which are outside of your role eg chair monthly admin meetings.

- As well as keeping your camera on, you need to speak up in meetings and take part in discussions.

- If someone needs help, offer your help.

- If your boss and colleagues are not contacting you, then you must contact them. It doesn't matter how busy you are – create a sense of connection, relatedness, belonging and inclusion. When we connect with others, our brains release oxytocin (bonding hormone) which gives us a reward feeling. The more oxytocin that's released, the more connected we feel, the more trust we feel and our relationships improve. Therefore, work to build up strong team bonds by scheduling regular one to ones. Also organize team lunches, team-building events, social events – there are many innovative ideas that can be done online such as treasure hunts around your house, wine-tasting evenings, cocktail making evening, guess whose baby photo is who and lots more. Inclusion takes thought, energy and intentionalism.

Barriers to good communication:

- Forgetting to communicate often enough! It's easier when you bump into staff daily in the corridor, kitchen or water cooler.

- Speaking too quickly, too quietly or both.

- Miscommunication.

Similarly, distance bias also works the other way round. **If you are not actively being inclusive of others then you will probably accidentally be exclusive.** This can cause misunderstanding and upset. Whenever we feel excluded, our brains treat it as a threat and we cannot think properly and productivity will decrease.

- Workspace

  - It's important that people working remotely have a specific and suitable area to work in, and ideally somewhere they can shut the door or close off at the end of the day and be able to differentiate between work and home life and make sure they have a proper work–life balance. There is a tendency when working from home to work longer hours which is not good for our mental and physical health.

- You need an ergonomically arranged workspace to prevent repetitive strain injury and to keep a healthy body and mind.

- You need the lighting to be right whether it's daylight or artificial lighting so you can be seen properly and not in shadow. Also be careful where you place the artificial lighting when you wear glasses so the light is not bouncing off them. Ideally any windows should be in front of you or at the side of you but not behind you.

- Consider your background as people are curious and may be looking at what's behind you rather than listening to what you are saying. You can use virtual backgrounds if you prefer but test it out before you go live as your body may disappear off screen when you move.

- Noise
  - Consider any jewellery you might wear, as the tinkling noise could be picked up by the microphone.

  - You may need to purchase a microphone and I prefer to use a mic on an extendable arm with a pop shield to filter any popping sound with P's and S's. If you do wear a headphone with mic, make sure you keep the microphone away from your nose and mouth as people will hear you breathe and it will prevent the popping sound.

  - Eliminate or move away from background noise: during a video conference you should close windows, move away from air vents, go to less noisy areas, close applications that may cause your laptop's fans to whirr. The correct etiquette is that everyone should be muted when not speaking and this will prevent some background noises occurring for everyone.

- Eye contact
  - To make people feel looked at and to give an illusion of eye contact, which is very important to help make them feel more involved, you need to look at the camera and not at the people on the screen, however tempting that might be. To help you remember to do this you can put a sticker or even a picture of a smiley face, near the camera lens as a reminder to look there when you speak.

It takes practice, but the more you do it, the easier it becomes as your neural pathways deepen and it becomes a habit. It's okay to look at the people when you are listening to others speak, and you have your team on screen.

- Meeting rules
  - These should be easily accessible for all, perhaps sent with the agenda or pre-read information.

Tips for successful remote working:

- Have a clear structure to your day – decide on start time, lunchtime and finish time and create realistic expectations and set boundaries. You should not be expected to be contactable 24/7 (unless you agree to this in special circumstances).

- Schedule daily check-ins with boss(es) even if only 10 mins, or as often as possible. Remember your meetings are crucial for you to understand what is critical to your boss on an hourly, daily, weekly, monthly and annual basis.

- Schedule weekly check-ins meetings with other assistants.

- After some meetings, use your judgement and think about leaving the channels open in case people want to chat as you would in an office environment. On the flip side – be careful at the end of the meeting of people who might still be online. You or your household might say something that you might not want people to hear so make sure you 'leave' the meeting first.

- Schedule weekly check-in calls/emails with direct reports.

- Use an instant messenger programme like Teams, Google Hangouts, Slack, WhatsApp etc to keep in touch with colleagues. These are great when have a quick question for your boss. When we have the messenger tool 'open', it gives a feeling of working alongside others and being connected. Psychologically this is important for the brain as social connection can lower anxiety and depression, help us regulate our emotions, lead to higher self-esteem and empathy and actually improve our immune systems.

- We often perceive real time communication as urgent and feel the need to reply straight away and this makes it difficult to prioritize workloads and complete tasks that require uninterrupted focus. Perhaps have set times when you are available and make it clear when you are not available in order to give yourself some uninterrupted time to concentrate and be productive.

- Find out what your organization provides in terms of communication tools to help with your productivity, for example certain cloud telephony solutions such as Nvoice for Microsoft Teams that enables user-defined call forwarding. With this communication feature, team members can set specific numbers that are allowed to contact them for a set period of time, while the rest can go to voicemail or be diverted to a colleague. Communications capabilities like these are perfect for helping you control your workload while remaining contactable to the right people, eg your boss, in case something urgent arises.

- With 'Zoom Fatigue' now a globally recognized term, an over-reliance on video conferencing has taken its toll on remote workers. It is important to avoid letting video calls become your default mode of communication or you risk exhausting your team. Another problem with video calls is the demand they can place on team-wide availability. If you are regularly struggling to align everyone's calendar or maybe your boss is spending so much time in meetings that it is affecting their ability to get through their work, you could record the call to catch up with later. Tools like Loom and Jing are great ways to achieve some of the benefits of video calling, without the need for everyone to be booked out for the same period of time. These tools allow you to more personally connect with people without having to do 20 different one to one calls.

- Organize regular social coffee catch-up chats, and discuss anything but work.

- Introduce a buddy system where colleagues can pair up and support each other.

- Ask to be included in appropriate leadership meetings, even if only as an observer, to keep updated on the vision, mission and goals of the organization.

- Health and wellbeing for mind and body are extremely important – make sure you are not on back-to-back video conferences.

- Plan regular 'brain breaks' away from your screen to reboot your brain and give your eyes a rest – you can practise a mindfulness exercise, go for a walk or do some ergonomic exercises to prevent musculoskeletal fatigue. (You can read more about ergonomic exercises in *The Definitive Personal Assistant & Secretarial handbook* Chapter 9.) Make sure you eat a nutritious lunch, drink plenty of water throughout the day and take a lunch hour so you can be more productive in the afternoon.

- Have realistic expectations of what you can achieve each day.
- Where possible, organize occasional office days where people work from the office for a day and include a teambuilding event or social drinks or meeting.

Develop a clear description of team values, behaviour and communication with ground rules for remote and hybrid working and document them and share them in a public place or shared document, intranet etc so that people can refer to them when needed. Include your team's suggestions when setting the ground rules and check in with your team at intervals to see if the rules of engagement need to be tweaked.

Suggested ground rules for discussion:

1 Limit the number of video conferences, they should not be back-to-back, all day. Ask are they really needed – could an email or phone call do instead? Who should attend – remember that attending meetings costs money and could their time be better spent on something else? Also the fewer people on a call the more they will be involved and participative.

2 Respond to emails within 48 hours.

3 Respond to phone messages within 24 hours.

4 Start and end meetings on time.

5 No meetings after 14:00 GMT on Fridays.

6 Conduct the weekly global team meeting every Monday at noon (GMT) and then rotate the time every quarter to incorporate different time zones fairly.

7 Make sure all work meetings have a formal or informal agenda so you know what is to be discussed to be sent out prior to the meeting.

8 Keep the meetings as short as possible – people will zone out if too long and the meeting will be unproductive – maximum one hour meeting.

9 What is the best way to reach each other – phone, text, email, instant messenger? How should team members communicate urgent questions that need an immediate response?

10 Decide on whether meetings can be recorded or not, whether minutes are required and whether you need a time-keeper to make sure the video conference does not run over.

11 Set clear communication hours when team members are expected to be available and respond to messages. When working on a project or unable to be contacted then make sure they change their settings to 'Do not Disturb' and uncheck it when available again. Develop a plan for urgent or time-sensitive communication outside of these hours.

12 Develop trust and allow some autonomy over working hours especially when team members are global and in different time zones. Having the ability to take two hours off in the afternoon to look after children or go to a medical appointment and then continue in the evening is empowering and motivating to do a good job.

13 Incorporate a video conference free day.

14 Culturally embed the importance of prioritizing your workload. It is important for remote workers to strike the balance between being contactable and productive.

Summary

Connection, relatedness, humanness are all critically important whether we are face-to-face or virtual. Focus on introducing some evolved or new approaches to mitigate exclusion and do everything you can to build inclusion in an intentional way. Setting ground rules in a collaborative way, discussing potential issues proactively and reaching agreement on the team values, behaviour and communication will avoid conflict and misunderstanding and set out a plan that you can all aim for. Close contact is important, but you also need to give employees the space to get their work done. Optimize remote working tools and communication for a team dynamic that is connected, efficient, streamlined, productive and engaged. The way we work and the tools we use are changing all the time so keep on learning and adapting and leading the way.

The key to the success of any team especially virtual teams is to build trust and social cohesion and to do that you need good collaboration and communication systems.

As a team leader you need to understand the different roles that make up a team as well as be aware of the different behavioural styles of team members. Understanding the five different stages that a team inevitably goes through and what you can do as team leader to help that process progress smoothly can be the make or break of an effective team. Using the Team

Charter, including guidelines for effective teamwork, should enable you to keep control of the dynamics of the team so that it can be the most effective and productive, and conducive for a fun and exciting place to work whether you are working virtually, in the office or hybrid.

Employee experience from recruitment to performance

05

This chapter is about best practice in an employee's experience including recruitment, onboarding, managing the performance of ourselves and others and how to give and receive effective feedback. It will give you the insight necessary to make your employee experience as successful as possible. It defines the role or job analysis of a 'professional assistant': what the characteristics, attitude, skills and behaviours are of the 'professional assistant' and you can find a downloadable Resource 2 of a sample 'person specification' for the 'professional assistant' which encompasses skills, attributes, and behaviours for this role for all levels, at www.suefrance.com under *The Definitive Executive Assistant & Managerial Handbook* 2nd edition resources. You can use the 'person specification' as a check list against your skills, discover where you might want to develop in certain areas and for recruiting purposes.

The chapter also includes tips on résumé writing, applying for jobs and interview techniques both from the recruiter and potential candidate's point of view.

There are tips on making onboarding worthwhile and memorable by using a structured onboarding programme so that you can help new recruits feel a part of the organization from the very beginning. It will explain how to create a 'standard operating procedures' binder and a work schedule for reference so anyone can step into your job if you are unexpectedly absent or plan to be away from work.

It discusses the evolution of performance management and how to give and receive effective feedback. I have also included information on the work of the World Administrators Alliance and the Global Skills Matrix that they have developed.

Performance management

Performance management is a strategic process that covers the whole life cycle of an employee, including recruitment, onboarding, engagement such as training and development, performance appraisal and promotion. It is about the assessment of performance as well as potential and it results in retaining the best and most effective workers.

Performance management is about having the right people in the right job, working with the right boss and the right team, with the right competencies, and making sure that they receive the right development tools in order to be effective (ie 'doing the right things') as well as efficient (ie 'doing things right').

Performance management is an essential ingredient for organizational success and depends on four critical factors, that everyone needs to understand:

- the mission and purpose of the organization;
- the strategic goals or key result areas that will lead to organizational success;
- how their individual roles and responsibilities fit with organizational objectives;
- aligning individual goals and objectives with their bosses' goals and objectives.

Recruiting

The ability to attract candidates depends upon how potential applicants view the organization, the industry or sector in which it operates and whether they share the values of that organization. The creation of an attractive employer brand is an important factor in recruiting especially with websites such as Glassdoor where you can find out people's opinions of organizations and whether you think you might be the right fit for that organization.

Recruitment is the process of getting the right person, in the right place, at the right time and it is crucial to organizational performance. Recruitment isn't always straightforward, as people might look excellent on their CV, but when you meet them your heart sinks because they just don't have that hidden ingredient that's right for your company, or when you meet them in person they do not portray what was on their résumés. Also, if you are the one being recruited, your hopes may be dashed when you realize at the interview that the job or company isn't right for you no matter how much research you may have done on it. Remember the recruitment process is a two-way process – both recruiter and recruitee have to believe that they are the right fit for each other. Recruitees need to find out and research thoroughly about the business before and during the recruitment process and consider whether the organization is one they would like to work for.

A popular way to recruit is through the internet and job search engines, including the social media networking site LinkedIn. In fact when you have an impressive and complete LinkedIn profile including recommendations for your work, achievements you have made and your career history plus what you post, any articles you write, videos, podcasts you make etc, then you are more likely to be headhunted for roles even if you are not looking for one! Other ways of recruiting are through internal applications, internal referral schemes, job fairs, newspaper advertising, job centres, networking, temporary work that becomes permanent work, word of mouth and recommendation. No matter how the hiring is conducted it is absolutely certain that any potential employee will have a search done on them via the internet, so do be careful about what you or other people put on all of the different social media websites about you, including pictures, if you want to be considered as a professional person and a potential new recruit. You should regularly 'Google' yourself to see what is out there about you!

The recruitment process involves working through a series of stages:

1 Defining the role/job analysis and creating a person specification.
2 Attracting applications.
3 Managing the application and selection process.
4 Conducting the interview and making the appointment.

All those involved in recruitment activities should be equipped with the appropriate knowledge and skills. As a team leader of executive assistants I was always involved in the second interview for hiring members for my team, the first interview being the screening interview conducted either by HR or an agency. It is at the recruiting stage that first impressions and the ability to build rapport instantly are so very important. It is very important that the line manager is involved with developing the job description and person specification as well as being involved in the third interview stage.

Job analysis

Before recruiting for a new or existing position, it is important to invest time in gathering information about the nature of the job. This means thinking not only about the content (such as the tasks), but also the job's purpose, the outputs required by the job holder and how it fits into the organization's structure. This analysis should form the basis of a compelling job description and person specification/job profile. However, I do not believe in keeping to 'job descriptions' to the letter – you have to be flexible and continually add to your job description where appropriate, in any case most job descriptions for assistants tend to have the curious addendum 'and anything else required'.

The job analysis leads to writing a job description. As well as explaining what the job entails, it helps the recruitment process by providing a clear guide to all involved about the requirements of the job. It can also be used to communicate expectations about performance to employees and managers to help ensure effective performance in the job.

Job description

Many people ask what are the duties, roles, job description, traits, skills, behaviours of today's assistant, and the answer is: it is about being proactive and making your role whatever you want it to be, and taking on new and exciting responsibilities at every opportunity. The potential for an assistant is absolutely massive! Of course there will be key skills and duties involved but this is only the base – the rest is up to you and your tenacity to improve and evolve, and as a leader you should encourage this in others.

There is much debate around what the differences are between the plethora of titles (over 100 and growing) for the role of a 'professional assistant'. The official name given to this role varies between countries, companies, industries and departments. Individuals in different countries and companies can be doing similar roles and have different titles.

There are also virtual assistants who work out of their homes who are self-employed contractors who do much the same work for clients on a freelance basis. They are their own boss like any professional entrepreneur and may also have associates and employ people.

The skills and attitudes of the assistant are so important. Resource 2: 'Example person specification', which can be downloaded from **www.suefrance.com**, outlines many of the skills, behaviours and attitudes of an assistant, although it is not exhaustive. I have set them out as a 'person specification' that can be used in recruiting and encompasses every professional assistant role, skill and behaviour I can think of, so it does not represent one job role but an amalgamation of many. I have also included many of the job roles that an assistant conducts, and if you are not currently performing any of these duties and would like to – then simply ask to see if you can get involved in these areas; remember 'if you don't ask, you don't get'.

Person specification

A person specification is written by the organization and outlines the type of person they want in order to match the right person to the job. It states the 'essential' and 'desirable' criteria to determine which competencies are absolutely necessary and which would be 'good to have', to help with selection purposes. By using Resource 2 mentioned above, you can find a list of competencies used in the variable assistant role.

In addition, the person specification might include some or all of the following:

- educational qualifications; technological certifications; professional certifications such as accounting, counselling, coaching, human resources etc;

- previous experience required; for example, how many years in the role as an assistant to a CEO etc;

- specialized skills; for example, ability to supervise/manage others, ability to manage projects etc;

- aptitudes; for example, verbal reasoning, analytical skills; numerical aptitude;

- interests; for example, social activities, sporting activities and hobbies;

- personal circumstances; for example, ability to work shifts, full or part time; preference for remote working, hybrid working, office based and flexible working hours;

- memberships; for example, member of a PA network, member of a Professional Institute etc.

Person specifications have to be prepared and used with great care. In particular, it is important to ensure that the list of essential or desired competencies does not lead to unlawful discrimination against potential employees. For example, in the UK we cannot discriminate against sex, age and disability.

Diversity and inclusion culture

Throughout the recruiting process, pave the way for a more diverse and inclusive workforce. Within the advertising, job description, person specification, recruiting procedures you should be inclusive of neuro diverse personalities and disabled workers. There should be no gender bias; racial bias; religious bias; sexual orientation bias or age discrimination etc.

Application forms

Unlike your résumé, application forms allow employers to ask a specific set of questions, rather than letting jobseekers choose the format and content of their application themselves. Your résumé can be attached to the application form so it is still important to have one.

Application forms allow for information to be presented in a consistent format, and therefore make it easier to collect information from job applicants in a systematic way and assess objectively the candidate's suitability for the job.

Résumé

The advantage of résumés is that they give candidates the opportunity to sell themselves in their own way. However, résumés make it possible for candidates to include lots of additional, irrelevant material that may make them harder to assess consistently. They should be no more than two pages long and typed up logically and attractively – you will find a plethora of templates on the internet to choose from.

All applications should be treated confidentially and circulated only to those individuals involved in the recruitment process. All solicited and unsolicited applications should also be acknowledged, and responded to. Prompt acknowledgment is good practice and presents a positive image of the organization.

Résumés should be tailored to the industry and to the job applied for, and therefore sending what is obviously a generic résumé does not show initiative or keenness. Always be truthful on your résumé as you will lose all credibility and trust when you get found out, which could be at the interview stage or even when you have the job, which will not do your career any favours. Recruiters want to know what you have achieved (work, community wise or personally), which shows your agility, diversity, business acumen, cost saving ability, creativeness and any other skill sets as well as your resilience and attitude. Include a short personal statement to explain why you are the best person for the job and this should be reflected in your cover letter.

Automated scanning programs

Many organizations use automated scanners to sieve through the résumés and could potentially miss suitable candidates simply because they did not use the words the scanner looks for. However, be aware also that some applicants write the words that the scanner looks for in white on the paper (so it cannot be seen by the naked eye). These words match the words in the job advertisement so that scanners will pick out their résumé. Therefore the scanner may pick out résumés of people who may not be suitable candidates but who have simply put the right words on their application.

When screening résumés and preparing questions for the interview, look for achievements and accomplishments that support applicants' claims about their behaviour, attitude, skills and personality and question them about these. For example look for statements and verbs that show their achievements such as: created, came in under-budget; increased; reduced; improved; developed, accomplished; researched; won and awards. Look for evidence – for example if they say they are motivated, a team player, outstanding, effective – what proves this? Also check for quotes from their leaders and supervisors that back up their claims to be excellent team leaders etc. Look to see if they have received any appropriate awards or any other forms of recognition.

Interviews

It is important for both interviewer and interviewee to have excellent communication skills and to be able to build rapport easily and quickly. Remember when reading body language that you can only read it well when you know someone really well and that you should take at least four or five different clues to really know what people are thinking.

The invitation letter should tell candidates that they should advise the organization in advance of any particular arrangements that need to be made to accommodate them on arrival or during the interview; for instance, ramp access.

Interview preparation

Structured interviews

Interviews should be structured so that questions are planned carefully before the interview to suit the attributes and behaviours required for the job and to ensure that all candidates for the same job are asked the same questions so you can have a fair and comparable assessment of each candidate.

Screening interviews and remote interviews

The screening interview could be done by human resources or the agency, which will sift through all the applications and choose the candidates that best match the person specification. They may even do software packaging tests at this stage as there is no point in putting someone forward for a second interview if they cannot match basic requirements eg Excel and PowerPoint expertise. Telephone interviews may also be the first interview to help screen applicants this helps the interviewer assess telephone etiquette skills as well as it being time and logistically effective. First interviews may also be conducted virtually using video conferencing technology.

As interviewer or interviewee, whichever method is used you need to make sure nothing gets in the way of your timely connection. If it is by video or phone you need to make sure technology is up to speed eg wifi connection, batteries charged, laptops plugged in etc and test the technology beforehand. Whenever I am conducting webinars I always connect by ethernet cable to make sure connection is never lost. Check beforehand which software conferencing will be used and download any applications required and test it out. As an assistant, if you fail at the first hurdle of using technology, then it does not bode well for a job offer! Make sure your microphone and camera are working and compatible with the software.

Make sure you have the right mindset, attitude and give off the right vibe whether on the phone or video. They can pick this up from your voice as well as your body language.

Set your stage in terms of background lighting and noise. Eliminate noise as much as possible by closing doors, windows, being in the quietest room and not putting your washing machine on! If you are not at home check in advance what your quietest option is. Make sure the lighting is good to make you properly visible and not in shade. Also be strategic in terms of your background if possible, either by choosing a place where it is ordered and tidy or choose a video background if the software allows like it does on Zoom or blur the background like you can on Skype.

You should present yourself and dress to the same standard as if you were going to a face-to-face interview (at least from the waist up).

The camera should be at screen height so you can see your head and upper body and when you speak, you should look directly in to the camera lens so they feel you are making eye contact. When they speak you can look at them if you want to. Giving eye contact (via the lens) will help build rapport and trust.

Print off a copy of your résumé and have it in front of you. Make sure you are solely focused on the interview and turn off all notifications and ideally set all systems to do not disturb mode.

If you want to make notes then check that is fine with the interviewer, and if you are the interviewer, let the interview know you will be making notes so both will know what you are doing when you are typing on another screen or looking down and writing.

As the interviewee, at the end of the interview make sure you have completely shut down or closed out of the application and mic and camera are off. After the interview send a brief thank you email for the interview, as it is not only polite but you will stand out as someone who is attentive, interested in the role and pays attention to detail.

Second interview

You should conduct the second interview and you may have the authority to hire or you may wish to bring back, for example, three suitable candidates for third interview for the assistant to meet with the manager(s) they will work with. These will be the candidates who have the right credentials, ethos and tenacity, and are suitable to fit in with the existing team of assistants and suit the personalities of the managers they would work for. When it reaches the third stage it is more about the 'personality fit' and whether they would work well with the manager.

You may want to have someone else with you in the second interview who will work closely with the candidate to make sure they are both happy to work with each other.

Before the meeting, read through the candidate's résumé again and make notes where you want to clarify any points, together with the pre-prepared list of questions that you need to ask.

Location of interview

Choose a quiet room where you will not be disturbed whether the interview is in person, telephone or video conference. When in person, you can position the chairs so there is no table between you (acting as a barrier) and put your chairs at 45° angles to each other so you are not facing each other directly as you would in a difficult conversation scenario.

The interview

Ensure that you have the applicant's résumé (with your notes) and covering letter to hand as well as a copy of the job description and person specification. Not only will they be useful for reference but they will also demonstrate to the candidate that you are fully prepared.

As the candidate, you should be a few minutes early if in person and on time if virtually and treat everyone with respect and dignity, be confident and keep eye contact (remember the camera lens tip above), actively listen carefully to the questions and answer the question asked, although you should also expand on your answer where appropriate.

Bear in mind the following tips:

- As the interviewer, you should welcome the candidate and smile using eye contact. Introduce yourself and any other interviewers. Begin each interview with an informal chat to help interviewees settle down. This will help to put the candidates at ease as they will always be nervous. Explain what format the interview will take and how long it will last.

- Taking notes is important for both parties as neither of you will remember everything. If you are conducting several interviews in succession, give yourself time to write further notes about the interview and your thoughts on the candidate, including your gut reaction, as it will be hard to review the results of the interview at a later stage without them.

- If the candidate asks to take notes either on a notepad or iPad etc, then realize that this is an initiative that the assistant will use within their role and is a plus point when discussing the successful candidate.

- This is an opportunity to describe the job and the responsibilities in more detail; assess the candidate's ability to perform in the role; discuss with the candidate details such as start dates, holidays, training provisions, and terms and conditions such as employee benefits.

- Give a brief overview of the company, the department and the role on offer. It is important to always give a positive impression of the company to the candidate as a 'good employer' because you should always take opportunities to enhance the brand of the company and you never know where they may end up working – it could be a client of your company. Even if you don't want to give them a job, you should still encourage them to think that they really want the job because it's a great place to work and they leave with a good impression of the company.

- Give plenty of 'talk time' to interviewees otherwise you will not find out enough about them. A huge mistake that interviewers make is that they talk too much and then wonder how they hired the wrong person for the job!

- Ask the candidates about themselves, being careful about how you phrase your questions (see more information on types of questions in Chapter 9, and remember to download Resource 3, 'Example questions for recruiting'. The resource can also be used by potential candidates to help them prepare for an interview.) You may need to consider relevant legislation when interviewing; for example, in the UK you are not allowed to ask for some personal information such as potentially discriminatory questions like: 'Are you planning to have children in the next few years?' Don't ask too many 'closed' questions but do ask open-ended questions that encourage the candidate to speak freely and remember to avoid leading questions.

  The interview questions need to give you a clear indication of not only the candidate's technical abilities but also their personality. The aim of the questions should be to answer the following: 'Will this person fit into the business from a work and personality point of view and help to increase company profits?'

- Take candidates chronologically through their résumés and take a quick tour of the candidate's roles from past to present. You should ask competency-based and behavioural questions relevant to the role. Pick out the key skills the candidate will need for the role – for example, creativity, leadership, resilience, time management – and ask questions around these attributes.

As well as asking questions you can also give the candidate a statement and then ask him or her to expand – for example 'You have had a lot of experience in managing teams. Tell me about it' – and be prepared to probe further.

- Remember to have fun. It is okay to use humour – it will put the candidate at ease. Do watch the time. I would give each candidate a maximum of an hour so that you can really get to know each other and to give a real chance to match and mirror, pace and lead as well as giving them time to ask questions. However if you know that the candidate is not suitable you can cut this time short (in a way that still leaves them with a positive impression of the company). You will find with the candidates you like and think are suitable, the hour will fly by and the conversation will be flowing and the opposite is true with candidates who are not suitable.

Growth and fixed mindset

Do you approach recruiting with a growth or fixed mindset? With a fixed mindset we believe that our talents are innate and static (we are who we are); with a growth mindset we believe that with effort and tenacity we can learn, develop and improve (we can do and become whatever we put our minds too). When you are of a fixed mindset and are recruiting, you will look for individuals who exhibit all skills and abilities that are required in the role from day one. If you have a growth mindset whilst recruiting, you will be looking for individuals who have some or most of the skills but who also show a great potential to be even better than what you can imagine.

You should also consider the mindset in the candidate.

- If they have a fixed mindset they will see effort as fruitless as talent is fixed, they may avoid challenges and have little tenacity when facing obstacles. They would be defensive against constructive/negative feedback and feel threatened by the success of others.

- If they have a growth mindset they will see effort as the pathway to mastery and self-fulfilment, they will enjoy taking on challenges, lead and embrace change, have pertinacity (a combination of persistence and tenacity), will search out feedback, learn from mistakes and find lessons and inspiration in the success of others. When questioning candidates with a growth mindset they easily answer questions on what they would have done differently and what they learned in difficult situations.

The limbic system and the amygdala when being interviewed

Most of us feel a degree of stress in an interview situation and being probed and examined is bound to increase anxiety levels. Having some stress is useful (adrenaline pumping through) as it can make you appear eager, excited and alert. When overly stressed (too much cortisol), our amygdala and limbic system activates, preventing our prefrontal cortex working therefore stopping us from being able to think properly and answer the questions in a way that we know we can when not stressed. Candidates cannot easily answer competency questions like 'tell me about a time when you …' as they cannot think of an example as their mind may have frozen or made them want to run away. So putting the candidate at ease at the beginning and even bringing humour into the situation, will help the interview process and enable the interviewer to have a more realistic view of the candidate's abilities.

When interviewing make sure you do not fall into the trap of making the following mistakes as every single human being has cognitive biases which are corner cutting mental shortcuts which are the bases of the following effects. The best way to combat them is to be aware of them:

- **Objectivism:** The implicit belief that our experience and beliefs are objectively true. For example, noticing biases in others but not in ourselves!

- **Confirmation bias:** Where we have a tendency to favour information that confirms our pre-existing beliefs. Interviewers may ask questions designed to confirm initial impressions gained either before the interview or in its early stages.

- **The stereotyping effect:** Interviewers sometimes assume that particular characteristics are typical of members of a particular group. The physical attractiveness stereotype is the tendency to assume that people who are physically attractive also possess other socially desirable personality traits. Studies have shown that people tend to think that they are also happier, outgoing, successful, kinder and many other positive traits.

- **The halo and horns effect:** A tendency to allow your judgement of the interviewee to be unduly influenced by an unfavourable (horns) or favourable (halo) first impression based on appearances.

- **The contrast effect:** Interviewers can allow the experience of interviewing one candidate to affect the way they interview others who are seen later in the selection process.

- **Similarity bias:** Interviewers sometimes subconsciously give preference to candidates they perceive as having a similar background, went to the same school/university, career history, personality or attitudes to themselves. We very quickly categorize people into our 'in-group' (people similar to us) or 'out-group' (people who are different from us). These decisions are made by very quickly by our subconscious amygdala (to keep us safe) outside of our awareness; but once categorized we respond positively to the in-group and less well disposed to the out-group.

- **The personal liking effect:** Interviewers may make decisions on the basis of whether they personally like or dislike the candidate.

- **The temporal effect:** Assuming that a candidate's behaviour at the interview, for example nervous, is typical of their general disposition.

- **The expectancy effect:** Giving undue influence to positive or negative expectations of a candidate formed from the résumé or application form.

- **The primacy effect:** Putting too much emphasis on impressions gained and information assimilated early in the interview.

- **Negativity bias:** Giving more weight to perceived negative points about candidates than to those that are most positive. We tend to pay more attention to, remember better, more frequently recall, and get more aroused by negative rather than positive experiences or information. So if a candidate explains a time when they made a mistake (even though they explained what they learned from it) the interviewer may feel concerned about some aspects when later discussing with colleagues whom they should hire. Therefore they need to actively remember the full answer and how they perceive the candidate to perform in the future.

Corner cutting biases can be mitigated by slowing down and engaging your prefrontal cortex (thinking, rational, decision-making brain) which comes back on board when you have calmed down your amygdala. Then carefully and objectively look at the data and logic related to the intuitive decision you made and check your assumptions.

The other way to mitigate bias is mindfulness. Research shows that the more mindful a person is, ie the more aware you are and open-minded to your situation in the present moment, the more able you are to label your emotions, neutralize the threat response of the amygdala and reduce unconscious bias.

You have to conduct structured interviews carefully so that they do not seem too rigid, and you have to be flexible because you will need to use probing questions depending on their answers, but at the same time each interview for the same job has to be comparable.

You may also use assessment centres, psychological and psychometric testing, 'in-tray' exercises, role-plays, giving a presentation, numeracy tests etc.

Closing the interview

It may be appropriate to ask what notice period the interviewee has to give. However, it is not advisable to offer candidates positions at the end of an interview or even let them know that they will be asked back for a third interview, because you need time to compare the different interviews and reflect on your thoughts and possibly discuss them with the first interviewer and your co-interviewer (if you had one). Let them know that they will be contacted in the next few days (and make sure you do this even for those who will not be asked back).

An informal chat often helps to end on a friendly note. Make sure that you have covered all your points and the candidates have covered theirs. If the interview was in person and the candidate has travelled a fair distance, this may be an opportunity to offer them reimbursement for their expenses. Your closing actions will have an impression on the candidate and it is important to make sure that they reflect well on both you and your company.

At the third interview, as well as the candidate having a 20–30 minute interview with the manager(s), it will be useful both for the candidates and the wider team to meet each other, even if it is over video conferencing if the whole interview process is conducted remotely. It would be preferable for the candidates to see the environment in which they would be working, if there is an office and the post is not totally virtual. Gaining the commitment of the immediate manager/supervisor by involving them in the selection process is vital to ensuring that the new employee is settled successfully into the organization.

Reviews and selecting the best candidate(s)

The review is a chance for you to reflect on the interviews. If you conducted the interviews with a colleague, it is a chance to compare notes and discuss individual candidate performances. If the candidate has come back for a third interview with the manager(s), then you should all be involved in discussing the three candidates to find the most suitable one for the job.

Sometimes managers need persuading and influencing if you firmly believe that one of the candidates is highly suitable, and you need to give reasons and examples. Be objective in your decisions. Remember the question you really need answering is: 'Will this person fit into the business from a work and personality point of view and help to increase company profits?'

Send each candidate an email/phone call as soon as possible to thank them for attending the interview and inform them of your decision. Most active job seekers will be making arrangements for and attending interviews for several different jobs so it is important not to allow too much time to pass after the interviews, especially if you are keen to employ them.

References

A recruitment policy should state clearly how references will be used, when in the recruitment process they will be taken up and what kind of references will be necessary (for example, from current and former employers and personal character references). These rules should be applied consistently. Candidates should always be informed of the procedure for taking up references. References are most frequently asked for after the applicant has been given a 'provisional offer'.

The purpose of references is to obtain information about a candidate's employment history, qualifications, experience and/or an assessment of the candidate's suitability for the post in question. Prospective employers may seek information on matters including length of employment, job title, brief details of responsibilities, abilities, overall performance, time-keeping and reason for leaving.

As well as taking references employers need to carry out other pre-employment checks – particularly, for example, if the job involves working with children or vulnerable adults.

Most companies will request references to be submitted in writing, either in the form of an 'open' unstructured letter or by use of a standard form. Requesting written references provides referees with more time to reflect on the questions and the wording of answers. It is important that any reference request is marked 'private and confidential' for the attention of the named referee.

Case law has resulted in a cautious approach from people giving references. All data given in a reference should be based on fact or capable of independent verification. As a guide, references should be fair, accurate and not give a misleading overall impression of the employee.

Medical requirements

Any particular physical or medical requirement should be made clear in the job advertisement or other recruitment literature. There will be different rules and laws in each country. Only essential medical issues should be discussed at this stage, such as requiring specialist equipment etc.

Employment offer

The selection processes should be based on a candidate's ability to do the job, ability to make a contribution to the organization's effectiveness and their potential for development.

Offers of employment should always be made in writing. But it is important to be aware that a verbal offer of employment made in an interview is as legally binding as a letter in the UK and possibly other countries. The recruitment process should be documented accurately, with access limited to recruitment staff as there are data protection issues. Unsuccessful candidates should be notified promptly in writing and if possible given feedback, including any psychometric test results.

If you have applied for a job and have not received any feedback then ask for it so you can possibly learn from it.

Onboarding programme and standard operating procedures

Cultivate great relationships with new team members. Building and fostering an open, honest, and respectful relationship with everyone on your team is critical to keeping them motivated to stay with your company.

You should have a structured onboarding programme in place that should be creative, engaging and fun, and do the job of reinforcing for people that they made the right choice. Make people feel warm and welcome from the first few seconds – remember first impressions are made in seconds and take weeks or months to change, so make the right first impression of both yourself and the organization.

Create an interesting standard operating procedure (SOP) binder which will be a physical binder as well as online, preferably on your intranet. That will have in it everything new recruits will require to enable them to do the job effectively, including a contents page so they can easily find what they need.

You can include standard organizational procedures: for example, how to claim expenses, how to set up Teams, Zoom, Skype video calls in different formats for different purposes for different amounts of attendees, all relevant telephone numbers, how to request IT help, information on how to order audiovisual equipment, stationery and catering, and the policies and procedures on how to book travel, as well as everything an assistant will need in your organization to help them do their job effectively.

You could include actual copies of forms required to do the job or screen prints of intranet instruction etc. The disaster recovery programme may also be included as well as a list of the official 'First-aiders' for the office and where they sit and their telephone numbers. You may want to include wellness and health and safety information such as ergonomic exercises you can do at your desk, mindfulness exercises and how to assess your desk for ergonomics, particularly when working remotely.

Include downloadable appendices from my website (www.suefrance.com) as well as from *The Definitive Personal Assistant & Secretarial Handbook*, 3rd edition, for example Appendix 3 'Personal development plan' which also contains a SWOT analysis and Appendix 11 on 'Event management'.

Make sure it is available in digital as well as print format.

Highly confidential information should not be contained within the SOP but must be stored securely. This includes information such as passwords and bank details etc.

The office based onboarding programme should include people sitting with the new recruit to go through different procedures so that they are not left simply to read the SOP for themselves. The SOP is there for reference later. The more people included in the onboarding the better so the recruit meets different people on a more personal basis and knows who are the 'experts' in each area. Below are some action points:

Put some thought and effort into trying to make recruits feel welcome and take them around for formal introductions to the different people and departments that they will be interacting with. You could perhaps hold a complimentary lunch for them to introduce them to their work colleagues/ peers in a social setting. When working remotely, introductions can still be made and virtual lunches can still be had via video conferencing. You could even have a meal sent to the new candidate to make them feel welcome.

At the beginning of team meeting where the new employee is joining for the first time, each attendee should introduce themselves and say a bit about themselves, what their role is and how they may help the new employee, eg being the person to go to for budgets or to learn about expenses.

The internal monthly assistant networking meeting, whether in office or remote, could be used to introduce the new assistant to each member and each of them say what their speciality is and how can they help, eg an expert in Excel spreadsheets or PowerPoint or the organization's systems etc.

The new assistant could be paired up with a 'buddy' whom they can contact whenever they have a question and the buddy can teach them different procedures etc. Remember that people can only retain so much information in one go. It may be worth spreading out the onboarding period over a week or two so they can digest it piece by piece. They of course should have their notepads, digital pads or voice notes apps with them at all times and note everything down that they feel they need to remember (unless it is already in the SOP).

Having an assigned 'buddy' is really useful especially when they are doing a similar role. It is also useful for the buddy to practise coaching skills and it is a way of making people's jobs more interesting and another useful addition for their résumé.

Make sure recruits understand the ethos and style of the company; to help them feel that they made the right decision and to help them settle in quickly and efficiently so that they start their new job committed, engaged and productive.

Most people start a new job excited and filled with anticipation and also have a natural feeling of anxiety about what's in store for them. Let them know what the company expects of them and find out what their expectations are. Be flexible, have fun and instil loyalty from the beginning because a great onboarding experience actually helps with staff retention. Your aim is for recruits to begin their jobs feeling reassured, well-informed and therefore fully operational quickly and truly feeling part of an organization that they can believe in, then any difficulties that may arise later on are far easier to deal with.

Work schedule

Once new recruits are settled into the role they can create a shared document/area on an intranet specifically for the assistants to share, containing the procedures and processes that they perform (which will be much more detailed than your official job description and different from the SOP in that it will be personalized to their particular role working with individual managers). The 'work schedule' could be kept in the SOP binder and may even be inherited from the previous employee, although if you are starting in a new role you should make the position your own, and in some cases change some procedures with the agreement of your manager. The best way to create a work schedule is to track your work as you do it; this will be on an ongoing basis so you will need to update it often to begin with.

It should include exactly what you do on a daily, weekly and yearly basis so that if you are not able to work, for any reason, especially if it is an unexpected absence, anyone could access your work schedule and be able to at least conduct the fundamental duties of your role to cover your absence effectively. It could include templates and forms, and screen prints to explain procedures and processes. It should include duties such as how your various bosses (if you work for more than one) prefer to receive their telephone messages, emails, post, how to access their calendar/emails, information on recurring meetings, how you deal with reminder systems and important telephone numbers. It can include reminders for daily duties and how often you have face-to-face and/or virtual meetings to catch up on the day's work etc. It could also include duties in your role as minute taker, team leader, project leader and so on, and everything else to help the person standing in for you to be able to do your job effectively in your absence. No one should be 'precious' about their role, and the best proactive assistants are those who share information and have contingencies in place to make sure the 'office' continues to run smoothly and effectively even when they are not there. It is also useful to train people up within your area who can cover for you when not there so that when you want to take annual leave or attend conferences webninars, and training courses, there will be no problem and nothing to stop you.

A work schedule is also useful to let your boss(es) know exactly what you do especially when it comes round to appraisal time. You may even want to ask your boss(es) whether there is anything that they would like to be included in either the work schedule or the SOP and they may even use it as a reference themselves.

The work schedule and the SOP are always work-in-progress being continually updated with new information. They are for you to use as much as for those who cover you to use, particularly for the things that you do not do regularly as they act as a reference, and checklists will be key to make sure all procedures are followed correctly.

Performance management

Performance management should be strategic and integrated – it should link various aspects of the business, people management, individuals and teams. As people are the greatest creators of value in organizations, it follows that excellent performance management is critical for an organization's success. Employees need to understand what's expected of them, have the necessary skills, resources, support, motivation and take ownership and be accountable to achieve those goals. Performance management aims to monitor, maintain and improve employee performance in line with an organization's objectives.

Performance management should incorporate:

- **Performance improvement**: throughout the organization, in respect of individual, team and organizational effectiveness.

- **Development**: unless there is continuous development of individuals and teams, performance will not improve.

- **Managing behaviour**: ensuring that individuals are encouraged to behave in a way that allows and fosters better working relationships.

It is also about ensuring that managers themselves are aware of the impact of their own behaviour on the people they manage and are encouraged to identify and exhibit positive behaviours.

Performance management is about establishing a culture in which individuals and groups take responsibility for the continuous improvement of business processes and of their own skills, behaviour and contributions. It is about sharing expectations. Managers can clarify what they expect individuals and teams to do; likewise individuals and teams can communicate their expectations of how they should be managed and what they need to do their jobs. It follows that performance management is about interrelationships and about improving the quality of all relationships and is therefore a joint process. It is also about planning – defining expectations expressed as objectives and in business plans – and about measurement. It is a continuous process operating as a continuous cycle.

Performance management should concern two major areas of measurement: performance and potential (ie what would be an employee's future performance, given the proper development skills and increased responsibility). All critical skills and learning processes should have success criteria and competencies against which employees should be measured.

When people are well managed they feel aligned, committed, on board and motivated. Their needs and wants are considered and their contributions are acknowledged. It really does help performance management if people know when there is a problem or difficulty at the time it occurs and not six months down the line at an official appraisal meeting. There should be no 'surprises' in such meetings as all problems should have been dealt with.

There is a mishmash of performance management systems and not one way suits all organizations. Each organization needs to find the right fit for them and whether they use a digital management systems or not may depend on the type and size of the organization but with more remote workers coming onboard, digitization is the way to go.

Some organizations have done away with annual appraisals completely and replaced them with regular agile appraisals or 'check-ins' or ongoing 'intelligent conversations'. My personal preference would be to have two formal, bi-annual appraisal reviews: one would be a 360 degree appraisal where everyone is appraised by their boss, their peers and the teams they lead; that appraisal would be used for calculating salary raises; and the other for discussing and organizing learning and development interventions on an individual basis so the budget can be set for the year. I would also hold semi-formal mandatory monthly performance check-ins and more when needed as situations arise. The check-ins need to work both ways so each person is able to feedback to the other no matter their position in the organization. There should also be the daily (if possible) or at the very least weekly boss/assistant catch up meetings for the day-to-day scheduling of work and priorities.

Day-to-day performance management involves dealing with people's confidence and morale and the feelings that go with that. Dealing with difficult issues requires a confidence in your own ability to handle anything that may come up.

Diagnosing poor performance

Before you can fix poor performance, you have to understand its cause. Does it come from lack of ability or low motivation? You can read more about motivation in Chapter 2.

There are five main ways to overcome performance problems associated with a lack of ability. Consider using them in this sequence, which starts with the least intrusive:

1 **Resources:** If an employee lacks time, money, personnel, or supplies to complete a task, they won't be able to complete it, no matter how much they want to. The employee should be reminded, however, that part of their responsibility is to take ownership and flag the problem up as soon as they realize there is a problem.

Retrain: Sometimes performance problems are due to a lack of skills required. Perhaps they took on a role before they were ready or have been given some new responsibilities. Provide additional training where appropriate including courses, webinars, elearning, mentoring, coaching etc. Given the pace of change, especially in technology, it's easy for people's skills to fall behind. Consider the many different methods of learning, including those which can be no or low cost. Good organizations sometimes help and encourage learning and development by offering free or subsidized college or university courses with the stipulation that people's new skills are to be used for the organization.

2 **Refit:** First consider expectations and if no clear parameters for a project have been set, or if the employee has misunderstood them, go over project goals and deliverables again and see if you can help clear up any confusion or miscommunication. If that does not work then consider refitting the job to the person including courses, webinars, elearning, mentoring, coaching etc. Are there parts of the job that can be reassigned? Have they been overloaded with additional people to look after when they already had a full workoad? This may involve rearranging the jobs of other people. Your goal is to retain the employee, meet operational needs, and provide meaningful and rewarding work to everyone involved.

3 **Reassign:** When refitting the job doesn't turn the situation around, look at reassigning the individual. Typical job reassignments may decrease the demands of the role by reducing the need, for example, of responsibility or technical knowledge or reducing how many people they are working for. Make sure the reassigned job is still motivating, challenging and stimulating. To ensure that this strategy is successful, demotion should never be used as punishment. It is simply that the person lacks the skills for the position or has been given too many people to work for and therefore cannot perform adequately to meet everyone's requirements.

4 **Release:** As a final option for lack of ability, you may need to let the employee go. Sometimes there are no opportunities for reassignment, and refitting isn't appropriate for the organization. In these cases, the best solution for everyone involved is for the employee to find other work.

You may need to consider contractual terms and restrictions; however, in the long run, this may be the best decision for your whole team. It may well be the conclusion that the individual has come to as well.

Giving and receiving effective feedback

Definition of feedback: Any verbal or written information received about prior behaviour. It can be about past behaviour deemed to be wrong in some way or it can be about things we have done well and are praise for.

Perceived definition of feedforward (an alternative word to use to 'feedback'): Any verbal or written information received about prior behaviour with a view to focusing on the other person's development for the future.

Whether you choose to call it feedback or feedforward, and whether it is from colleagues, friends or family, it's about understanding the effect past behaviour had as well as focusing on how to do things differently, improve and move forward in both personal and professional lives.

Only talking about what went wrong does not help us improve for the following reasons:

- **It shuts down the thinking, rational, decision-making conscious part of our brain**
  When we get negative feedback about something that we can't change or control (we can't change the past), we release the stress hormone cortisol, which triggers our threat response; the amygdala flares up and we go on the defensive and we are prevented from using our thinking, creative, decision making, rational part of our brain. We are then only working with our subconscious reactive part of the brain.

- **Feedback during performance management appraisals tends to focus primarily on ratings and not on development**
  When we give feedback we often overlook the essential goal of feedback which is to create a positive and lasting improvement.

- **It reinforces the negative**
  When we hear negative feedback that is what we ruminate on and remember for longer. We cannot change what has happened in the past and we therefore feel helpless, possibly regret, guilt and even embarrassment and we feel there is nothing we can do now because it has already been done! We forget about looking forward to the future and committing ourselves to improvement, we tend to hold onto this debilitating view of who we were and are, instead of focusing on who we can become!

Feedback/feedforward should always be given about someone's behaviour and not their personality, therefore avoid saying 'you are…' or 'you were…'. Individuals can accept feedback better when it is about something they said or did, ie an action or behaviour. Always give an example of their behaviour so they can relate to your comments.

Here is a quick and easy model to help you give constructive feedback/feedforward.

'BOOST' Model:

Balanced: Address both positive and developmental aspects not just one or the other. Be sincere and empathetic – people need direction and we need to preserve our relationships. When we focus on what we can do differently it supports a growth mindset and behaviour change.

Observed: You must always base your feedback on what you have observed, rather than on what you think about it or your feelings about an issue. It should be first hand observations, ie not reports from others.

Objective: When giving feedback, don't refer to the personality of the receiver but only the actions and behaviours.

Specific: Make sure that you back up your comments with specific examples of the observed behaviour and not just vague statements.

Timely: Always endeavour to give your feedback as soon as possible after the activity. Doing this ensures that you capture the observed action(s) as accurately as possible.

Feedback/feedforward is best received when a person asks for it

Feedback expands your understanding of your personal impact beyond your own point of view. We cannot always see ourselves as others see us. Feedback is an essential component in our personal and professional development. It gives insight into ourselves that we may not be aware of.

When asking for feedback you may want to give them time to think about it. This way their feedback is well-considered and measured.

Remember to thank a person for both positive and/or negative feedback as it is not easy to give and expressing gratitude will help people to do more of it.

Individuals benefit from having a reliable and robust feedback model to understand and follow so I am introducing you to Viktor Cessan's EPIQ Feedback Model.

The EPIQ Feedback Model including The Four Intentions Model by Viktor Cessan

This is my interpretation of Viktor Cessan's EPIQ Feedback Model.

The EPIQ Feedback Model includes four primary dimensions to help you craft and deliver effective feedback: **Intention, Position, Quality and Empathy**.

Intention

Before you start giving feedback you need to understand your intention and purpose for the feedback and then be able to communicate it. You need to know what you want to say and why you want to say it.

The Four Intentions Model

Most feedback has one of four intentions:

1 **Improving performance** – This is the intention to help someone master their craft or profession. It has nothing to do with the relationship or helping someone learn about themself. The focus is the other person's performance and results. 'Critiquing' without considering all the components of the EPIQ Feedback Model can often turn into criticism which harms performance and the relationship. Truly great feedback gets the message across while keeping the relationship and morale in tact.

2 **Develop the relationship** – This is the intention to improve collaboration and the relationship. The focus is on how someone's behaviour affected your relationship with them. This type of feedback is when you say: 'When you…, I felt…, I wish you would…'.

3 **Raise self awareness** – This is the intention to help someone learn about their personality and cognitive abilities such as their reaction to stress, thought patterns, emotions, etc. Be careful when giving this type of feedback as we don't know what a person may discover about themselves and unless you are a trained therapist, you could do harm.

4 **Boosting and energizing people** (confidence, self-esteem, inspiration, motivation) is all about showing appreciation. There's no hidden agenda

or wish for change to happen with this kind of feedback. It's purely used to show someone that you appreciate them or want to encourage them. Feedback with this intention sounds something like 'Thank you for...' or 'I appreciate ...'.

You may have multiple intentions within the same feedback session so pick one to focus on at a time in order of how important each intention is to you.

Your ability to clearly communicate your intentions has a huge impact on the outcome.

Questions to ask yourself regarding your **intention**:

1 Which of the Four Intentions is your intention here?

2 Why do you want to give feedback?

3 What do you hope to achieve with your feedback?

4 If your feedback were to be successfully delivered and received, what would you like to see happen?

5 For who's sake are you considering offering feedback?

Position

Position consists of **power dynamics, permission**, and the strength of the **relationship**.

1 **Power dynamics** are *always* at play and especially when giving or receiving feedback. Our self-esteem and backgrounds predispose us to have the need to feel either superior, inferior, or equal to our peers. The preference toward superior, inferior, or equal power dynamics differs across cultures and individuals, so it's important to be aware of the power dynamics that could be at play when formulating your feedback. Whenever we want to offer someone feedback, we risk challenging the power dynamics, so it's important to consider how your feedback may affect that dynamic. When feedback does challenge the dynamics the receiver is more likely to go into defensive mode.

2 **Permission** – it's important to ask for explicit **permission** before you offer someone feedback to make sure you get started down the right path towards effective feedback. Asking for permission sets expectations and creates psychological safety where both of you are more comfortable speaking openly.

Depending on the intention you have, you need to ask for permission in different ways. If your feedback centres on helping someone increase their performance, you might ask 'I have made an observation that I think will be helpful to you, may I share it with you? Or you could ask 'May I offer you some advice?'

If your feedback relates to developing the relationship, you might ask 'May I offer you feedback about our relationship?', or, 'May I offer you feedback about how your behaviour in our latest meeting affected our relationship?' If your feedback is related to boosting someone, you could ask 'May I offer you some encouragement or appreciation?'

Effective feedback takes into consideration the receiver's openness to new information and how it is given, in order not to put them on the defensive or close up.

Questions to ask yourself regarding your **position**:

- Does the other person expect feedback from you, and, if yes, what type of feedback?
- How are you planning on getting permission to give feedback?
- How are you planning on starting the feedback discussion?
- How might this feedback affect your power dynamics/status?

3 **Relationship** is comprised of **expectations** and **trust**. When the expectations of the feedback giver and receiver do not match, the likelihood of misunderstandings and defensive behaviours increase. If you, for example, **expect** your peers to boost you but they continue to give you advice or critique you, eventually you're bound to clash.

Trust is about considering whether or not you have the necessary trust built up to have the conversation you plan to. If they trust you, they are more likely to listen and act but if they don't trust you the feedback will not be effective.

Quality

Quality can be broken down into **clarity, format,** and **purity**

1 **Clarity** comes from making sure the other person fully understands your message and meaning. For some, this comes from giving more context, and for others, it requires making the feedback more concrete and concise. Without clarity, you dilute your message and the meaning can change.

2 Format is about matching the feedback format to the intentions. What's most effective will come back to your intention. If you want to improve your relationship with someone then use relationship feedback.

3 It's also important to note that 'feedback' has many meanings and that there may be cultural elements at play so explore whether you have the same view on what feedback is.

4 Purity is about your ability to distinguish between fact and interpretation. Keeping the two separate is crucial for ensuring that your feedback is real feedback. It's easy to blur the lines between what actually happens and how we interpret something. For example, if I'm five minutes late to a meeting, we can all agree I was five minutes late. But do we all place the same meaning on it? Some may perceive me as lazy or disrespectful. Others may think I am overcommitted and unorganized. When these people then find out that I was early for the meeting but the cables in the room didn't work so I went to fix them, they may see me in a different light. Effective feedback starts with being able to distinguish between what happened and what we've interpreted.

The better we are at separating this type of 'intake' from the inter-pretation, the purer and more effective our feedback becomes.

Questions to ask yourself regarding **quality**:

- Replay the situation you want to base your feedback on. What objectively happened, ie what was visible to anyone looking, and what was your interpretation?
- If someone else observed the situation, what would they see?
- What are two other ways you can interpret the event/behaviour/situation?
- What format best fits your intention?

Empathy

Empathy – To give great feedback, you need to have at least some empathy towards the person you want to offer your opinions. There are three types of empathy: **emotional, cognitive,** and **perspective**

Emotional empathy is when you feel and exhibit the same feelings as your co-worker/friend when they are telling you about how they feel. You feel what they feel.

Cognitive empathy is understanding how the other person is reasoning and thinking about a situation, you understand why the feel they way they do.

Perspective empathy is about understanding how those feelings belong to your co-worker/friend and not you. Even if you can relate to and experience the same feelings, you understand they are their feelings about a situation.

Before you offer someone feedback, it's important to self-assess whether or not you have thought things through from an empathy standpoint. When you don't access your empathy towards a person, it increases the chances that you design feedback that will be perceived as blunt or disrespectful. This can make the conversation feel unsafe for the receiver, who will go into defensive mode, and prevent you from delivering effective feedback.

Be aware of which type of empathy you have for the other person. If you feel emotional empathy but you're unable to distinguish between your feelings and the other person's feelings, their reality may become yours. This may lead you to avoid offering feedback. Not being able to distinguish between feelings may also lead to the feedback not being about the other person but being about you.

Questions to ask yourself regarding **empathy**:

1 Put yourself in the other person's shoes. What do you think was going through their mind at the time?

2 What do you think the other person's goal was?

3 What would make you behave that way?

4 How do you think the other person was feeling?

5 Think back to a time when you felt that way. What was going through your mind at the time?

6 What were you feeling in that situation?

7 What type or types of empathy (emotional, cognitive, perspective) do you have towards the other person?

8 What type or types haven't you considered?

Feedback/feedforward conclusion

When an organization fosters psychological safety then asking for feedback and giving feedback could become the norm, it becomes less of a negative event and links to a growth mindset culture. It is better to ask for feedback than to be given unsolicited feedback. The more we practise giving feedback/feedforward the easier it becomes and the better we get at it. When done well, using emotional intelligence, feedback/feedforward promotes learning, development, confidence; improves engagement and working relationships. It gives rise to change, fuels growth and gives people a sense of purpose and looking forward. If we can create a culture of asking for, giving and receiving effective feedback/feedforward, organizations would be better places to work and we would all be better people.

The World Administrators Alliance

The World Administrators Alliance is a non-profit trade association, representing administrative associations, networks, professionals and industry partners across the globe. The aims of the World Administrators Alliance are to guide, influence, develop and elevate the administrative profession and to have one voice. They have developed a generic Skills Matrix for different levels of experience of assistants which you will find below as a guide to help you with your career.

Skills Matrix

The Skills Matrix does not specify job titles or job descriptions, as many organizations already have their own internal frameworks and sector specific duties for their administrators. Nor does it include recommendations for remuneration because this will vary dependent on geography and sector. However, it does form a basis for much-needed discussion on all these areas within individual organizations.

It is assumed that each higher level includes the skills of the previous level(s). So, for example, the skills listed in Level 3 are in addition to those in Levels 1 and 2.

Figure 5.1 Global Skills Matrix

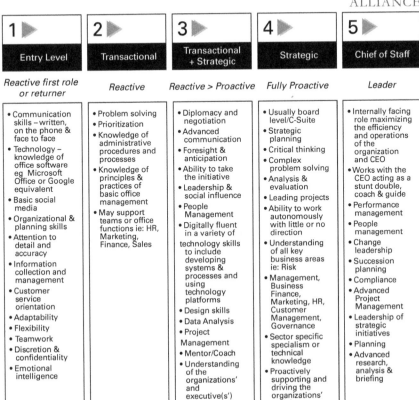

SOURCE World Administrators Alliance, 2021

Task Matrix

The Skills Matrix should be used in conjunction with the Tasks Matrix. It should be noted that this is not an exhaustive list of tasks. It is purely a guide to provide a basis for discussion when creating job descriptions and career plans.

It is assumed that each higher level includes the tasks of the previous level(s). So, for example, the tasks listed in Level 3 are in addition to those in Levels 1 and 2.

Figure 5.2   Global Task Matrix

WORLD ADMINISTRATORS
ALLIANCE

1 ▶	2 ▶	3 ▶	4 ▶	5 ▶
Entry Level	Transactional	Transactional + Strategic	Strategic	Chief of Staff
Reactive first role or returner	*Reactive*	*Reactive > Proactive*	*Fully Proactive*	*Leader*
• Answering the phone to take messages or redirecting calls to appropriate colleagues • Filing • Data entry • Creating spreadsheets • Creating/ updating presentations • Producing word documents • Covering reception • Processing and directing mail and incoming packages or deliveries • Prepare outgoing mail • Monitoring stocks of office supplies (toner, stationary etc) and reporting shortages • Assisting with copying, collecting and distributing office paperwork • Booking meeting rooms	• Calendar management • Travel management • Email triage • Organizes meetings • Expenses • Minute taking • Preparing documents for meetings and business trips • Sets up conference calls/virtual meetings • Schedules own priorities • Works with realistic time estimates • Can juggle multiple tasks	• Event/meeting/ conference management • Finds ways to improve personal administrative processes • Assists project teams in timely completion • Answers basic emails on behalf of principal • Manages and maintain basic budgets • Manages a small team of transactional administrators • Mentors/coaches more junior administrators • Maintains and updates administrative and personnel databases, correspondence, supports human resource functions including managing, recording and maintaining employee leave time records • Manages multiple managers effectively • Presents at meetings • Implements or maintains a disaster recovery plan • Prepares systems to track workflow & responsibilities • Responsible for meeting administration including preparation of agenda, papers and minutes • Confidently participates in online meetings/video calls • Research & recommend suppliers • Design skills, including formatting & proof reading	• Oversees and supervises all administrative functions including training recommendation s, identifying frustrations, implementing improvements in process • Attends leadership meetings as part of the leadership team to support principal • Prepares and maintains company documents and reports • Answers complex emails on behalf of principal • Reviews and approves expense reports • Leads projects • Takes the lead in preparation of project documents, reports, brochures and budgets • Manages and coordinates employee recruitment, performance evaluation and termination processes • Prepares and maintains office procedures • Manages and maintains budgets • Responsible for governance meeting administration including preparation of agenda, papers and minutes • Research and compile basic briefing documents • Confidently analyses data	• Takes meetings on behalf of CEO • Acts as communication arm for CEO with staff • Takes over projects the CEO is too busy to do • Takes customer tours to conduct research • Works with CEO's direct reports to ensure projects are delivered on time • Challenge ideas and offer a different perspective • Prioritizes for the CEO to ensure they are working on the most important items • Helps complete priority items for the CEO • Keeps the CEO accountable for commitments • Keeps the CEO accessible and open to new ideas and proposals • Asks the right questions • Research new revenue streams/projects • Research and create complex briefing documents • Manages rhythm of the business eg recurring leadership meetings • Employee satisfaction • Prioritize across team • Reviews company processes • Explores frustrations • Recruits and hires for high level positions • Manages strategic budgeting processes

SOURCE World Administrators Alliance, 2021

Summary

Performance management, appraisals and regular check-in meetings are strategic tools to drive learning and organizational results. There is a constant pressure to improve performance as the world is changing fast and we need to be on top of our game; competition is getting stronger; technology is hurtling us along into 'smart' connected and data driven, digitization, gamification, automation, artificial intelligence, bots, virtual reality; eradicating the repetitive side to our roles and leaving humans to deep thinking, being creative, solving problems and taking action!

> **'We need to develop a future ready mindset and future proof the human skills of our roles.'**

'He who stops being better stops being good.'

OLIVER CROMWELL

Think about development and how performance can be improved. What new skills are needed for the future? What is required to adapt to any new situations? Is training, personal coaching or mentoring required? Seek practical, cost-effective solutions that will increase the performance and motivation of individuals and teams. Remember to read Chapter 2 on 'How to motivate yourself and your teams' and Chapter 6 on 'Coaching' to help you with performance management.

Performance problems need to be fully addressed and learning and development promoted as this creates a positive environment where people feel supported to maximize their potential and makes everyone feel valued.

Become proficient in giving and receiving feedback and remember to practise professional etiquette. Treat everyone with respect and dignity throughout all the processes and procedures as this is an indicator of your level of professionalism, whatever role you play.

Coaching 06

This chapter will explain coaching in detail, and provides a brief overview of mentoring and counselling. You will be able to enhance the working environment and your own self-esteem, and help others by providing encouragement, experience and expertise and promoting learning opportunities for colleagues and to realize the possibility of being coached, mentored or having counselling is a route you may like to take. I will also explain how you can use neuro-linguistic programming tools and techniques in coaching.

As a leader, assistant, colleague, even mother, father, wife, husband, daughter or son, you will have come across many times when you wish you knew the right thing to do and say in order to help someone, whether you should say something or not and whether you should be mentoring, coaching, or counselling somebody.

> Everyone has the capacity to change. Their ability to learn and change is rarely a function of capacity, but of choice. The coach helps the learner recognize the choices they have.

You will learn the differences between mentoring, counselling and coaching; however the crucial point is that once you have understood the benefits of each you have to decide which is right for you both for giving and receiving. To explore your reasons for wanting to help others in these areas and whether you want to take this type of commitment further, ask yourself the following questions:

- Do you want to contribute to other people's growth and success?
- Do you want to share your knowledge and experience with others?
- Do you enjoy encouraging and motivating others?
- Are you comfortable asking challenging questions?
- What type of person do you ideally want to mentor/train/coach or counsel? Can you describe the professional and personal qualities of this

person? Do you want someone from the same profession or the same career path as you?

- In what areas are you willing to help? Are there any areas that you don't want to go near?
- How will helping others contribute toward your own career goals?
- How will it add to your sense of contribution and community?
- Are you prepared to invest your time on a regular basis?

Clarifying your reasons and motivations for becoming a mentor/coach and/or counsellor will help you assess your compatibility with a potential mentee/coachee.

Helping others can be a rewarding experience for you, both personally and professionally. You can improve your leadership and communication skills, learn new perspectives and ways of thinking, raise your profile, advance your career and gain a great sense of personal satisfaction.

Mentoring

Widely used in organizations, mentoring provides a mechanism by which experienced managers can pass on their wisdom – helping to shape their mentee's values and beliefs in a positive way. This is in contrast to coaching and counselling, where the emphasis is on getting people to come up with their own solutions. Mentors often give advice and guidance.

Mentoring is an essential leadership skill. In addition to managing and motivating people, it's also important that you can help others learn, grow and become more effective in their jobs.

You may not only want to be a mentor but you might also like to have a mentor yourself, so you need to know which kind of mentor you prefer. Having a mentor will also help you be a better mentor to others as you will have a better understanding of being a mentee.

Mentors help you advance in work and life, and you should be proactive and seek out people who can help you. The first step is to figure out which mentor will best meet your needs:

- The **co-mentor** can be a colleague or a friend.
- The **remote mentor** is someone outside your organization or office who can offer objective advice. You may need a remote mentor if you are looking for a fresh perspective and you've already exhausted closer resources.

- The **distant mentor** does not even need to know s/he is your mentor! Distant mentors are people who stand out from the crowd from any walk of life. They will be someone you admire even from afar, someone with integrity and who demonstrates very specific attitudes that you wish to emulate.

Counselling

Counsellors, like coaches, create a space in which the coachees can talk about their issues. The key difference is that counselling deals primarily with helping people overcome problems whereas coaching is concerned with enhancing performance. Counselling generally tends to focus on the past in its search for reasons for why we behave the way we do. The goal is to assist people in understanding the root cause of long-standing issues. Counsellors might use 'why' questions such as 'Why do you keep doing that?' whereas coaches more often ask 'what' questions such as 'What would you like to do instead?'

In comparing coaching and counselling, the former might be seen as solution focused and action orientated, while counselling is more meaning based. Coaching addresses aspirations, objectives and tasks, while counselling focuses more on feelings. Coaching tends to be more structured while counselling can have a more free-form approach. Coaching puts greater emphasis on gaining clarity about what people want and how to achieve it, whereas counselling aims to help people to understand themselves better.

Coaching

A coach helps people to perform better than they are currently doing and develops their skills and confidence over a period of time. Coaches work in the certain belief that people have vast reserves of potential that are rarely used and that it is the coach's job to draw it out.

Whether you are a sports coach, life coach or business coach, the role is very similar. Coaches are committed to their individual coachees: they concentrate on improving performance without imposing limits on the performance of individuals or teams; patiently work with individuals on the details of their performance; help to reduce stress; offer a unique perspective to solving complex problems; stand back and let others take the credit; and continuously learn from situations and people.

In each situation a coach has the opportunity to learn and grow as well as the coachee as every situation will have its own unique scenarios, problems, quirks and demands. Coaches need to be open minded and agile as what worked in one situation may not work in another. Coaches will not only learn from their experiences of coaching others but will need to be agile in their approach to their own self-development and continual learning by reading, attending courses, belonging to a professional coaching institution and ideally being a certified coach. They need to continually upskill in areas they may not be familiar with, such as technology and neuroscience (how the brain works). New discoveries, ideas, tactics and scientific research are being developed all the time so keeping updated in soft as well as hard skills is important. A coach with laser sharp interpersonal skills and deep expertise can make a difference to people's lives.

Coaching can take place informally on an ad hoc basis or formally, for example at a specific scheduled appointment agreed by both parties.

There are many reasons for coaching to take place:

- Your advice is sought by others.
- Someone tells you they can't do a particular job.
- Your opinion is asked or a decision is required.
- You see a job or task can be done in a better, cheaper or quicker way.
- Mistakes are made.
- Extra benefit as part of rewards/benefit package.
- We see a talent in them and want to develop them.
- Indefinite ongoing coaching to get things off your chest.
- As part of a culture change programme.
- Coaching to change mindsets. For example: it might be to increase diversity and inclusion in an organization – coaching is much more effective than simply writing a new policy!

In fact in any situation where individuals are required to raise their current levels of skills, abilities and overall performance, coaching can be appropriate. It is important to have a structure that follows logical steps and use coaching models that suit you and your coachee's situation.

Coaching structure: 'ARE WE READY?'

Agreement	Agreement for the confidential coaching to take place and to foster a growth mindset. Awareness of the current situation and purpose for the coaching with a unique approach in every situation.
Reflection	Reflection, realization and connecting the dots through provocative questioning and observation.
Empower	Empower and inspire creative, goal-oriented solutions, focusing on the possibilities and the positives, using positive psychology to disperse mental roadblocks and visualizing the future.
Way forward	Clarification of decisions made and create an action plan. The coach instils confidence and motivation in the coachee to commit to taking decisive action.
Engage in feedback	Follow up and discover the results of the coaching; what transformations have taken place and any lessons learned. Discuss what future coaching may be required. (See Chapter 5 on 'Employee experience from recruitment to performance' for detailed information on giving and receiving feedback.)
Ready	Both coachee and coach need to be **ready** to foster a strong relationship, connecting on a deep level of trust and psychological safety; to remain open minded and flexible throughout the process; to plan and schedule the sessions and be **ready** to face some hard challenges; be creative, curious and collaborative, helping the coachee to realize Aha! moments and then be **ready** to take action!

Coaching upwards

There is often a mindset that the boss knows best, but in today's fast changing world, with flatter structures, remote working and cross-functional working, this isn't always the case. Individuals need to break this mindset and view their bosses differently. They need help, support and to be challenged just as much as everybody else. To coach upwards you will need all the skills described below, and in particular: know what it is that you want to achieve and why; use your knowledge of the individual and your personal judgement of how best to approach them; make sure that they have confidence in you as a credible person and remember to choose your moment, as timing is very important.

Skills required to be an effective coach are:

- Excellent interpersonal skills in the areas of building rapport, asking questions to gain information, listening, summarizing, giving and receiving feedback, persuading, influencing and encouraging others.
- Observation skills are key for coaches as they need to be able to spot what's happening and what's not happening.
- They help people change their negative beliefs; for example believing they 'can't...' limits their ability to perform (beliefs strengthen and uphold values or what is important to people).
- They think on their feet and tackle situations creatively.
- They have empathy – seeing things from others' point of view.
- They are confident in their own abilities and at the same time know their limits.
- They are patient and willing to make time for people.
- They have sensitivity, especially knowing when to step in and when to be quiet.
- They have a sense of humour.
- They are able to keep confidentiality.
- They must be able to show that they genuinely care about the best interests of others. The best way to radiate concern is to ask lots of questions, to engage others rather than lecture them.
- Curiosity – the best coaches are superb listeners and absorb whatever they hear. By remaining accessible, genial and supportive, such coaches motivate by offering a safe, non-judgemental sounding board.
- They help others paint a picture of a higher level of performance.
- Highly effective team facilitators and team coaches understand what drives human behaviour.
- They have the ability to plan what they are going to do as far as they can.

> Understanding others does not mean that you have to agree with them.

Alternatives to face-to-face coaching

Face-to-face sessions are preferable as the most effective way to conduct coaching sessions, because studying body language and facial expressions is extremely important in communication and it's easier to build relationships. However, time available, geographical location and having a remote work-force may mean that you have to conduct some or all coaching sessions virtually or by phone. The technologies are there so put them to good use. It can help you if you have already met face-to-face first, but it's not essential.

A coach needs the hard skill set of understanding different technology and methods they can use such as online video conferencing, podcasts and webinars. Virtual coaching can be carried out by such tools as Skype, Google Hangouts, FaceTime, Zoom and many others. It not only allows flexibility and variety but global reach as well. The human element is critical and tech-nology cannot replace the necessity to build relationships and it is important that you can see each other and have your cameras on to get the full benefit of coaching and having the ability to see reactions, facial expressions and body language. A hybrid mix of face-to-face, video and telephone is a great way to build your relationships, keeping in touch as often as necessary and you can even provide podcasts as a way of reminding them of their commit-ments, motivating them and for deeper learning. You may even want to record sessions so they can act as reminders for the coachee. Recorded ses-sions may also help the coach to critique themselves, reflect and learn. Of course confidentiality is paramount and all precautions for privacy, safety and agreements with the coach should be decided upon and set out in the coach/coachee contract, whether you choose a formal written contract or informal verbal contract.

When using video conferencing, you can make the session more interest-ing by using tools such as videos and PowerPoint to help illustrate points. Using visuals of different coaching models and images may be useful depend-ing on your coaching style and the requirements of each session.

Telephone coaching

You may be pleasantly surprised how focused and effective telephone coach-ing can be.

When you cannot see the person, the key challenge is in picking up on the nuances in the absence of visual communication. Effective coaching is dependent on proper engagement and rapport, and this is a lot harder to achieve when we can't actually see the other person. More summarizing and checking understanding can counteract this. For example, when you ask a person a question that requires a degree of reflection and you are in the same room as them, you can tell whether they are actually thinking and considering their response. On the phone, you have to listen more intently for tone of voice, volume, pauses and energy in the conversation. The skill is in understanding the silences – is the pause a sign that the coachee is reflecting, or is s/he struggling? You will begin to understand these types of things the more you coach over the phone. You should give particular attention to the words you choose to use and your tone of voice. You should listen to people's pitch, pace and choice of words and maintain relationships by matching them.

Practical things are important too, like the quality of the telephone line and using a headset so you are not restricted by the telephone or mobile. Make sure you're not going to be interrupted by visitors; get yourself a supply of drinks (remember to visit the bathroom before you start); have your phone on hands-free, so you can write notes. It could be helpful to first ask coachees about their own environment so you can get a picture of where they are; imagine yourself in that environment with them.

An advantage of telephone coaching would be that you could have reference material around you; this can be helpful, especially when you are just starting coaching. Another benefit can be a lessening of inhibitions if the coachee is not having to watch your body language too.

You should have an agenda and share it with the coachee. It is also worth considering recording the calls and possibly providing a transcript that can be sent as an audio file and a PDF transcription.

Whilst on the phone, you should focus and expect the other person to do the same. Concentrate purely on the conversation and don't be tempted to do anything else whilst on the phone, like checking emails or eating etc. Treat the telephone meeting just as you would treat a face-to-face meeting.

> Coaching is unlocking people's potential to maximize their own performance.
> It is more often helping them to learn rather than teaching them.
>
> John Whitmore, author of the GROW Model

One proven approach that helps with coaching is the GROW Model. GROW is an acronym standing for Goal – Reality – Options – Will. The model is a simple yet powerful framework for structuring a coaching or mentoring session.

The GROW Model – for solving problems and achieving goals

The power of GROW is that it is easily understood, straightforward to apply and very thorough, and as a behavioural model it is suited to the world of work. In addition, once you have an understanding of how it works, it is possible to apply it to an amazing variety of issues in a very effective way. Even complex, multifaceted problems can be tackled with GROW and it often enables individuals to make progress on issues even when they have been stuck for a long time.

The GROW Model works well because it provides a structured, effective process for goals and challenges. It enables you to break down an issue into its constituent parts. Once these are clear it becomes straightforward to develop solutions yourself, so it is likely you will be committed to carrying them through.

A useful metaphor for the GROW Model is when you plan an important overseas driving journey for a business meeting. First, you would start with a map and together with your colleague you would decide where they are going (their Goal) and establish where they currently are right now (their current Reality). Then you explore various ways (the Options) of making the journey from where they are to where they want to be. In the final step, establishing the Will, you ensure your team member is willing and committed to making the journey and is prepared for the conditions and obstacles they may meet on their way; remember – 'where there is a will – there is a way!'

In its traditional application, the GROW Model assumes that the coach is not an expert in the coachee's situation, and therefore the coach must act as an objective facilitator, helping the coachee select the best options and not offering advice or direction. However, when leaders coach their team members and they have relevant experience, expertise and often common sense, then I believe people would like to hear some practical suggestions and solutions that they can mull over and consider – or you can at least plant a seed in their mind. You then become more of a trainer or mentor. It's your job to guide the selection of options that are best for your organization and the coachee and to ignore any options that may have negative consequences.

Having said that, you must try and get the coachees to diagnose their own problem first and draw on their own resources to help themselves, as many people actually know the solution but it just needs teasing out of them. This way it becomes more of a collaboration between coach and coachees and the coachees will have more 'buy-in' to the solution if they are the ones who thought of it (or at least think they thought of it first). The approach also depends on the subject matter and whether it is something practical or personal.

You can use GROW for yourself or with the support of another person. However, working through a difficult issue with other people often helps, as they do not have the same emotional attachment that we have to our own issues.

Use the following steps to structure a GROW coaching session:

Establish the **G**oal

In order to have an effective coaching session you should have already established a rapport and built a relationship. Throughout the coaching session you should continue to mirror, match, pace and lead to maintain your rapport. Together with the coachee, you must define and agree a 'SMARTER' goal (detailed information on goal setting and how to write SMARTER goals is also in *The Personal Assistant & Secretarial Handbook*, 3rd edition and you can download a goal setting proforma with full explanation as a resource for the afore mentioned book at www.suefrance.com) or outcome to be achieved and make it inspiring and challenging. Business goals should be aligned with the organization's goals and your boss's goals. A goal that is personally framed within the organization's goals will make a difference. In doing this, it is useful to ask questions like:

- How will you know that you have achieved that goal?
- How will you know the problem is solved?

Examine current **R**eality

Then you ask the coachee to describe their current Reality – where they are at now. This is a very important step: too often, people try to solve a problem without fully considering their starting point, and often they are missing some of the information they need to solve the problem effectively. As the coachee tells you about his or her current Reality, the solution may start to emerge. The use of open-ended questions is the primary tool that enables reality to be understood. The intention is to help the coachee to probe into things, see things clearly and specifically, clarifying meaning, strip away assumptions and judgements, use precise language and provide real-world examples.

The most important condition for the most effective coaching question are:

- It moves the coachee forward.
- It has a future focus.
- It gets to the heart of the issue.
- It deepens the coachee's understanding.
- It's personal – it's all about them.
- It's expressed clearly without ambiguity.

Useful coaching questions include:

- What, who, when, how often?
- What is happening now?
- What is the effect or result of that?

Explore the options

Once the coachee has explored the current Reality in rich detail, it's time to explore what is possible; your role is to help the coachee to generate and discuss as many options as possible to move forward and help solve the problem. This is a natural process of self-discovery and in most cases they will amaze you by their capability of seeing their way through issues. Let them talk as much as they want to and only add suggestions if appropriate. Start by asking open-ended questions, remembering that they may not be coming out with lots of new ideas but instead bringing forward previous thoughts into sharper focus; then you need to discuss which are desirable and which are not. After the baseline questions, coaches can become more creative with their questioning style. At this stage coachees would probably like to hear your perspective, especially if they can't think of any more solutions or the ones they have generated are inadequate. Your aim is to flush out a variety of options to be pinned down or discarded in the 'will' phase.

Typical questions used to establish the options are:

- What are the benefits and downsides of each option?
- What if this or that constraint were removed?
- What factors will you use to weigh up the options?
- What else could you do?

Connecting the dots and finding the Aha! moments

Keep the coachee fully involved by using their knowledge and their wisdom to connect the dots by sharing observations, asking forward thinking, powerful and provocative questions whilst keeping them focused on solutions and their goal. Challenge them to stretch their thinking and give them the space to reflect to encourage new connections and possibilities where they can experience insights or Aha! moments that lead to creative actions!

> Self-discovery, self-realization and self-learning are the golden nuggets to successful coaching and achieving the Aha! moments that motivate the coachee to move forward and take action!

Establish the **W**ill and the **W**ay forward

By developing a goal, examining current reality and exploring the options, coachees will now have a good idea of how they can achieve their Goal. If they have several options that they are still considering then you can help them narrow these down by asking further questions. Ask them to describe the reason for their choice(s) of solution as it tests their thinking and provides greater clarity about the level of certainty and confidence they have in taking action. You can help them break down the action into specific steps and to seriously think about evaluating the implications of the action, its practicality, any obstacles that could arise and any support they may need. Now coachees need to commit to specific actions, writing their goals down and specifying when they will take each step, who will be involved and when they will be reviewed.

This is when taking a challenging approach can be supportive. Using a variety of closed questions and feedback can ensure that a coachee has thought of everything. In so doing, you will help them establish their will and motivation.

Useful questions:

- What could stop you moving forward?
- Will this address your goal?
- So what will you do now, and when?
- And how will you overcome it?
- How likely is this option to succeed?
- What else will you do?

A great way to practise using the model is to address your own challenges and issues. When you have a problem you can use the technique to coach yourself. By practising on your own challenges and issues, you will learn how to ask the most helpful and skilful questions. You will also be able to use the model in an unconscious-competence way (just as when you have been driving a car for years – you no longer have to think about how to do it).

The two most important skills for a coach are the ability to ask skilful questions and truly actively listen, allowing the coachee to do most of the talking. I have added a comprehensive list of coaching questions for your use in Resource 4, 'Coaching questions'. You can download this from **www.suefrance.com** under Resoures for *The Definitive Executive Assistant & Managerial Handbook* 2nd edition. Remember that silence is valuable thinking time and you don't always have to fill silence with the next question.

Coaching, however, is not just about asking questions and actively listening; it is also about summarizing what people have said, offering feedback, rephrasing, confirming, considering and sometimes getting them to reframe what they have said. Remember that coaching is always a conversation.

Active listening for coaches

Highly developed listening skills are a core requirement of effective coaches. A coach who truly listens attentively will feel tired at the end of the session because of the intensity and effort they have to put in. A coach has to listen from the perspective of the coachee and demonstrate they are listening.

> Most people do not listen with the intent to understand; they listen with the intent to reply.
>
> Stephen Covey

There are three levels of learning (also look at Chapter 9 on 'The art and science of effective negotiation' for more on questioning and active listening skills such as 'the Echo' technique):

Level 1: **Listening to speak** – Listening to your own internal voice with your own agenda and thinking what you will say to reply and so only half hearing what the coachee is saying. This is our default mode of listening so coaches have to be intentional about their listening skill set and not fall into the trap of missing key information to be able to understand the coachee's situation.

Level 2: **Listening to hear** – Focused listening with laser like attention on the coachee and being present on what's happening for them. Most of us can listen like this in situations where we are motivated to do so. You have to listen non-judgementally and with an open mind.

Level 3: **Listening to understand** – Listening to the coachee for subtle cues and the context. Be receptive for more information using all your senses, tuning into their body language, tone, pace and pitch. This high level of listening needs intentional practice to listen not only to the words they are using but what they mean. Listen for the potential, what they are being vague about, their intonation, their emphasis, their thoughts, feelings and emotions behind their words. Zone in and be present with them in their situation. The coach needs to give encouraging signals to the coachee to let them know they are listening and it's okay to carry on so they can glean as much information as possible. **Without understanding we cannot coach!**

It is important to be aware of the barriers to listening:

- we think much faster than we talk – so we often think guess what people intend to say, as they are speaking (hence people finish other people's sentences off);
- We may feel overwhelmed by the amount and complexity of the content;
- Cultural barriers;
- Physical environments and distractions;
- Mentally challenging or disagreeing with the other person;
- Making assumptions;
- Selective listening – only picking out some of what is being said as you start to form opinions.

It is recommended that you take brief notes during the conversation, with the agreement of the coachee, and complete them after the meeting.

Using different frames

Representational systems are the way that we represent experience. They are typically described as visual, auditory and kinaesthetic (feelings). Reframing can be used in different ways, depending on our preferred representational system. When coaching it is easy to pick up the coachees' representational systems from the language they use. You can read more about this in *The Personal Assistant & Secretarial Handbook*, 3rd edition. Here are some examples.

- I **see** what you mean – **visual.**
- That **sounds** about right – **auditory.**
- I **feel** unsure about that – **kinaesthetic.**

Looking for patterns and repetition of visual, auditory and kinaesthetic words, as well as context and content, helps you to select the most helpful reframing tool for the coachee. Below are some examples and how they might be used.

A person who has a preference for a 'visual' representation will have created a picture in their mind's eye of a particular experience. As a coach you can suggest that they try to make the following changes to the image they have in their mind's eye and then reflect on how this alters their experience of the situation. If it is an experience they want to feel better about then ask them to:

'Change the picture'; if it's colour then change it to black and white; if it's bright then change it to being a dull picture; 'Make the picture smaller', 'Change the frame around the picture', 'Adjust the contrast', 'Add in some humorous imagery' etc.

If it is an image and experience that you want to remember, enhance and feel good about then you can:

'Change the picture', 'Change the colour to vivid colours', 'Make it brighter', 'Make the picture larger', 'Change the frame around the picture', 'Adjust the contrast', 'Add in some humorous imagery' etc.

The new perspectives offered by these changes may influence the feelings that the coachee has about the situation. In this way a potentially daunting meeting with 'the boss', for example, can be adjusted so that it becomes a more pleasant experience or even one that the coachee looks forward to.

Reframing the internal dialogue

Our internal dialogue is the voice we hear in our heads; it can be positive or negative so when coaching you can ask coachees to think about what they are saying to themselves at certain points during the coaching session. This helps them to notice what their inner voice is saying and whether it is helping or hindering their progress. For coachees with 'auditory' preferences, you can ask them to change the negative thoughts to positive ones; ask them to try the following and reflect on how this alters their perception:

'Turn the volume up or down'; 'Add some funny music'; 'Change the pace or tone of the voice.'

As with changing the picture, this process also has an impact on the feelings about the experience.

Looking at the situation from a different perspective

We get bound up with the events, issues and concerns about how to tackle a relationship or a situation in our lives. This often leaves us trapped in a cycle of non-productive behaviour. A useful way of helping coachees to reframe these types of situation is to get them to view their experience or an event from another person's shoes, often described as being in second position or even third position. You should ask questions like: 'If you were the other person, what would you notice about your behaviour/approach/manner?' 'If you were an observer watching the event/discussion, what would you notice?' 'What would your mentor/manager/best friend/coach do in this situation?' It is also useful to ask coachees to physically sit in different seats as they do this exercise, imagining that they are someone else and truly empathizing and observing what is going on from somebody else's point of view.

The process of stepping into another's shoes can help to take the heat out of a potentially fraught situation, help the coachee to see a relationship in a different way, identify alternative ways of tackling a problem and offer a variety of different ways of responding to situations.

Support and challenge

Coaching is a combination of being supportive and challenging as it creates the best space for a coachee's high performance.

Support

1 Ensure the coachee understands it is a **confidential conversation** so they feel psychologically safe to share things, and know there is no need to be afraid of any consequences.

2 The conversation is **non-directive** because it triggers critical thinking in the mind of the coachee. It is powerful because the solutions generated are from the caochee and therefore are more likely to be followed through. They feel empowered and have full autonomy over their decisions.

3 The conversation will be **non-judgemental** – the coachee will neither be judged positively or negatively, will not be agreed with or disagreed with. The role of the coach is to help them gain clarity and facilitate their journey of self-reflection and self-revelation to help them move forward.

You could reflect their feelings with sentences like 'What I am sensing is …'.

Challenge

A coach will challenge the coachee with questions which may make them feel uncomfortable at times but when we are uncomfortable we are learning and discovering. Challenging questions results in reflective learning. You could ask questions like 'If you were able to … what would it look like? 'As you hear yourself say … what are you thinking?' 'On a scale of one to ten, how committed are you to do this?'

When a coachee has a high level of support and a high level of being challenged then they will enter into a state of flow and even though they may feel uncomfortable they know that everything will be alright and so they can be innovative and try things out and feel safe whilst doing so.

Wheel of Learning/timeline

The Wheel of Learning is an extremely powerful coaching tool for helping people see where they are at currently and where they want to be – see Figure 6.1 (which you can also download from www.suefrance.com) This particular Wheel of Learning concentrates on your work–life balance so that you can take some time out to think about yourself. It will also help you clarify priorities for goal setting. You can use Resource 5 in conjunction with Resource 8 to write down a brief description for each category as if you were feeling total satisfaction and achievement. Imagine what it would look and feel like and what you would hear if each category was marked with a 10! This downloadable resource can easily be changed to suit any adaptation of the wheel that you choose. See Resource 6, 'Blank "Wheel of Learning" – to use creatively'.

Figure 6.1 Wheel of Learning

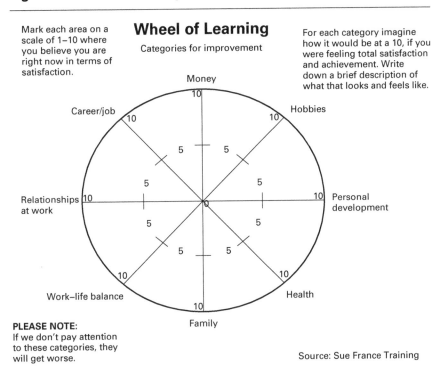

Mark each area on a scale of 1–10 where you believe you are right now in terms of satisfaction.

Wheel of Learning
Categories for improvement

For each category imagine how it would be at a 10, if you were feeling total satisfaction and achievement. Write down a brief description of what that looks and feels like.

PLEASE NOTE:
If we don't pay attention to these categories, they will get worse.

Source: Sue France Training

Instructions on how to use the Wheel of Learning tool

Think about what success feels like in the different areas (career/job, money, relationships at work, hobbies, personal development, family, work–life balance and health), then rank your level of satisfaction with each area of your life by placing a value between 1 (dissatisfied) and 10 (extremely satisfied) against each area to show how satisfied you are currently with these elements of your life. This will be portrayed by drawing a line across each segment.

An example of how the wheel may look once charted can be found in Resource 6, 'Blank "Wheel of Learning" – to use creatively'.

Studying the Wheel of Learning that you have charted, you will see where you may need to spend some time working on it to improve the situation.

Ask yourself the following questions:

- Are there any surprises for you?
- How do you feel about your life as you look at your Wheel?

- How do you currently spend time in these areas?
- How would you like to spend time in these areas?
- Which of these elements would you most like to improve?
- How could you make space for these changes?
- Can you prioritize which you will work on in order?
- Can you effect the necessary changes on your own?
- What help and cooperation from others might you need?
- What would a score of 10 look like?
- What would you need to do to make each area a score of 10?

Adapting the Wheel of Learning to suit your needs

The Wheel of Learning can be adapted and used in many different ways in coaching others and yourself. For this purpose you can use Resource 6, which is a blank Wheel of Learning that can be completed to suit your requirements, taking into consideration some of the ideas below or any ideas you can think of that suit the person you are coaching and/or for yourself.

When coaching others you may wish to collaborate with the coachee and decide on what each section should be called (ie the areas you wish to work on). Alternatively you may wish to pre-fill some of the sections and leave some blank sections for coachees to complete, thereby getting their buy-in.

The Wheel of Learning as a performance management tool

You could use the Wheel of Learning as a performance management tool and complete the sections to show how you perceive the person you are coaching/mentoring.

Alternatively you can use it in a 360° appraisal and have the boss as well as peers and anyone reporting to them/you complete a Wheel of Learning for them/you. The people you ask to complete this should be trustworthy and those whose opinions they/you value; they should know the coachee/mentee (or you) well as it can be helpful to see how others perceive you. The coachee/mentee (or you) can complete the Wheel of Learning and compare it with the ones others complete on them/you. This will give an all rounded overall view of how others perceive how you are performing and how they/

you perceive they/you are performing, which can be quite enlightening – which is why you have to trust and value the opinion of the people completing this for you. The coachee/mentee should be allowed to choose the people who complete this for them.

The sections for a performance management tool will be the skills and competencies used in your role and can be as detailed as you like, or have other Wheel of Learning exercises with 'chunked down' (detailed) sections.

For example: you could have a 'Competency Skills Wheel of Learning' with the following eight sections: leadership skills, communication skills, social media skills, stress management skills, networking skills, organizational skills, public relationship skills and technology skills etc.

Each area could be broken down, and using a blank wheel you could input the following sections for a 'Leadership Skills Wheel of Learning': Leadership could be 'chunked down' for example to: problem solving, decision making, delegating, negotiating, emotional intelligence, persuasive and influencing skills, coaching and mentoring skills and motivational skills etc.

A 'Communication Skills Wheel of Learning' could be 'chunked down' to the following skills: questioning skills, listening skills, body language skills, business writing skills, assertiveness, giving and receiving feedback skills, linguistic skills (eg NLP and visual, auditory and kinaesthetic) and presentation skills.

Again each of these areas could be further 'chunked down' in, for example, a 'Presentation Skills Wheel of Learning': understanding learning styles, research and preparation skills, continual self-development, understanding personality styles, handling difficult people skills, motivational skills, confidence skills and time management skills.

Remember: 'If you always do what you've always done, then you'll always get what you always got' and the only way to make a difference is to TAKE ACTION.

Yes you've guessed it – you can also use the Wheel of Learning to help you take action!

Action-planning Wheel of Learning

Using Resource 6 you should write a 'SMARTER' goal or required outcome at the top of the page. Then complete each section with an action that helps you achieve your goal. If you wish to create more sections then please do, as the downloadable Resource can easily be changed. You should also put a date against each action showing when it will be achieved. You can also use the sections or 'pieces of pie' to record the per cent complete for each area and date that too.

The opportunities to apply the Wheel of Learning in many different guises are immense. Be creative, find what works for you and your organization and continually review and update and most of all learn, improve and enjoy.

Measuring your coaching skills

Remember to measure your own outcomes and the success of your coaching efforts. Be in control of your own goals and don't just serve your coachees. To do this you have to be clear about what you want the coaching to achieve. This is where setting clear outcomes, at the early stage of the coaching process, is critical. Focus on what your coaching has achieved; in other words, look at the outcome or effect rather than the way that the coaching was carried out. Ask yourself what people have done differently as a result.

Summary

Coaching accelerates the individual's progress to unlock potential and maximize performance, by providing greater focus and awareness of possibilities, leading to more effective choices. Coaching concentrates on where individuals are now and what they are willing to do to get where they want to be in the future. Coaches recognize that results are a matter of the individual's intentions, choices and actions, supported by the coach's efforts and applications of coaching skills, approaches and methods. The coaching process depends on the people being coached taking responsibility for taking action and making their own decisions, not on the coach providing solutions.

Individuals who engage in a coaching relationship can expect to experience fresh perspectives on personal challenges and opportunities, enhanced thinking and decision-making skills, improved interpersonal effectiveness and increased confidence.

As a mentor, coach or counsellor, you will typically help your team members to solve problems, make better decisions and learn new skills.

Whilst formal training and certification in these skills is preferable you can develop your knowledge by reading this chapter and using the proven techniques, finding opportunities to practise and learning to trust your instinct. This will help you to become a better coach and enhance your team's performance, adding value to yourself, your boss, your colleagues and the organization. However, you must recognize your limitations and when your skill set and experience is not at a level required in certain situations, where clinical expertise is needed then you must advise and help them to get the support they need.

Find a coach for yourself as well as helping others achieve their potential, knowing that both you and they have a source of unlimited growth potential and are not just a resource to get the job done. Being coached will give you insight not only into your situation but also into coaching itself, helping to make you a better coach. Coaching others will help you to develop yourself too and at the same time enhance your self-esteem and self-confidence and have the wonderful feeling of personal satisfaction and empowerment that comes with being able to empower others.

How to communicate with different personality and behavioural styles

07

This chapter will enable you to be an effective team member, supervisor and leader. Leadership is about making informed, emotionally controlled and educated decisions. The chapter also covers how to motivate and inspire people into taking action on the decisions. This chapter will help you to understand yourself and the people you work and live with in order to effectively engage with them, build relationships and influence them. It will teach you how you to:

- interact with others for the best outcome;
- communicate effectively;
- get the best out of different types of personalities and behavioural styles.

Have you ever tried to communicate something to someone and they just don't understand what you mean?

Or perhaps you cannot understand why someone should act in a certain way or say the things they do? Some people simply understand immediately, whilst for others there can be continuous misunderstandings. Understanding different personality styles will help you communicate better but of course there are several things that can affect this, including how busy you or they are, however it does give you an advantage.

Filters and perception

We use our memory and past experiences as the filter through how we judge other people's behaviours. Our primitive reaction is to decide quickly whether someone is a friend or foe so we stereotype people, judging them by how they stand, how they dress, their hairstyle and so on. Our perception profoundly changes how we feel about people.

We need to understand why we judge and perceive others the way we do and find out why other people do and say what they do and say. We can do this by fully exploring the alternatives of what we see, hear and feel and what maybe we could see, hear and feel if we looked at it differently. The ability to see things from the point of view of another is a key skill in understanding people.

One way to accomplish this is to use the NLP technique of the 'Three Perceptual Positions' as follows.

Three Perceptual Positions technique

This technique is very useful when there is a conflict as it allows us to have multiple perspectives in any situation so that we can have greater understanding, empathy and flexibility. You don't need the person you have a conflict with to be present as it is an exercise where you can figure out a solution by yourself.

Place three chairs in a circle – each chair is a 'perceptual position' and you have to sit in each chair/perceptual position for each stage as follows:

First position (sit in first chair)

Looking at the world from your own point of view, through your own eyes. This is your own perceptual position as you really experience it: feel it, see it, and hear it. You should be fully in it and living it as if it is happening right now. You should be totally associated and not taking account of anyone else's point of view.

Think: How does this affect me?

Shake yourself and disassociate yourself from the first position.

Second position (sit in second chair)

This is the perceptual position of another person. Looking through another person's eyes, appreciating the other point of view. How would this appear to them? This position can be in direct communication with first position. That is, if you adopted second position, and spoke to yourself in first position, you would address yourself as 'you'.

The stronger the rapport you have with another person, the easier it will be for you to appreciate their reality of the world and how they perceive things – remember we all delete, distort and generalize the same scenario completely differently from each other. You really have to 'get into their skin' and think how are they seeing this problem? What do they feel? What do they hear?

Shake yourself and disassociate yourself from the second position.

Third position (sit in third chair)

This is about observing the feedback of first and second positions from a dissociated position. You see the world from an outside point of view, as an independent observer with no personal involvement in the situation. How would this look to someone who is not involved? This is a useful position for gathering information and noticing relationship dynamics going on between them. In the third position, if you were to refer to yourself in the first or the second position, you'd use third person pronouns such as 'he', 'she' or 'they'.

This creates an objective viewpoint from which you can generate and evaluate some useful choices in a difficult situation.

All three positions are equally important and the purpose is to be able to move between them freely, taking the information gained from each, to see if you have gleaned any new insights from the different positions; if you need to go and sit back in one of the seats again then do. You must only state from that other person's point of view, or from the observer when sitting in the appropriate chair/position.

Your personality will also have an effect on the way you think, perceive things and communicate. There are several models and systems that help to explain our behaviours, the words we choose to use and our preferred style of communicating.

In order to help you with understanding your own and others behaviours and how best to interact for the most effective outcome, I will describe and explain:

- the Flock Personality Model;
- Transactional Analysis – the ego states.

The Flock Personality Model

I have created my own behaviour model called the Flock Personality Model, which which contains four bird types: Passionate Parrot, Diplomatic Dove, Orderly Owl and Eager Eagle. I have used the personalities of birds to reflect how we might behave to make it fun and memorable. When I teach this in my workshops people get it immediately as they already know the perception of the personalities of the birds and it is much easier than having to remember a combination of letters or what personality is which colour.

Background

In the 1920s, Carl Jung, a Swiss psychiatrist, conducted in-depth work into psychological types that became the foundation for many works to follow, for example Myers-Briggs, Keirsey, Lowry, Berens, DISC, Insights Discovery, and mine – the Flock Personality Model. Jung described the four personality types as being Intellect directed, Body directed, Feeling directed and Intuition directed.

Extravert vs introvert

Carl Jung's most important contribution to the study of human personality was his theory of introversion. In common terms, introversion relates to reserved personalities and 'extraversion' (Jung's preferred spelling) to outgoing personalities. However the types can also be described as how individuals who are energized (ie extraverts) tend to seek stimulation from outside themselves while introverts seek stimulation from within.

Introverts tend to be more focused on what they are doing or thinking. They look at a subject in more depth. They can be quieter, but not necessarily all the time. They are more likely to have only a few people that they call their close friends.

Extraverts get their energy from the outside world and other people. Having to sit quietly by themselves is what drains their energy. They need to socialize with people and they have many close friends and acquaintances.

I believe that developing successful relationships is about choosing the way we respond and knowing and understanding the Flock Personality Model you will be able to choose your response effectively.

In each of the two following behavioural tools, not everyone will fit the descriptions all of the time. In fact we all have every behavioural style within us that we can and do use at different times, with different situations and also depending on our own mood and the outcome we are looking for. However, one or two behaviour style tends to be dominant – a set of behaviours that we are more adept at, feel comfortable with and use frequently and will fall back on when under stress or overwhelmed.

By reading the descriptions of each personality you will be able to recognize which ones are more like you and which ones are more like your boss and colleagues. You may then have some aha! moments and realizations of why certain things are said or actions taken or behaviours displayed or any clashes you may have had or how and why you particularly get on with certain people more than others.

After reading this chapter you will have a better insight and understanding of yourselves as well as of those around you at work and at home. You will understand the strengths and weaknesses; recognize and appreciate the differences between people's personalities and how best to approach and influence your boss, colleagues and family. Having this knowledge will allow you to 'read' their verbal and non-verbal clues to their personalities and behavioural styles so you can adapt your behaviours in order to influence, persuade and be better able to communicate on the same wavelength.

You will learn and understand each of the four behavioural styles to understand yourself and others better. It will help you to choose the right style for the situation you are in at any given time and it is the key to unlocking empathy, solving conflict and being an exceptional rapport builder who is known for building excellent working relationships.

How the Flock Personality Model can help assistants and office managers be leaders in their everyday role

We should not describe people as an Orderly Owl, Passionate Parrot, Eager Eagle or Diplomatic Dove as we are much more complex beings than having just one or two of these styles. It is important to remember that we all have all of these styles within us to a more or lesser degree and one or two styles will probably be dominant and be able to be perceived by those around us. There are a few people who may also be fairly equal across all four styles and I am one of those people, although most people say they perceive my highest dominant style is a Passionate Parrot. However, it is fair to say they are observing me when I am training or networking so it is the style I bring to the fore in those circumstances. It is true to say we are all capable of flexing our style to be able to match and mirror our bosses and people we wish to support, build rapport with, manage, influence and help them and ourselves to shine.

To enable you to understand the different behavioural styles of the Flock Personality Model, I am going to describe each bird personality style and the behaviours they display; how best to approach and influence each style; how to negotiate with each style and describe what irritates each style so you know how to avoid conflict with them. I will also give a case study illustrating how each style would behave when organizing a charity event. By reading through the descriptions and their reactions, you may recognize yourself and may be able to identify your boss(es), members of your own team and colleagues.

Characteristics of a Diplomatic Dove:
(Famous Diplomatic Dove: Saint Mother Teresa)

- tend to be introverted;
- people oriented;
- slow paced and steady;
- sociable;
- inclusive;
- value good working relationships;
- amiable and friendly;
- calm;
- reliable;
- loyal;
- collaborative;
- supportive;
- kind;
- dependable;
- go with the flow;
- good listeners;
- considerate of others' feelings;
- nurturing;
- informal;
- adaptable;
- follow rather than lead;
- team focused;

- patient, tolerant;
- accommodating;
- harmonious;
- trusting;
- natural peace-keeper;
- avoid conflict;
- empathetic;
- encouraging.

Possible negative perceptions of a Diplomatic Dove:

- they can seem insecure around change and uncertainty;
- can be indecisive;
- stubborn;
- docile;
- sensitive to criticism;
- dependent (need the support of someone in order to exist and do their job);
- permissive (allows behaviour others may disapprove of).

Body language of a Diplomatic Dove:

- tend to lean back;
- some facial expression;
- good eye contact;
- regular gestures;
- tone of voice = caring, informal, reassuring.

Characteristics of an Eager Eagle:
(Famous Eager Eagle: Margaret Thatcher)

- tend to be extraverted;
- task oriented;
- fast paced;
- results oriented;
- like challenges;

- pragmatic – take action;
- competitive;
- direct;
- independent;
- assertive;
- questioning;
- forceful;
- formal;
- manage time well;
- resourceful;
- quick thinkers;
- like to take charge.

Possible negative perceptions of an Eager Eagle:

- can be insensitive;
- dominating;
- intolerant;
- poor collaborators;
- poor listeners;
- over reactive;
- they don't express feelings much or convey warmth;
- blunt;
- disinterested in you as a person;
- can lack empathy;
- impatient.

Body language of an Eager Eagle:

- their posture is upright;
- direct eye contact;
- they walk purposefully & fast;
- facial expressions tend to be more serious and intense;
- tone of voice = authoritative, assertive, matter of fact.

Characteristics of an Orderly Owl:
(Famous Orderly Owl: Bill Gates)

- tend to be introverted;
- task oriented;
- slow paced and steady;
- stable;
- accurate;
- cautious;
- likes a challenge;
- curious;
- pedantic;
- systematic;
- reserved;
- formal;
- detail oriented;
- private;
- solitary;
- high standards;
- precise;
- perfectionists;
- focused on facts and figures;
- logical;
- strong advisors;
- conscientious;
- clear communicators;
- serious;
- methodical;
- values competence in themselves and others.

Possible negative perceptions of an Orderly Owl:

- can be stubborn;
- perceived as cold;
- take time making decisions;

- analysis paralysis;
- overthinking and not wanting to commit;
- can appear preoccupied;
- worriers;
- reserved and cautious;
- critical, judgemental;
- bureaucratic;
- hard to please;
- detached;
- fearful of mistakes.

Body language of an Orderly Owl:

- tend to lean back;
- limited facial expression;
- limited eye contact;
- limited gestures;
- tone of voice = conversational, questioning, factual.

Characteristics of a Passionate Parrot:
(Famous Passionate Parrot: Richard Branson)

- tend to be extraverted;
- positive;
- fast paced;
- warm;
- inspiring;
- people oriented;
- like to take action;
- collaborative;
- enthusiastic;
- lively;
- motivational;
- spontaneous;
- optimistic;
- persuasive;

- seek recognition;
- love to have fun;
- talkative;
- informal;
- seek variety;
- full of ideas;
- dynamic;
- visionary;
- natural networkers;
- helps to build morale;
- likes to be centre of attention;
- likes to be liked;
- energized by challenges.

Possible negative perceptions of a Passionate Parrot:

- easily distracted;
- unfocused;
- impulsive;
- disorganized;
- poor time manager;
- can be quite loud;
- excitable and can be hasty;
- out of control;
- impatient;
- impulsive;
- can be perceived as overwhelming;
- act first and think later;
- can be perceived as manipulators.

Body language of a Passionate Parrot:

- they tend to lean forward;
- good eye contact;
- use lots of gestures;

- facial expressions are highly communicative;
- tone of voice = cheerful, friendly, enthusiastic.

CASE STUDY Organizing a corporate social responsibility charity event

A charity event must be organized to support the company's corporate social responsibility. This is all the information that has been provided. The following is how the different elements may react to the news that they are to organize a charity event, and how their preferred style can contribute to the success of the event.

Eager Eagle

- Would have made the decision to host the event in the first place.
- Will already be thinking about potential business or networking opportunities that may come out of it.
- Will provide a brief that is short and without detail; however, if you ask questions they will provide structure and detail to provide good results.
- Are goal orientated – they would measure the success of the charity event by the amount of money raised and the amount of supporters gained.

Orderly Owl

- Are internally focused and will sit down to plan the event, making detailed lists and schedules.
- Will anticipate any hiccups and have multiple back-up plans in place.
- Are not prone to being emotional so others may perceive them negatively, as they worry more about resources than who will benefit from the charity.
- Appreciate clarity and will ask lots of questions relating to cost, practicality, insurance etc.
- Will be on board with the project and give it 100 per cent as that is what they have been asked to do.

Diplomatic Dove

- Would love the concept of organizing a charity event as it involves helping people.

- Will want time to consult everyone about which charity to support.
- Take a long time to make a decision, as they take everyone's thoughts, suggestions and concerns on board.
- Are calm. They will pull out all the stops to make sure the event goes to plan without stress.
- Would aim for a smooth running event, want everyone to have a wonderful time and want to make lots of money to help the charity.

Passionate Parrot

- Would be very enthusiastic and already thinking about the venue, balloons, beautiful invitations, what outfit they will wear and about standing on stage to greet all the guests, as they love to be the centre of attention.
- Will want to get everyone involved and excited about the event.
- Do not like boundaries so would have to be carefully managed by others to make sure they stay on budget.
- Are creative, and will come up with good ideas on how to raise money. They will use their hands a lot when talking about their ideas and are easily distracted.
- Will enjoy the whole idea of organizing a charity event and will even organize a celebration event when it's successful.

How to influence an Eager Eagle style

When you talk to an Eager Eagle, they want to know what's in it for them and what the purpose is. You should be firm, assertive, direct and to the point, and at the same time be confident both in what you say and how you say it. At the same time, respect the fact they need to feel need they are in control and that you understand that failure is not an option. Use your pertinacity to help them achieve goals by showing your competency and focusing on the measured outcome you want. Your body language should be congruent to what you are saying and your head should be held high. You should make eye contact when you speak directly with them. If you are going into a meeting with an Eager Eagle, make sure you have just a page of bullet points prepared and keep it short and to the point and know which are the top most important things you definitely need to talk about before they dismiss you! They don't want long reports but prefer tables illustrating what you mean or pie charts that are quick and easy to read. They simply want to get the job done! They want you to think ahead for them and be ready for any eventuality. Admire their achievements, their leadership and their status if appropriate.

Do not expect long-winded conversations with an Eager Eagle as they are not interested in small talk about how their weekend went. Neither are they interested in asking you about yours! They do not want you to ramble on about things or be touchy-feely. Don't take it personally that they are not interested or that they may be blunt – it is just their style so don't take it to heart. They can lack self-awareness and you need to be aware not to expect empathy from them, especially if your preference is the Diplomatic Dove style, who are the most people oriented. They enjoy recognition, praise and acknowledgment but they may forget to give it. In meetings, be brief and be gone!

Your Eager Eagle boss is motivated by a measurable success and would want you to align your goals with theirs and the organization's. They expect you to help them achieve their goals, and align your goals with their goals. Remember they are not averse to taking risks.

Questions you might ask an Eager Eagle in order to 'connect' with them and guide the conversation to a positive outcome are:

- What specifically are the results you are aiming for?
- This is a big challenge – how can we face this head on?
- This may be a bit risky but what do you think about...?
- I've got two points we have to discuss and then would you like us to make it happen straight away?

How to influence an Orderly Owl style

As time frames are important to Orderly Owls, discuss what needs to be prioritized in order to reach their objectives and deadlines. Make sure you clearly communicate lots of detail to them in a logical sequence and speak slowly and precisely so they clearly understand. Orderly Owls could be inclined to micromanage unless you give them constant feedback and the detail they crave. Let them know you understand how the details fit into the big picture. When you are listening to an Orderly Owl, stay focused on what they are saying, take notes and ask questions for clarity. You should allow them time to ask their own questions, give them time to think and time to make decisions. They want your help to achieve accurate results. They like tidiness, so if your desk is messy they may think you are out of control. To communicate effectively, be precise and focused and have reasons and facts at the ready to answer questions. Demonstrate that you value high standards and are ready to cross the t's and dot the i's. However, be aware that they may go past deadlines due to being perfectionists and over cautious to get everything right. Show you are dependable and always be prepared. Make sure you have effective reminder systems for each step to help them keep on track. Recognize and acknowledge the need for structure and rules so make sure their parameters are clear and keep Standard Operations Binders and procedures up to date.

They do not want you to demand immediate action but prefer to have time to think things through from every angle – including the human angle. They don't want you to exaggerate or overgeneralize. You will lose them if you change subjects too quickly.

Clarify the desired result and outcomes, and support Orderly Owls by making positive suggestions but avoid displays of emotion. Encourage them and their abilities by letting them know you know they can do it.

Questions you might ask an Orderly Owl in order to 'connect' with them and guide the conversation to a positive outcome:

- What do you think about this?
- How much more time would you need to...?
- What steps would you take to overcome this?
- Can you explain the logic behind this?

How to influence a preferred Diplomatic Dove style

To influence Diplomatic Doves and communicate effectively you should focus on the needs of the team as a whole, the department and the organization. Where possible avoid unnecessary changes and avoid conflict. Remember to share information and let them know what's coming in advance and avoid pushing or rushing. They would like you to communicate calmly and considerately and be aware of their feelings. Speak slowly and softly, smile with your eyes and look as if you care. They are kind and sensitive and expect kindness in return. Explain what you need and why, and help them to make decisions. Admire their hard work, loyalty and kindness, and remember to thank them for their efforts. You should value their contributions and include them in everything and offer to help them whenever you can. Keep it personal and explain values and meanings when you give advice. They are 'people-people' and always think of others. Be open and interested, listen attentively and build trust, which helps to build strong working relationships. Be reassuring and supportive, steer away from conflict and consider what might be fair and equitable. Ask them about their family and tell them about yours as they are genuinely interested. Diplomatic Doves love to chat and may get carried away, so you may have to steer them back on track.

Diplomatic Doves do not want you to be too loud, bold, demanding or discourteous. Give them as much of your time as you can as they love to be around people, and also give them time for processing their thoughts. Be prepared to share your thoughts and ideas with them.

Questions you might ask a Diplomatic Dove in order to 'connect' with them and guide the conversation to a positive outcome:

- How do you feel about...?
- Do you want to include everyone in this?
- Shall we send a survey out to get everyone's buy-in first?
- Shall we tackle this problem together?

How to influence a Passionate Parrot style

Enthusiastically communicate with Passionate Parrots and speak quickly, varying your intonation. Smile and inspire them, point them towards a bright future and give them hope. Keep your energy up, give options and remain positive. Acknowledge their feelings and have a sense of fun about you. Give them the big picture and not too much detail. Try not to set them boundaries or structure them. Be animated when you talk to them and be optimistic and even adventurous – they like to be consulted. They want you to be open to ideas and to be trusting. They love feedback and the more positive the better, though constructive criticism is much appreciated. Inject a sense of fun where appropriate to keep things alive and moving. Have new ideas and be spontaneous, inspirational and visual. Focus on possibilities and opportunities. Admire their ideas, creativity and their popularity. They want you to recognize their efforts and they would love it if you praised them publicly as that would motivate them. When you communicate with them, they need positivity and excitement to keep their interest.

When you are creating presentations for them, make them as interesting and 'whizzy' as possible. They want you to be open to new ideas and make suggestions where appropriate.

You may notice that they have a fear of loss of control, being taken advantage of and vulnerability, therefore when an occasion arises, reassure them that they are not being taken advantage of and that they are still in control. Questions you might ask a Passionate Parrot in order to 'connect' with them and guide the conversation to a positive outcome:

- What possibilities and opportunities can you see in this?
- How will this help us to reach our vision?
- Who else will be involved in this project?
- Shall we celebrate the end of this project?

Factors that irritate each style

If you are irritated by something that somebody else is doing, take a step back, pause and reflect to understand why you feel like that by looking at your own personality traits and then look at the other person's personality traits. Understand exactly what is irritating you and ask yourself how you can solve it, can you empathize? Can you let it go? Do you need to discuss it with the person?

Forewarned is forearmed – if you know what irritates the people around you, you can tailor your communication and behaviour accordingly to avoid any kind of conflict and conversely also know what actually makes them feel contented.

Orderly Owls are irritated by:

- unpredictability;
- overly emotional displays;
- carelessness;
- illogical decisions;
- hustle and bustle;
- social occasions with no higher function;
- criticism;
- lack of information – they like to know all the detail and they like to plan;
- untidiness as they like order.

For example: an Orderly Owl would be irritated by a messy and incomplete stocked stationery cupboard so if it is your responsibility to keep it stocked and tidy then make it a regular habit and be pedantic about it.

Passionate Parrots are irritated by:

- rules – being forced into a situation where there is no flexibility;
- routine;
- slow processes;
- low tolerance to risk taking;
- obligations;
- rejection;
- having freedom curtailed – they like spontaneity and want to do what they want to do and when they want to do it.

For example: a Passionate Parrot might think 'I don't like being asked to explain my behaviour'.

Diplomatic Doves are irritated by:

- loss of security;
- no offers of help;
- negative criticism;
- broken promises;
- lack of social opportunities;
- insensitivity;
- insincerity;
- impatience;
- being forced into public situations;
- conflict which they avoid at all costs.

For example: a Diplomatic Dove might think 'I expect people to be nice to each other and am disappointed when they are not'.

Eager Eagles are irritated by:

- inefficiency and having their time wasted;
- small talk;
- a haphazard attitude;
- turning up to a meeting unprepared;
- people who do not follow through;
- indecision;
- last minute changes;
- having control taken from them;
- trivial discussions of no consequence to the end goal.

For example: an Eager Eagle might think 'Why do I need to know that? And how does it affect me?'

Your irritation is often more about you than it is about someone else. Remember you have choices how to respond.

How to negotiate with each style:

Tips on how to negotiate with an Eager Eagle:

- show respect – turn up on time;
- talk about the thrill of a new challenge;

- talk about rapid results and financial rewards;
- be specific and let them know you are doing what is right;
- research the competition and update them;
- give an overview and not too much detail;
- plan to discuss actions;
- use facts and logic;
- use assertive body language and tone of voice;
- when necessary, disagree with facts rather than opinions;
- keep it business-like, efficient and to the point;
- personal guarantees and testimonials are least effective – better to provide options and facts;
- do not invade personal space;
- plan for a short meeting.

Tips on how to negotiate with an Orderly Owl:

- come with details and talk about how this will solve problems;
- talk about creating systems and procedures;
- create a schedule with a step-by-step plan;
- apply formulas, calculate risks (they avoid them);
- calculate costs;
- think through all ideas and have answers ready;
- stick to specifics;
- their decisions are based on facts and logic;
- they can often be very co-operative, but need time to establish relationships;
- consider telling them what the product won't do or the downside to something. They will respect you for it and they will have spotted the deficiencies anyway;
- discuss reasons and ask 'why' questions;
- 'go by the book'.

Tips on how to negotiate with a Diplomatic Dove:

- take some time to build relationships – small talk;
- find out about personal interests and family;

- work jointly, seek common ground;
- be patient and avoid going for what looks like an easy pushover;
- use personal assurance and specific guarantees;
- focus discussion on who will be involved, who it will affect and how it will affect them;
- suggest talking about seeking other people's input and assurances;
- give them an opportunity to share their ideas;
- actively listen to them and let them know you value their ideas;
- give them testimonials of what others have said;
- demonstrate low risk solutions;
- they tend to use their heart and not their head;
- don't take advantage of their good nature.

Tips on how to negotiate with a Passionate Parrot:

- talk about the possibilities and opportunities;
- check out the competition;
- discussion should be about people, as well as fact oriented;
- be enthusiastic and looking to the future and possibilities;
- keep summarizing, work out specifics on points of agreement;
- try short, fast moving experience stories;
- remember to discuss the future, as well as the present;
- look out for the impulse buy;
- negotiate in a friendly way;
- bring some humour;
- improvise if you have to;
- they tend not to think about the money and have the mentality of if you've got the money use it.

Conflict management

We work with people with different behaviour styles all the time and our different ways of going about tasks and getting results can blend together very effectively. One of the factors that determines how well individuals and teams function together is how well they deal with conflict. It is inevitable that sometimes conflicts and misunderstandings occur.

When you have a conflict with another person it's often about the differences you have in personality as well as the differences in values that cause the problem. Your personality style is a huge factor in the way you approach tasks and interact with others, and when you encounter someone who doesn't share your approach, it can be annoying and vice versa and this may be because of a lack of empathy and only seeing the world from your own perspective. Understanding your own style and the style of others gives you the choice to flex your style so that they feel understood and you are able to work out a solution together.

Below are tips for resolving conflict, based on the personality style of the person you are dealing with:

If you have a conflict with an Eager Eagle:
Strong-willed Eager Eagles can be a bit intimidating but they will respect you for approaching your disagreement head on and being direct. Let them know that you will not waste their time and you want to support them to reach their goals. They will be assertive and want to deal with conflicts as they arise. Argue about facts not feelings and allow them to have their say and actively listen to their suggestions. They will typically respond positively and prefer to tackle conflicts to get them out of the way and then move on towards their goal. To avoid conflict they must have mutual respect and understand each other's boundaries.

If you have a conflict with Passionate Parrots:
You need to deal with issues in a no nonsense but friendly manner and plan some extra time to talk things through. They love interacting with people and are genuinely happy to talk with anyone. If you have a conflict to discuss with them, perhaps start off with a compliment or praise as they are looking for recognition most of the time. They like to be liked and do not like to feel rejected so approach the issue as if it is about a task or behaviour but not their personality. You could start the conversation about the way they are doing something well and suggest if they did ... it would be even better. Use humour and keep it personable and make suggestions that make them look good. Actively listen to their ideas and be open minded.

If you have a conflict with a Diplomatic Dove:

Approach the Diplomatic Doves in a friendly, sensitive and easy going way and chat first about how things are going – take it slow and steady and make sure there is a feeling of trust between you. Appreciate what they do well and then approach the problem and state that you wish to find a solution together for the good of the team. When you talk to Diplomatic Doves about a problem, start by focusing on things you agree on, not where you disagree, and try working together to find common ground. They value harmony and will act as peace-makers between others so you may need to bring into the conversation how solving this problem will help the harmony of the team. They want everyone to be happy and working together collaboratively in an inclusive and positive way. Offer a good compromise which will include a great outcome for everyone.

If you have a conflict with an Orderly Owl:

Approach them formally and privately and praise their methodical way of working and procedures. Orderly Owls are perfectionists and take complaints personally because they put a lot of time and effort into researching, planning and getting things right. This makes them difficult to confront about tasks they have done. Approach them by being well prepared and presenting facts clearly and logically. Listen to their concerns, reasoning and suggestions and work through the problem giving all the details step by step, taking it steady and slowly.

Even though they may be critical of others they do not like being criticized as they put so much time and effort into their work to ensure accuracy. Make it clear that you appreciate all the effort they put into getting things right and that you're bringing something to their attention that they may not have thought about or has only just occurred and which they need to think about in the future. Perhaps focus on parts of the problem which may be out of their control or have only just come to light. Remember to tackle the problem not the person. Give them time to make decisions and come to their own conclusions. They are not wanting social talk or to be friendly so be rather more clinical and matter of fact. Expect them to ask questions about what you present to them and be ready with any answers that you should have anticipated and thought about beforehand. Give them time to reflect and analyse before making a decision.

Remember:

- When conflicts have reached the point where they interfere with the quality of work, it is necessary to have discussions to solve the issues.

- Even during conflict stay professional, calm and considerate of other personality styles.

- Not everyone thinks the same way as you do and your way is not always the only way or the right way.

- Accept that other people have their perspective on things which is just as valid as your perspective on things.

- It is good to have different personalities on a team as you can work together to create different ideas and solutions.

Transactional Analysis – the ego-state (or Parent–Adult–Child) model

In addition to the analysis of the interactions between individuals, Transactional Analysis (TA) also involves the identification of the 'ego states' that lie behind each and every transaction.

Have you ever thought that you were communicating in one way and later learned that you were perceived in a completely different way? Have you ever asked a question at a meeting and then felt about five years old? Have you ever told someone off and then felt like kicking yourself for it later? Do you often find yourself feeling defensive about your ideas or point of view? Do you feel that you have to take care of too many people who should be taking care of themselves? Have you ever used the same technique to get what you want from your boss that you used as a child with your parents? Now you will understand why you do and say what you do and say.

Transactional Analysis is a model of people and relationships that was developed by Dr Eric Berne. It is based on two notions: first that we have three parts or 'ego-states' to our 'personality' (parent, adult and child), and second that we communicate (transact) as a parent would communicate, as a child would communicate or as an adult communicates.

As a practising psychiatrist in Carmel, California, Berne treated hundreds of patients. He consistently noted that all people change over the course of a conversation. The changes would not necessarily be just verbal; they could involve facial expressions, body language, body temperature and many other non-verbal cues.

The following are detailed descriptions of the three ego states, and you may recognize your own behaviours as well as the behaviour of others that are portrayed some of the time.

Parent

The Parent represents a massive collection of memories of external events experienced or perceived as a child.

When in Parent mode we talk to people as if they are children. This behaviour comes from what we observed as children in our parents and other figures of authority. The Parent state is where people behave, feel and think in response to an unconscious mimicking of how their parents (or other parental figures) acted, or how they interpreted their parent's actions. For example, a person may shout at someone out of frustration because they learned from an influential figure in childhood the lesson that this seemed to be a way of relating that worked.

It is worth noting that, while remembering these events, the young child has no way to filter the data; the events are 'recorded' in his or her brain without question and without analysis. You can consider that these events are imposed on a child. The Controlling Parent says things like 'Never talk to strangers'; 'Don't show off'; 'Always eat with your mouth closed'; 'Look both ways before you cross the street' and 'Sit up straight'.

There are two forms of Parent state that we can use:

- The **Nurturing Parent** is a loving parent, permission-giving, encouraging, security-giving, caring and concerned. They seek to keep you contented and encourage you, offering a safe haven to calm people's troubles. They can appear comforting, making excuses and making allowances for you, and can even be suffocating. They gesture with open arms and are likely to give you a pat on the shoulder or back for doing a good job. They may call you 'poppet' or 'sweetheart' and say things like 'are you ok?'; 'I'll take care of it for you'; 'don't worry about it'; 'well done'; 'what a shame'; 'take care'; 'remember to...'; 'I'll help you...' and 'It won't take me long to...' They simply want to look after you and make sure everything is alright for you. They use words like 'good' and 'nice' and will often smile.

- The **Controlling Parent** is a restricting parent who disciplines you and tries to make you do what they want you to do, perhaps transferring values or beliefs. They may wag their finger and their eyebrows may go up or they may have their hands on their hips when they talk when in this state. They may also pound the table or shake their heads. Their facial expressions may be scowling, hostile, disapproving and frowning. They lay down the law and can lecture you. They can appear patronizing, sneering, condescending, judgemental, concerned, strict, sometimes sarcastic and even disgusted. They will say things like 'You must always...'; 'make sure you...'; 'you should...'; 'how could you be so stupid as to...'; 'it's dangerous to...'; 'we have got certain standards and procedures to follow.' They use words like 'right/wrong', 'good/bad' and 'never/always'.

When we feel, think, talk and behave in the way we remember our parents doing, then we are adopting the Parent state. So at work we might say things like 'The way to act in this situation is...' (Controlling Parent) or 'Leave it to me I'll fix it' (Nurturing Parent).

When you are in a Controlling Parent state, you will have a strong personality and probably will find it fairly easy to get people to do what you want. In this state you have to be careful to not make enemies and you should try and give people the impression that you do respect them.

When you are in a Nurturing Parent state you can create a strong positive impression being seen as a helpful and caring person. However an exaggerated concern for others can inhibit them and even take away their influence. It can also result in you taking on too much yourself, impinging on your time in a desire to do too much for others.

When you express your Parent state you:

Give advice   Nurture and protect

Discipline   Make rules and regulations

Criticize   Teach

Moralize   Judge

Adult

In the Adult state we behave much more logically, basing what we do and say on facts and an objective analysis of the situation. It is the 'grown up', rational, thoughtful, calm person – we talk reasonably and neither try to control nor react aggressively towards others. The Adult is comfortable with him/her and is or should be our 'ideal self'. We can think through different situations, be able to assert ourselves and negotiate effectively, leading to clearly effective workable solutions.

The Adult stance is normally standing up straight with good eye contact and head held high. The facial expression would be thoughtful and alert.

Understanding Transactional Analysis will help you to learn to strengthen the Adult state within you, which is the ideal state. It is often the attitude rather than the actual words that reveal the different states.

Adults are likely to use what, why, when, where, who, how questioning and find out whether the matter in hand is practical and logical. Their attitude is one of being interested, detached and evaluative. It is the mature and intentional part of the personality where our actions and words are sensible and well considered, as opposed to the almost automatic reactions of the Parent or Child states. In the Adult state we collate information, evaluate it, work out possible solutions and resolve problems in a logical and calm way. We concentrate on the facts rather than emotional feelings and prejudices.

Adopting the Adult stage as your dominant behaviour can be advantageous in many circumstances. In difficult, stressful or conflict situations you should stick to the facts, be sensible and analytical, looking at things from everyone's perception and viewpoint in order to make a rational decision. If you are respected as a well-balanced person who can think logically and objectively then people will turn to you for advice. However, if you are in the Adult state too much, there is a risk that you will not have much fun.

You use your Adult state when you:

Plan	Evaluate
Check alternatives	Estimate probabilities
Make decisions	Set limits
Reason.	

Child

Stored in the Child state are the emotions or feelings 'recorded' in our brains from our own childhood and upbringing, and we behave, feel and think similarly to the way we did in childhood. For example, a person who receives a poor evaluation at work may respond by looking at the floor and crying or pouting, as they used to when scolded as a child. Conversely, a person who receives a good evaluation may respond with a broad smile and a joyful gesture of thanks. The Child is the source of emotions, creation, recreation, spontaneity and intimacy.

There are three types of Child state that we use: our patterns of behaviour, feelings and ways of thinking, which can be functional (beneficial or positive) or dysfunctional (counterproductive or negative). Sometimes it is stated that there are only two types of child state: the Free Child and the

Adaptive Child, but here I have separated the Free Child state into two parts:

- The **Natural Child** (Free Child) is largely not self-aware; in this state we are carefree, playful, uninhibited (and undisciplined) and creative. The Natural Child is energetic, loose limbed and casual, and speaks with a loud tone. When we are in a Free Child state, we have a joyful twinkling expression on our faces.

- The **Little Professor** (also part of the Free Child state) is the curious and exploring Child who tries out new things (often much to their Controlling Parent's annoyance). When we are in our Little Professor state, we are intuitive and understand things and people in a way that is different from Adult logic.

- The **Adaptive Child** reacts to the world around them. When we are in this state, we either change ourselves to fit in or rebel. We can be obedient, resentful or manipulative. In this state we may become withdrawn, going quiet after being told off, or we may become angry. An example would be someone stomping out of a meeting and slamming the door behind them! You would say things like 'please let me...'; 'I won't!'; 'It's not fair' 'You always try to...', 'I can't...', and 'why me again?', 'please' and 'thank you'. Someone in an adaptive child state might say they are not going to listen to you, agree with you or do what you want. They can rebel indirectly by forgetting, procrastinating and doing things differently or badly. The gestures of the adaptive child could be slumped, dejected, nail-biting or eyelash-fluttering. They could use tone of voice in a whining, sulky, defiant or in an aggressive way. Their facial expressions could be fearful, pouting, wide-eyed or innocent.

If you spend time in the Child state as your dominant state then you will have intuition, spontaneity and inspiration, which are all useful traits when you want to be creative and generate ideas. You will be able to inspire and motivate people emotionally to get them to accept your proposals and suggestions. However be careful not to be perceived as being aggressive, resentful and sometimes selfish.

The Child state is observable when you show:

Fear   Compliance

Curiosity   Aggression

Creativity Sulking

Trust   Self-indulgence

Anger   Rebelliousness

In an attempt to explain Transactional Analysis, Dr Thomas Harris developed the following simplified summary.

Parent – taught concept

Adult   – learned concept

Child   – felt concept

We each have internal models of parents, children and also adults, and we play these roles with one another in our relationships. We even do it with ourselves, in our internal conversations. They all have their uses, have their strengths and weaknesses and are appropriate in different circumstances. For example Free Child (Natural and Little Professor) is particularly useful if we want to generate lots of new ideas in a brainstorming (brain-dumping) session. Using the concept of ego states gives us a method of checking our behaviour and consciously selecting the most appropriate option for our current goal.

Analysing transactions (communication between people)

When analysing transactions it is important to note that when identifying which ego states are involved we have to take into consideration not only what is said but how it is being said: for example, accents on certain words, tone and volume of voice, the choice of words used, non-verbal body language such as facial expressions and so on.

Types of transactions

The first thing you say is called the 'stimulus'. If someone says to you 'You look good today' (you perceive it as an Adult comment) – and what you say back is the 'response' – 'Thank you' (Adult).

You have to recognize there are different types of dynamics – it's about perception. If someone answers you back in the Child state, think about why they answered in that way. It's because of their perception of you. If you have just said something they perceive as Controlling Parent (ie judgemental or criticizing), they hear the Controlling Parent in you and can come back with a Child response.

Their filters and their past can cause them to misunderstand and mis-translate your words, and thereby cross-miscommunication begins and conflict can occur.

For example: someone might say to you 'You look good today' (and you perceive it as Controlling Parent) and you reply 'Oh, this old thing – I have had it ages and I just threw it on' (Child).

There are basically three kinds of transactions:

- reciprocal/complementary (the simplest);
- crossed transactions;
- ulterior.

Reciprocal/complementary transactions

These transactions occur when both people are at the same level (Parent talking to Parent, etc.). For example:

A: Have you been able to write the report yet? (Adult to Adult)

B: Yes – I'm about to email it to you. (Adult to Adult)

A: What do you think of the new filing system I've devised? (Adult to Adult)

B: Tell me more about how it works – is it colour coded? (Adult to Adult)

A: Would you like to skip this meeting and go watch a film with me instead? (Child to Child)

B: I'd love to – I don't want to work anymore, what should we go and see? (Child to Child)

Crossed transactions and conflict

Conflict arises and problems occur in crossed transactions, where each is talking to a different ego state. For example, an adult supervisor/leader may take on the Parent role, and tell an adult employee off as if s/he was a Child.

For example:

A: Have you been able to write that report yet? (Adult to Adult)

B: Will you stop hassling me? I'll do it in my own time! (Adaptive Child to Parent)

A: What do you think of the new filing system I've devised? (Adult to Adult)

B: It must have taken you ages to do all that – how clever of you. (Nurturing Parent to Child)

A: What do you think of the new filing system I've devised? (Adult to Adult)

B: If I were you I would spend less time messing about on things that don't have top priority. (Controlling Parent to Child)

Crossed transactions are likely to produce problems in the workplace. Sometimes a message is sent from one ego state and the sender expects it to be sent back from the same ego state, but it's sent back from a different one. The transaction is crossed; communication is non-effective.

A: You messed that document up – it's full of errors and typos. (Controlling Parent – Child)

They will have expected a response like 'I am sorry, I'll make sure it won't happen again'. Instead they get the response:

B: That's rubbish, it's your fault because you can't understand or use correct English. (Controlling Parent to Child)

A: The deadline is tomorrow and we will need to stay an extra half an hour to finish it. (Adult – Adult)

Expecting them to say 'Yes that's fine I know it has to be done'. Instead they get the response:

B: If you didn't always leave things to the last minute that could have been avoided! (Controlling Parent to Child)

The Parent is either nurturing or controlling and often speaks to the Child, who is either Adaptive or 'Natural/Free' in their response. When both people talk as a Parent to the other's Child, their wires get crossed and conflict results.

The Nurturing Parent in a warm friendly tone naturally talks to the Natural/Free Child within you and may ask for some solutions, ideas and creativity that the Natural/Free Child will respond to. The Controlling Parent naturally talks to the Adaptive Child within you. The Controlling Parent may ask the Adaptive Child to come up with some ideas and solutions and ask them to sort the problem out, and the Adaptive Child may think to themselves, 'They are asking me for some solutions – well I don't think so.' In fact these parts of our personality are evoked by the opposite. Thus if I act as an Adaptive Child, I will most likely evoke the Controlling Parent in the person I am speaking to. The nature of transactions is important to understanding communication.

To improve situations where conflict happens, first go to the state that the other person is, in order to talk at the same level; then move yourself and the other person to the Adult level.

Ulterior transactions

Ulterior transactions are when a person communicates at two levels, social and psychological at the same time. The communication seems to be going smoothly on the surface but actually it is a cross-transaction for all practical purposes. This is because even though the ego states are complementing one another (the social level), at the psychological level the contradiction takes place. The psychological level will be conveyed non-verbally, for example, through eye contact, facial expressions and body language, and emotional energy will be expressed through the words people use. Non-verbal language is likely to be key in determining the outcome of the communication.

You need to ensure that your non-verbal language is congruent with your language, your intent and your ego state.

When in Parent mode (standing straight, with head up and looking confident) you could ask to see one of your team members for a meeting and you would say something like: 'I want to see you in my room tomorrow at 10.00 am as I need to have a meeting with you to go through the proposal for next week; remember to be on time and bring the completed documents with you.' The team member might say (in a whiny voice with a slumped posture, head looking down) as they go into Child mode: 'I know you want to see me at 10.00 am but is it okay if I come at 11.30 instead please as I really need a bit more time as I have not quite finished them yet?'

Instead of being in a Child mode the team member should be in an Adult mode and the reply should be in an assertive and strong tone (not aggressive), with a confident posture (ie head held high, shoulders back) before assertively saying: 'I know how important the meeting is and it does need to be held tomorrow; however, I require the morning until 11.30 am to complete the document. If you are free for 11.30 I will definitely be there on time and with the completed documents and we will still have enough time to get the proposal off in the evening post – is the timing ok in your diary?' The response will be 'That's great, thanks for preparing the documents so thoroughly. I'll see you tomorrow morning at 11.30' (Adult).

We are likely to have preferred states or a tendency to adopt some states more than others, and some people have a dominant habitual ego state and find it difficult to behave in any other way. For example: the constant Parent who always criticizes or helps others; the constant Adult who is always rational, unemotional, analytical, preferring facts to feelings; the constant Child who always operates under strong emotions, anger or guilt, looking to indulge themselves, manipulating people and situations and often feeling helpless and dependent.

As a mature person, we need a healthy balance between the three (Parent/Child/Adult). To build relationships and connect with all people you can be particularly influential if you convey some Parent support, some Adult options and some Child warmth. This would then tap into the positive aspects of all ego states of the other person (remember people like people who are like them).

Internal dialogue

The ego states also apply to internal dialogue where your Controlling Parent may tell you not to do something because you won't be good enough (I call these thoughts negative Gremlins). This has come from our early years of childhood and listening to our parents and authoritative figures guiding us. You should realize that these rules no longer serve you well. You can use your Nurturing Parent and your Adult ego state to change your mindset and know you can do whatever you put your mind to.

Key points

At any one time you will have one of the ego states established (often described as your mood), which is dictated by prevailing influences.

You choose which ego state to adopt when you are dealing with someone by the words you use, your tone of voice and the behavioural actions you take.

Your reaction and carefully crafted response to them will bring about change and success.

The ideal line of communication is the mature and rational Adult–Adult relationship and as you remain in the Adult ego state, others will eventually join you.

Summary

Remember you have a choice of how you respond, and choice makes us feel good. When you are in control you can make it work. Do what you need to do, look at it from different perspectives, do it consciously and make active choices.

If you accept that people are different, you can start to communicate differently and match their thinking and receptive styles and stimulate them to achieve better results.

Think of someone you know is difficult. Write down how their approach differs from yours (eg task oriented, people oriented, results driven). Think what you can do to accommodate their traits, knowing that people are all different and look at things differently from each other. Also remember that other people may feel frustrated by your behaviours!

Disagreements will occur sometimes but it's okay to have healthy debate as it often leads to more creativity and better outcomes. However, understanding models like the Flock Personality Model and Transactional Analysis helps us make sense of our own and other people's behaviour and actions and paves the way for controlled and healthy debate rather than conflict. Understanding will also help you to influence and persuade!

Think about the way people interact and behave, and adapt your behavioural style to theirs, remembering you cannot change other people but you can change yourself, even if only for the time you are conversing with them. Remember people like people who are like them! Think about whether they are reacting from a Parent, Adult or Child mode and carefully respond in a way that moves things forwards. Focus on solutions and determine how the other person thinks and what you can do differently to get a more positive outcome.

We can all think situations through differently and clearly in order to have effective working relationships to enable a productive working environment that we are pleased to work in every day. Keeping a solutions-focused mindset will help ease personal conflict, because it isn't personal, its work.

Managing projects

08

This chapter is for everyone who organizes projects in any format, from small office moves to events for thousands of people. Project management is already a part of the assistant's role in many guises, from one-off projects to regular events. If a task requires planning, assessing options, organizing activities and resources to deliver a successful result on time and you are accountable to others, then you are already a project manager – even though you may not have an official title or even have had official training. Project management is a key component of what assistants do for their organizations and in their personal lives too.

This chapter will prepare you on the fundamentals of project management, the role of the project manager, understanding project management terminology, and the common problems that can occur and how to avoid them. You can increase your effectiveness as a project manager by knowing the different stages, processes and tools that will give you a good grounding in project management, thus enabling you to actually manage any project with or without technology.

> To further your knowledge, you should consult *The Definitive Personal Assistant & Secretarial Handbook*, 3rd edition, which includes information (in Chapter 7) on 'Organizing meetings and events'. And a very useful Appendix 11 can be downloaded from www.suefrance.com – a 'Comprehensive generic checklist for organizing meetings and events', which complements this chapter very well.

The neuroscience of project management

I am going to explain the neuroscience of project management to help you get inside the mind of projects. When you start to understand your own and everyone else's biases, attitudes to risk, perceptions of value, then you start to understand why people behave the way they do. One of the main reasons why projects fail in any way, is due to the behaviours of the project team as well as the quality of leadership skills.

We need to pick up on the subtle dynamics like group think; which is the practice of making decisions as a group resulting typically in unchallenged poor quality decision making. In this case decisions are often made with conformity or the desire for cohesiveness.

If you have ever thought about speaking up in a meeting and then decided against it because you did not want to appear unsupportive of the group's efforts or led a team in which the team members were reluctant to express their own feelings and opinions, then you have been a victim of group think.

The VUCA (Volatile, Uncertain, Complex and Ambiguous as described in Chapter 1 on 'The leadership challenge') world we live in, applies to projects as well. Embracing this as well as social dynamics and their consequences is essential. We are often charged with delivering projects in a relentless ever-changing environment and parameters and goal posts are being moved regularly. When things are not conforming to expectations it can cause feelings of frustration and bewilderment as to which path to take to move the project on to a successful outcome. It can be a myriad of problem solving and decision making in an ambiguous environment. I hope this chapter gives you some insight into the workings of the mind in managing projects as well as the people involved and some practical tools to improve your project outcomes by learning how to balance your attention to technical skills as well as the behavioural and social skills.

Definition and terminology of project management

A definition of a project is: a series of interrelated activities undertaken to achieve specific goals with a timed end result – it has a start, a middle and an end. It usually has a sponsor and a project manager.

Project management techniques and project planning tools are useful for any tasks in which different outcomes are possible – where risks of problems and failures exist – and so require planning and assessing options, and organizing activities and resources to deliver a successful result.

Examples of projects that you may organize are:

- reorganizing the office to be Pandemic safe;
- reorganizing employees to work virtually from home;
- exhibiting at major national exhibitions and conferences;
- running a residential conference or training course;
- moving the office to another location;
- designing new systems and procedures;
- annual general meetings with people attending from different offices and countries;
- many different types of meetings;
- events such as client seminars and conferences;
- team building events;
- voluntary organizations' projects such as organizing conferences for assistants, for example International Management Assistants;
- charity events;
- and much more including personal events such as weddings and celebrations, whether organized for themselves or the executive they work for.

Below is a glossary of project management terminology that will make it easier to understand this chapter and to understand the terminology when speaking with others who work in project management.

Glossary

Sponsor: A sponsor is usually part of the senior management team, is ultimately responsible for the project and has the final say on it. Sponsors will have sufficient authority over all parts of the organization that are impacted by the project. They are unlikely to play an active part in the day-to-day management of the project but they will: set the objectives for the project in line with the strategic plan; ensure that appropriate resources are committed; resolve issues where necessary, as well as chairing the project board meetings. They are sometimes known as the 'project director' or 'project executive'.

Deliverables: The expected outcomes over the life of the project – what it is that is going to be delivered.

Milestones: A milestone is a significant event in a project that occurs at a point in time. The milestone schedule shows only major segments of work; it represents first estimates of time, cost and resources for the project. Milestones are important control points in the project. They should be easy for all project participants to identify.

Project initiation document (PID): Also known as 'Terms of reference' or 'Project charter'. The PID gives a clear path for progression by stating what needs to be achieved, by whom and when and should include success factors/risks and restraints. The PID defines the:

- vision, objectives, scope and deliverables (what has to be achieved);
- stakeholders, roles and responsibilities (who will take part in it);
- resource, financial and quality plans (how they will be achieved);
- work breakdown structure and schedule (when it will be achieved).

Project stakeholders: Project stakeholders are individuals and organizations who are actively involved in the project, or whose interests may be positively or negatively affected by the project.

Scope: The project scope sets the stage for developing a project plan for how you are going to run the project. It clearly states the project's objectives and deliverables. The scope definition should be as brief as possible but complete. A poorly defined scope leads to project failure. The development of the scope must involve the project manager, sponsor(s) and beneficiaries.

Work breakdown: A key project deliverable that organizes the team's work into structure: manageable sections/tasks.

Definition of a project manager and his/her role

A project manager can be defined as: the individual or body with responsibility for managing a project to achieve specific objectives. A project manager must lead, inspire and motivate team members to perform at their best. When a project manager takes on servant leadership style behaviours by putting the focus on the interests of the team members (see Chapter 1 for more information on servant leaders) they build trust, engagement and commitment to perform difficult and complex tasks, increasing the success of the project. The greater the risks, the greater value servant leadership provides.

Project managers need to ensure that their team and stakeholders are involved as early as possible in the planning of the project and have a say in decision making as the opportunity to make choices create a sense of autonomy and empowerment. Setting clear guidelines that allow team members to make personal judgements within the guidelines increases commitment, creativity and the likelihood of project success.

Neuroscience knowledge is an advantage in project management

It is crucial that project managers have an understanding of how brains operate. They need to learn how to keep their high level thinking brain (prefrontal cortex) working in times of stress, uncertainty, ambiguity, complexity and difficulty. During these times, our thinking brain shuts down and our amygdala takes over, as explained in Chapter 3 on 'Developing emotional intelligence'. When this happens we are working with our unconscious and autopilot mind and are unable to make informed and well thought out decisions.

Project managers need to look out for this in their team and help themselves and their team get back on track by being mindful which means understanding what is happening in your brain and taking back control. Often our mind is hijacked by our thoughts, emotions and concerns as well as our worries for the future and regrets from our past. Developing mindful awareness is about paying attention to the present, in a non-judgemental way and on purpose. This reduces the tendency to work on our autopilot, unconscious part of the mind and shift it to the conscious thinking brain.

You may also have physical symptoms, eg your chest might feel tight, your breathing becomes shallow, your stomach may feel like it is knotting, you may feel your face getting hot and going red or you may be clenching your jaw or fists. When you find your mind being taking over by your unconscious emotional brain, then use the STOP method explained in Chapter 3 and take a few rhythmic breaths and bring yourself into the present moment. You could physically move to a different location, or take a walk in the fresh air or do a three minute mindfulness exercise, whatever it takes to calm your mind – learn what works for you best. If you are in a meeting you could ask for a comfort break to take back control of your mind. You will then be able to choose how you respond and be able to think clearly and make informed decisions.

You need to be socially aware and capable of tuning in to your team members and able to realize when they need help to take control of their minds.

When you build effective working relationships, with open, honest and transparent communication and where they feel psychologically safe, they may feel they can tell you how they feel and ask for your help.

Project managers should also be conversant with **the 'The SixEss Threat/ Reward Model'** explained in Chapter 10 about how the brain can be triggered into an away from (avoidance) or towards (reward) mindset.

It would be useful for all team members to understand how their brains work and how they can be self-aware and learn how to regulate their behaviour. This could be part of the project manager's role to educate and advise so that they can all look out for each other and create a collaborative, innovative and results oriented team dynamic.

Stakeholder analysis

Project managers are accountable for the success of every project they manage and are responsible for identifying the needs, concerns, wants and interests of all the stakeholders. They should conduct a stakeholder analysis of those people who may significantly influence the success of the project. A stakeholder analysis can be used to anticipate the kind of influence, positive or negative, these groups will have on your initiative, develop strategies to get the most effective support possible and reduce any obstacles to successful implementation of your programme.

The final step is to consider the kinds of things that you could do to get stakeholder support and reduce opposition. Consider how you might approach each of the stakeholders. What kind of information will they need? How important is it to involve the stakeholder in the planning process? Are there other groups or individuals that might influence the stakeholder to support your initiative? Record your strategies for obtaining support for or reducing obstacles to your project.

Project managers should set themselves up for success by being constantly aware of the following three different activities that run concurrently during any project:

- **Content:** Day-to-day decisions.
- **Structure:** Four stages of the project: definition, planning, execution and delivery/close.
- **Processes:** Management skills.

As the project progresses it is a common mistake to become submerged in the 'content', which is what managers are generally good at, and lose sight of the other two equally important activities – the 'structure' and the 'processes', which could be a huge mistake that could make the project fail.

Content

'Content' refers to the day-to-day decisions that have to be made as the project progresses. This is a key activity and no project would achieve success without it. The content is often the main focus for discussion, either through informal encounters, or through more formal project team meetings.

For example, what would need to be discussed if you were planning to exhibit at a major national conference?

Content discussions would focus on such topics as: Where do you want the stand? What banners do you want on the display? What products do you want to promote? What freebies will you give away? Who will attend? What should they wear? Are they going to use a scan gun? Are they going to advertise in the promotional booklet?

Structure

The life of the project typically passes through four stages: definition, planning, executing and delivery/review/close.

As project managers you need to understand what the stages are and make sure all aspects are covered. You also need to understand that even during the execution stage you may still be required to do some planning if things change or barriers are put in your way. The starting point begins the moment the project is given the go-ahead (for a formal project this is when a contract/scope agreement is signed).

Stage one: define

Once the project has been conceived, you will need to work closely with your sponsor. Your first task will be to define the scope and purpose of the project. It will help you establish a clear focus on what you have to do and why. You need to establish your project initiation document, identify any major constraints and define the critical success factors for a successful outcome. By the end of this stage you will have established the project's objectives and the project teams are formed (see Chapter 4 on 'Leading effective office based and virtual teams to success'). Responsibilities will be assigned and objectives written, and the initial strategy will be created. This will help you estimate the resources you need to achieve the results identified.

The three steps described below provide a planned approach for collecting the project information necessary for planning, scheduling and controlling the project. These are:

- defining the project scope;
- estimating costs and developing budgets;
- creating the work breakdown structure.

The five steps of project start-up: sequence of events

Step 1: sponsor initiates the project

The sponsor gives the initial brief and business case to the project manager. The business case will set out how the project fits into the business strategy of the organization, where the project will lead to and the purpose of the project.

Step 2: strategic investigation

As project manager you then need to understand the brief and business case and make sure that what you are doing is right, minimize any risks or threats and search out any opportunities. You should carry out a strategic 'PESTLE' investigation (Political, Economic, Social, Technological, Legislative and Environmental considerations), which will enable you to understand any restraints on the project.

When applying PESTLE you should look at it from an external as well as an internal point of view. 'Political' could be changes in government and political stability, or who is in what position within the company, their power, vision and goals, or organizational in-house politics. 'Economic' could be the state of the economy, interest rates, exchange rates or salary rates, recession and the cost of living. 'Social' could be cultural aspects, including the population growth rate, division of wealth in society, health and safety, what is and is not acceptable within the culture, working hours, charitable work and so on. 'Technological' could be research and development activity, innovation and recent technological developments, and automation or new technology within the organization. 'Legislative' could be what is happening with changes to legislation that may impact employment, access to materials, resources and imports/exports, or changes to employment law, recruitment, visas and the like. 'Environment' could be the weather, which may affect industries such as tourism and insurance, or the space available within the office, what can or cannot be moved where and so on.

This will enable you to understand any restraints on the project and ensures you do not waste time doing things you should not be doing. It can be used as a prioritizing tool as there may be things you have to do before you can do something else.

To help with this process, the 'PESTLE' can be combined with a 'SWOT' analysis. The 'SWOT' analysis is an important part of the project planning process and is a strategic planning tool used to evaluate the Strengths, Weaknesses, Opportunities and Threats of a project. It involves specifying the objective of the project and identifying the internal and external factors that are favourable and unfavourable to achieving that objective. The strengths and weaknesses usually arise from within an organization, and the opportunities and threats from external sources. See Table 8.1, SWOT analysis.

Step 3: findings and confirmation

After the research and understanding of the scope and business case, the project manager can then informally go back to the sponsor to explain the findings and agree on any changes they need to make. This stage gives you the opportunity to correct the business case before you commit yourself. You can then confirm that both sponsor and project manager have the same understanding of the project. This will help build trust between the sponsor and the project manager, especially if the sponsor did not expect such thorough strategic research, and the sponsor will feel comfortable with empowering this project to you.

Step 4: project initiation document (PID)

The project manager then formally prepares the PID (sometimes referred to as 'terms of reference' or 'project charter'). The PID is a guide to the project

Table 8.1   SWOT analysis

←————————Helpful————————►◄————————Harmful————————►

Strengths (Internal factors)	**Weaknesses** (Internal factors)
How can we use our strengths? What are the attributes of the organization that help achieve the project objective? What strengths can the project team or wider organization bring to the project?	How can we address each weakness? What attributes of the organization might stop achievement of the project objective? What factors within the organization can hinder progress/success on the project?
Opportunities (External factors)	**Threats** (External factors)
What external conditions might help achieve the project objective? How can we exploit each opportunity? What benefits will be gained from completing the project? What opportunities may present themselves once the project is a success?	Are there any external conditions that could damage the project? How can we guard against each threat? These may be external factors that we have no control over but need to be aware of.

and clearly lays out its justification, what its objectives will be, and how it will be organized. This is where you bring together all of the information needed to get your project started and communicated to the stakeholders. With a well-defined and detailed PID you can let everyone understand where the project is heading from the outset, answering the questions What? Where? Who? Why? When? and How? The PID is supported by other detailed planning documents that may not be entirely completed by the time that it is prepared. The PID is the outcome of the business case and scope and helps secure funding (if required).

Your organization may have its own template for project initiation documents that you are requested to use.

The PID can be split into three sections:

- project overview, including project scope and business case;
- project approach;
- project approval.

Project overview

Project title and description (identification)

Write a description of what the project is so that all stakeholders can identify the project. Give it a formal name as well as any other terms that might be used to identify the project. If this project is a new incarnation of a previously cancelled or abandoned project, it's a good idea to reference the name of that as well.

Project background and history

Give any background information, explaining how the project came about. What is the context of the project?

Project purpose and justification

The project justification describes how and why your project came to be, the business need(s) it addresses (its relevance), the scope of work to be performed or problem to be resolved; how it will affect and be affected by other related activities, and why it is timely. The project justification needs to be clear and precise and show how the project benefits the business. You should derive the project justification from the strategic objectives, for example:

- market demand;
- business need;
- customer request;
- technological advance;
- legal requirement.

If applicable, include details of why existing tools or products are inadequate. If you have supporting documents for any of these reasons, you can list them here and include them as appendices to the PID.

Business case

The business case should have been given to you by the sponsor and you can include it as an appendix in the PID. It describes the effect the project will have on the business and supports this with a detailed account of the risks that should be considered. It may state options and other courses of action that were considered when the project was designed and developed. It should provide a breakdown of project costs and related financing including a cost–benefit analysis, which is used to work out how the costs of the project are balanced against the expected returns – return on investment (ROI).

Assumptions

What assumptions are you making at the start of the project? If necessary, schedule time to confirm these assumptions.

Measurable project objectives and goals

This section addresses how the project ties into the organization's strategic goals, and includes the project objectives that support those goals. The objectives need to be measurable.

What specific outcomes will be achieved, and how will you measure these outcomes? The project objectives must address all the work within the project, including cost, schedule and quality measures. Remember to use the 'SMARTER' goal-setting technique, which you will find in *The Definitive Personal Assistant & Secretarial Handbook*, 3rd edition, as a downloadable Appendix 5.

Hard measurable objectives are typically difficult to quantify. Easily measurable objectives have a unit of measure (for example a percentage of change, a specific amount of money or value, a unit of time).

Examples of hard measurable objectives include:

- improve client satisfaction;
- increase product quality;
- improve process flow;

- increase employee productivity;
- improve information flow.

Examples of easy measurable objectives include:

- increase sales by a defined percentage;
- reduce costs by a defined percentage or specific cost amount;
- reduce product production waste by a defined percentage;
- reduce manufacturing time by a defined period of time on a per unit basis.

A project manager should encourage the sponsor to convert hard measurable objectives to easy measurable objectives; for example, instead of 'increase product quality' you could say 'reduce defective products by 10 per cent'. Instead of 'increase employee productivity' you could say 'increase the number of calls handled by each person by 5 per cent, allowing us to handle more calls with the existing staff'.

Project sponsorship and major stakeholders

Name the project sponsor and stakeholders and eventual project owners. In addition, identify the role of each individual listed so that there is no confusion concerning responsibilities later down the line.

Pertinent documents and references

List any related documents or other resources that could be helpful in understanding various aspects of the project, such as the business case, and include them as appendices to the PID.

Product acceptance criteria

The process and criteria for accepting completed products, services, or results.

Constraints

You must take into consideration anything that will influence your deliverables and schedule. Think about which restrictions can limit what you can achieve, how and when you can achieve it, and how much it will cost to achieve it. These are external variables that you cannot control but need to manage.

Project scope and limitations

The scope is one of the most important sections of the PID because if it is not written in detail to begin with, it can be the source of argument later on in the project. It should include what the boundaries are for the project for example, type of work, type of client, type of problem, geographic area covered and so on.

The scope usually has three parts, which are:

- project scope statement;
- in scope;
- out of scope.

Project scope statement

A well-written scope is crucial to a project manager's ability to make intelligent decisions, and the more information you can gather in the early stages of a project the more adaptable you can be if you should have to deal with obstacles that might appear during the project. Scopes outline the results the project will produce and the terms and conditions under which the work will be performed.

Of course predicting the future is impossible, but the scope statement represents your project commitments, based on what you know now and expect to be true in the future. If and when situations change, you have to assess the effect of the changes on all aspects of your project and propose the necessary changes to your sponsor. Your sponsor has the option of either accepting your proposed changes (allowing the project to continue) or cancelling the project.

Your scope statement should include the following information:

- Describe what is 'in scope'
  You will find that the more specific and detailed this section is, the less confusion and argument about the scope there will be later on in the project's life. It should be clearly detailed so that all parties involved are very aware of exactly what the project includes as well as what it doesn't. It is better to write more than less, and you may need to get clarification

from the sponsor or at least cover any limitations in the section on what is 'not in the scope', and these can be discussed when you go for sign-off.

For example, it could say that 'this project is for the human resources department and all other departments are out of scope.' In other words it defines what is relevant to the project you are working on. The people who requested the project and the project key stakeholders should agree to all terms in the scope statement before actual project work begins.

- Describe what is 'out of scope'
  List any areas excluded that you believe stakeholders might assume are included, but are not. It is crucial that you identify work that might fall outside the project scope (ie what you will not be delivering), as well as how the project work might interact with other projects. Identifying the exclusions is important because it enables you to set expectations with your sponsor, project team and stakeholders. The more specific you are, the less opportunity there is for misunderstanding at a later stage in the project.

  Examples of what might not be covered by the scope could be:

  - any upgrades required to other systems to enable them to work with the new system;
  - all advertising and marketing required for launch and on an ongoing basis will not be delivered or paid for by this project;
  - any recruitment required or resources once the new system has been launched.

A comprehensive scope statement is a key document that binds you, your project team, the project sponsor and the customer. It is an agreement that defines the work of the project and the customer's business objectives. A comprehensive scope statement can help you identify changes in scope after the project has started and help you plan for any modifications or adjustments that might be needed during the life of the project.

Project approach

This gives a high-level overview of how and when the project will be completed. There are several standard components that normally comprise this section.

Project deliverables

List what the project will deliver as outputs. Where you can, describe deliverables as tangible items like reports, products or services. Remember to include a date when each deliverable is expected. List the major deliverables of the project and include the milestones and when these goals should be achieved, and remember to monitor the milestones.

Responsibilities and roles

You may feel it appropriate to create a diagram of the project organization structure showing the lines of authority and reporting for each project team member:

- Name the project sponsor who has the ultimate authority and control over the project and its implementation.
- Name the project manager, stating his or her responsibilities.
- Name any other key stakeholders.

Project team members

As the project manager you then identify and select an effective and efficient team (if you have the choice). Remember to read, digest and understand Chapter 4 on leading effective teams to success regarding stages of team development, Belbin® team roles and the Flock Personality Styles. It is important to understand how they react in different situations, how to communicate effectively with each style and how to influence and negotiate with each style.

For example, the 'Eager Eagle results oriented' team members tend to be natural leaders and are pragmatic and keep the team grounded towards a successful outcome; the 'Diplomatic Dove relationship focused' team members are approachable, foster trust and respect and are considerate and inclusive of other team members; the 'Orderly Owl process and rule follower' team members are detail driven and will analyse results and will cross the t's and dot the i's and make sure procedures are followed; and the 'Passionate Parrot innovative and disruptive thinker' team members are imaginative, creative and big picture thinkers.

Having a good balance of team members would make a skilful and effective team, whereas if you have a team of Eager Eagles they will be fighting over the leadership role; a team of too many Diplomatic Doves may prioritize getting on with each other rather than challenging each other to get the results; a team of Passionate Parrots may generate lots of great ideas but not take them to the next stage and will just want to party; a team of Orderly Owls will get bogged down in detail and take too long over making decisions, causing scope creep.

Understanding Flock Personality Styles as well as Belbin team roles will help you to form a well balanced team with complementary skill sets so that you have a fighting chance of having a compatible, high performing and dynamic and successful team.

Identify who the key members of the project team are and their roles and job descriptions. Include contact details – phone numbers and email addresses. Set out who they should report to on a daily basis.

List the required skills and expertise that each individual brings to the project as well as each person's responsibilities. You need to be clear about roles so that you don't duplicate responsibilities, but you do need to have back-up so people may have a primary role and a secondary role as a contingency plan. Everyone needs to be clear about what's expected of them. If this is a long-term project, you may even consider developing job descriptions for team members.

Project resources

In addition to the human resources, what other resources will be needed for satisfactory completion of the project? Provide a list of equipment such as computers/laptops, software and applications, raw materials, working space and any other resources that might be required. If certain resources will only be needed during specific phases of the project, make a note of that as well.

Risk management overview

Risk analysis: identify, assess, manage, monitor, action

Identify the risks within the project; then you will need to assess them and decide how you will manage, monitor, accept or take action upon them. Describe what you are going to do to manage risks. Where you can't prevent risks, what are your contingency plans for dealing with them and what likely impact will they have on the project? What actions will you take should the risk materialize? What processes do you have in place to routinely assess the risks associated with your project? Are the risks low, medium or high? Low risks are generally ignored, medium risks you have to keep an eye on, and high risks should have contingency plans.

For example, unquantifiable objectives, such as customer satisfaction, can involve high risk.

Our brains treat social pain (the feelings we experience when we don't feel valued, are misunderstood or feel disconnected from a group), whether real or perceived, the same way as physical pain. So social pain feels the same way as a physical slap in the face, causing the fight or flight syndrome to activate and our cognitive ability to diminish. We then become less able to evaluate and manage high risk complex projects and risks may rise. Project managers need to be aware that what they and their team members say, how they say it and how they act, can cause social pain and need to be able to spot and address these problems instantly to mitigate risks.

Project's life overview

Give a basic breakdown of the project's life and list the various stages that your project will go through. Make sure to include the objectives of each stage and why the stage is necessary.

Basic project control and communication plan

The project control component explains the tools that will be used to assist the project manager in tracking the project's progress. It also serves as a communication device for communicating the project's progress to the project team, project sponsor and project stakeholders.

Project schedule

Provide a basic schedule overview that lists, among other things, the key milestones and stages of the project. Various documents such as a Gantt chat, including the associated work breakdown structure, should be included. It can be quite advantageous to use a project management software tool to produce a schedule that can be monitored and adjusted as the project progresses, or this can be done on a spreadsheet like Excel.

Project approval

List all of the names and roles of the major stakeholders ready for their signatures, indicating that each of these individuals is satisfied with the details included in the PID.

In addition, if the project will require resources from other departments or groups, a representative from each of these divisions should be listed in the approval section as well. The signatures of these individuals will signify that they accept their own responsibilities for successful completion of the project and agree to provide needed support.

Step 5: PID sign off

The project manager then formally organizes for the PID to be signed off by the sponsor, the end user/customer (internal or external), stakeholders and themselves, which effectively means that all parties are happy for the project to go ahead.

Stage two: plan

Having established what your project has to deliver and you're clear about what its scope is, you now need to do some planning. Whether your project is big or small, one of the first challenges of project planning is to break the overall deliverable down into manageable chunks to determine the project sequence of activities and time frame. Later, you will use this to work out the schedule, identify the resources you'll need and work out the budget.

Provide information about how the project will be implemented, including timelines and resources. What major tasks (with milestones) will be completed during the project?

Prepare a Gantt chart (see below) or similar schedule of the timeline. Consider how many days' activity will be needed to complete the project. How many support staff will be needed? Will you need to bring more people onto the project team? How will the progress be monitored and communicated? What quality-control procedures will you put in place?

If you have been given a fixed deadline, plan to meet it earlier, and work back from that earlier date. However, err on the side of caution and build some 'cushion'/leeway into each phase of the project. Ambition and aiming high are good attitudes but exercising realism at the outset of a project regarding financials and timescales can save an enormous amount of trouble later.

There may be a number of sub-projects that you will have to coordinate to meet your overall objective. You will need to break down each sub-project and prepare a detailed specification of who does what by when. You will have to agree these details with the team members assigned to carry them out and provide clear direction concerning budgets and other resources.

Work breakdown structure (WBS)

A work breakdown structure provides an opportunity to structure the project in a systematic and logical manner. It is useful for all small and large meetings, events and projects. It is a way of showing, in an easy-to-understand diagram, how the project breaks down into the key and supporting activities. Once you have generated a list of activities and tasks required in order to deliver the project, you can organize them in a hierarchical way where each lower level supports the ones above.

A frequent technique to use is backward planning, so put the end date at the top under the project outcome and work backwards from there. You should take a flip chart (or put several pieces together if it is a large project) or use a whiteboard, and start at the top with the overall project title at the top.

You then use Post-it notes that already have the activities and tasks written on them as this will make it easier to move your ideas around until you have finalized your WBS.

Each main activity is then broken down into its supporting activities, which have to be completed in turn to achieve it. The process is repeated until all the key tasks have been identified. The completed diagram gives an overview of the project and the interrelation of the activities involved. Having already identified many of the activities it should be easy to sequence them into a systematic structure.

All the work that needs to be done to make the project a success will have been identified. The WBS helps establish the sub-projects that are necessary to meet the overall project objective. It will form the basis of a timed programme of activities, showing the most efficient and economical way forward for the project.

Work breakdown structure example

We will create a new training programme using a WBS.

Brainstorm what major intermediate/final products/deliverables are needed to produce and achieve the project's objectives (for this example these are not exhaustive by any means but are just used to illustrate the WBS structure):

- training programme needs statement;
- training programme design;
- participant workbooks.

Then divide each of these major deliverables into its component deliverables in the same manner. Choose any one of the deliverables to begin with and work your way through each one. For this example I am choosing 'Training programme needs statement'. I need the following intermediate deliverables so I can create the needs statement:

- interviews with potential delegates;
- a review of materials discussing the needs for the programme.

Divide each of these work pieces into its component parts. I choose to start with 'Interviews with potential delegates' for my illustration. The deliverables I must have in order to complete these interviews are:

- select interviewees;
- interview questionnaire;
- interview schedule.

I have then taken 'Interview schedule' and broken it down to show just one of its components (ie 'Select interviewees').

Once you get some activities and tasks drilled down, put some dates/ deadlines in. A critical path analysis is a diagrammatical representation of what needs to be done and by when. Timescales and costs can be applied to each activity and resource. Look to see where your milestones are. Putting the dates in gives it a sense of urgency and you know when you have to have things in place by (Figure 8.1).

The Gantt chart

The Gantt chart (named after Henry Gantt, who developed the procedure in the 1900s) is a useful tool for analysing and planning more complex projects. It helps you to think about people, resources, dates, overlaps and key elements of the project. It allows you to predict the outcomes of time,

Figure 8.1   Work breakdown structure: creating a new training programme

cost and quantity. When a project is under way, a chart helps you to monitor whether the project is on schedule. If it is not, it allows you to pinpoint the remedial action necessary to put it back on schedule.

Gantt charts can be produced on Excel spreadsheets or you can use software that is simple and easy to use. It is a horizontal bar chart that graphically displays the time relationship of the steps in a project. Each step of a project is represented by a line placed on a chart in the time period when it is to be undertaken. When completed the Gantt chart shows the flow of activities in sequence as well as those that can be underway at the same time.

Sequential and parallel activities

An essential concept behind project planning (and critical path analysis) is that some activities are dependent on other activities being completed first. As a shallow example, it is not a good idea to start running a training workshop before you have designed it, produced workbooks and practised it.

These dependent (sequential) activities need to be completed in a sequence, with each stage being more or less complete before the next activity can begin. Other activities are not dependent on completion of any other tasks. These may be done at any time before or after a particular stage is reached. These are non-dependent (parallel) tasks.

It is well worth your time finding out more about Gantt charts either via the internet or by asking project managers in your office to show you.

Stage three: execute

'If you fail to plan, you plan to fail!' Once you have planned well it is easy to execute your well-defined plans to achieve a successful outcome. You will be involved in monitoring to make sure that the project keeps on target. If the sequence of events is not proceeding to your plan, you will be involved in problem solving and decision making. This often means modifying the project plan in light of new evidence and the response to change. Remember to get the sponsor's approval to any changes in the scope. Be prepared to introduce a contingency plan where appropriate.

Common problems that can occur in project management and how to avoid them

- **Scope creep:** Recognize that every piece of work you get is a potential project and that people not directly affected by the project will want you to add things to it. Check with the sponsor before proceeding. Make sure you use all the time management tools and techniques in order to hit all the milestones on target. Time management should be a high priority for everyone involved. Scope creep can happen when things change.

- **Poorly defined roles:** Make sure every team member understands who does what and what their role is within the project team.

- **Lack of documentation:** Ensure that all details are written down in the PID and Gantt charts, which should be accessible and visible for all to see, that minutes are written up and all communication channels are open appropriately with all key stakeholders. It is important to keep everything documented, and to keep the documents even after the project is finished in case questions come up later.

- **Over-budget:** Budget with educated estimates rather than 'guesstimates'. Keep an eye on spending or put someone with the appropriate skills in charge.

- **Over-dependency**: As project manager you should make sure that people have cover and that you don't rely too heavily on one person for any particular role. Train people to double up for the different roles.

- **Poor team morale**: Make sure the team is motivated (see Chapter 2). There may be lack of clarity, which can cause confusion and lead to people pulling in different directions, building up unrealistic expectations, and having unnecessary worries and fears. Developing a detailed PID at the initiation of the project can help people understand the what, why, where, when, who and how of the project.

- **Changeable deadlines**: Deadlines are agreed in the project schedule; however, some may be brought forward or delayed for different reasons beyond your control, even if risks have been addressed. Be ready with Plan B and calmly sort out alternatives.

- **Mistakes**: No matter how good the planning, and even with the existence of contingency plans, mistakes will happen as we are human. Good leadership, flexibility, support and team development may be required.

- **Resistance to change**: The nature of the project may be alien to what an organization is usually involved in. This may cause resistance amongst the work force, affording slower than possible activity. In severe cases this may lead to sabotage.

- **Priority changes**: If the project is part of a larger programme there may be a pecking order for each project. The projects may be fighting for a pot of central funds. Even within a project there may be prioritization of resources that can seriously affect key areas, so you have to have contingency plans in place and use flexibility and proactive problem solving skills.

- **Changed objectives**: This will mean different processes, analysis, methodologies, team requirements and sometimes even suppliers. Visibly using and enforcing the scope will help you get a Request for Change signed off by the project sponsor, and helps ensure those eventually paying for the work have a better sense of the impact of later changes on project costs, timescales and the ultimate quality of delivery.

- **Insufficient people** (either of the right number, the right experience or the right capability): You need a good mix of experience, enthusiasm and energy, and must make sure your sponsor is aware of resource issues and the consequences. These might include overrunning time, undermining quality, and probably stress and possibly burn-out.

Stage four: deliver/review/close

This is the stage where the project reaches its close. You will need to check that all that you set out to do has been done. Was the eventual outcome acceptable to all those concerned? Highlight what was successful, as well as areas where you feel you could have performed better. You may need to train the end user on whatever your project has produced. You will need to lead a review on the outcome and overall results.

One of the greatest things about formal processes is that you can look back at lessons learned, which helps us to do an even better job next time.

You will need to produce a written report in which you summarize the results and give recognition to the project team for their achievements, and then it is time to celebrate with the team.

Processes

Whilst the content and structure are happening you also have to take care of the processes. Whether you are leading a large or small project, the process is still the same. The benefits of having processes include saving time that you can use elsewhere in the project. They will reduce errors, allowing you to see what might go wrong, helping you to minimize or avoid it ahead of time. A process is also reliable as you know that when you do something you will get a certain result, allowing you to move on to the next phase. There is a degree of confidence that comes from understanding a process, because as you use a process repeatedly your skills improve and your confidence increases.

If you are currently a team member of a project and you would like to be the project manager one day, then practise these processes regularly, even if it is on a small meeting. You will then be able to transfer your skills into larger more visible projects that you may get involved in. Take the time to learn and do it right.

If you don't have the time to do it right, then when will you have the time to do it over again?

A good process will also help with communication in terms of where you are in the project and understanding what you should be working on next. This makes a big difference to teams working together.

All project managers face problems – efficient and effective project managers are working on next week's or even next month's problems.

Leverage artificial intelligence, data analytics and machine learning

Artificial intelligence (AI) is a computer/robot/machine that can mimic human intelligence. They also have the ability to learn, interpret events, support and automate decisions and take actions.

Machine learning is a subset of artificial intelligence whereby computers are programmed to learn automatically and improve as they encounter additional data. Much of the focus of machine learning is to create programs and software that can learn to make predictions and decisions without being directly programmed to do so.

Data analytics is the science of analysing data to find trends, answer questions, and draw conclusions.

By examining data, they can identify patterns, highlight trends, make informed decisions, help to create forecasts and predictions based on existing data to help future planning and provide valuable and actionable outcomes. AI, machine learning and data analytics can be beneficial in project management for automating such tasks as scheduling, monitoring, budget planning and resource planning.

Project management software embedded with AI and data analytics will become a staple in the project manager's toolkit.

Agile or hybrid project management approaches

Our fast-paced world often demands speed, flexibility and agility and if you have small projects which are loosely defined and need a fast turnaround, that do not need the traditional project management steps outlined above, then you can use Agile project management. Agile project management is a philosophy that helps teams continuously improve and believes in incremental development to help teams respond to change and deal with uncertainty. It uses methodologies such as Kanban and Scrum as project management frameworks.

Kanban – the Kanban framework is a visual way to plot out projects and workflows using columns and digital cards. It helps to manage continuous processes by working on digital Kanban boards of 'do', 'doing' and 'done' and you will see your team move tasks from 'do' to 'done'. It helps teams see the progress made, and spot anything blocking progress that you can give immediate attention to. You will also be able to see whether team members are operating at optimal capacity or overburdened. It is an effective method to drive improvement and cultivate transparency within the organization.

It is possible to create Kanban boards on the Asana tool and you can use Scrum on Kanban boards.

Scrum – is an Agile framework that helps teams collaborate and complete high impact work. It establishes specific ways teams can continuously improve through tools like 'sprints', 'stand-ups', and 'retrospectives'. It provides a blueprint of values, roles and guidelines to help your team focus on repetition of a process and continuous improvement. 'Sprints' are usually two-week long working sessions with a specific deliverable at the end. There are two additional Scrum events which are the daily 'stand-ups' that happen once a day for 15 minutes to co-ordinate daily activities. The second Scrum event is the sprint 'retrospective' run by the 'Scrum master' who could be the project manager where the team analyse their work techniques and reflect on their 'Sprint' and make adjustments for continual improvement.

Hybrid project management takes advantage of project management techniques from both traditional and agile methodologies and is detailed and fast. It combines the traditional methods and thoroughness of some of the traditional project management tools such as work breakdown structures with the Agile method of speed and lean.

Project managers need to continually learn and upskill to use new and emerging management frameworks and technology to adapt to the unique needs and demands of different projects and be relevant as proficient project managers. You will need to research any methods you are interested in, take some training and keep on looking for what's new in the project management world.

Summary

For a project to be successful, it's not enough simply to manage the project competently and deliver a good-quality product on time and within budget. To avoid failure, make sure you have identified the right business requirements, created an achievable business case/scope, communicated effectively with all key stakeholders including the project team members on a timely basis, managed a high-quality execution, focused on outcomes and monitored your changing environment. You also need to use excellent people skills to manage your team effectively and build trusting relationships ready for the next project that you manage.

Importantly, you have to manage the expectations of your sponsor, stakeholders and team members so that they stay supportive and endeavour to take the project to success.

Enlightened project managers understand the need to balance out the different skills that individuals bring to a team so they complement each other. They also understand the need to create a psychologically safe and respectful environment as this is key to ensuring that teams work well together; individuals feel safe to speak up, which encourages innovation, collaboration and successful outcomes. Well informed project managers understand how social threats triggers a pain response in the brain and they also know how to avoid this and are able to manage individuals in a way that encourages, motivates and inspires excellent performance.

As a final point, with today's digital communication and technological world where people work virtually, information moves fast: we share documents via 'clouds'; we can sign off electronically, you need to keep up to date with new technology and be aware of what is available such as how AI and data analytics can be utilized to take some of the drudgery out of project management and help you become a better project manager. Embrace the change in technology – keep on top of what's new and have fun using it. It is also important that project managers are armed with the right human skills to lead their teams such as empathy, emotional intelligence, trust, communication, leadership, flexibility a psychologically safe space for teams to work in. Share your knowledge, raise your profile as you never know what you have that could be extremely valuable to others and where in your career these skill sets might take you.

The art and science of effective negotiation

09

Negotiation is both an art and a science. It involves the systematic analysis of problems (the science), understanding how the brain works (neuroscience) and the interpersonal skills an individual needs to deal with people (the art). It's the art of influencing your counterpart(s) to change their mind and making them think it's their idea! It's getting their buy-in and getting them to agree with what you want for their reasons. Therefore you need to approach the conversation through their negotiation lens. The ability to negotiate is a skill relevant to most areas of our lives. We all negotiate every day and most of the interactions we have in and out of work have a negotiation element in them. We negotiate with our bosses, colleagues, spouses, children, family, vendors, customers and clients.

We negotiate about workload, deadlines, calendars, prices, time, goods, services, activities, schedules, solutions, ideas, approach and relationships.

Remember the **problem/issue** is your 'opponent', not your counterpart(s)! If you adopt a 'me vs them' mentality, your body language, choice of words and tone will unconsciously project an air of competitiveness.

Assistants and leaders in particular will need to negotiate on deadlines and procurement, and deal with colleagues on many issues, such as coming to an agreement on how the business should be run, which tasks should be prioritized or negotiating change management. Effective negotiating will enable you to meet your needs and the needs of others without causing conflict and help you persuade people to help you, over whom you may or may not have direct authority. Virtual assistants will particularly use negotiation skills whilst conducting their business.

This chapter will give you the interpersonal and communication skills as well as practical tools to prepare for the different stages of negotiation. You will understand the different negotiating styles as well as how to negotiate best with the Flock Personality Styles and the tactics and techniques available to you, including effective questioning skills and how not to ask questions. You will learn how to communicate effectively and pick up on verbal and non-verbal cues from the other party. You will learn the 'The SixEss Threat/Reward Model' which is a brain based model to effectively collaborate and influence others. It will consider information-handling skills, which includes being knowledgeable about all the issues involved and possessing the ability to use that knowledge flexibly and with discretion. Judgemental skills allow you to make decisions on behalf of your organization using your own discretion. It will enable you to achieve successful win–win outcomes, whether negotiating for the best deals with venues and suppliers, negotiating contracts, engaging in conflict resolution or negotiating with members of your own team, your boss and your colleagues.

When you don't want to do something, consider negotiating instead of saying 'Yes alright then' or 'No I won't do it.' The first is too weak, the second too aggressive. In both cases you'll come out better if you negotiate the deadline.

Most people have a particular negotiating style, and when you learn the tactics you will be able to recognize these in other people and understand how they think, and therefore know how to counteract their tactics. You will be able to read their body language and use your body language and verbal language to help you gain successful outcomes.

The skills used in negotiating, such as interpersonal communication, will help in many situations. Ethical influencing – persuading, negotiating and convincing – is the foundation of successful leadership, relationship building and customer service.

Definition of negotiation

A successful negotiation is a strategic discussion between two or more people that resolves an issue in a way that both parties find acceptable. Each party tries to persuade the other to agree with his or her point of view. An ideal outcome is to reach a win–win where both parties make gains, where both may concede certain items, where relationships are preserved and everyone feels satisfied with the outcome.

Negotiations can be formal, informal, planned and unplanned and whatever the negotiation situation is, you need to have the skill set to create a positive outcome.

Negotiation styles

Learning about the different styles that negotiators use and understanding how to use them appropriately will ensure that you approach people in the correct way to achieve a positive outcome. Some people negotiate quickly whilst others take risks, and some take their time and try to avoid risks. Some negotiators can be quite intimidating to the point of being rude whilst others are quite passive and easily manipulated. To negotiate with all these different types, we need to be able to adapt our behaviour and be flexible in our approach.

A popular model for explaining the approach to different typical behaviours of negotiation styles is the Thomas–Kilmann Conflict Model developed by Kenneth W Thomas and Ralph H Kilmann. They state that there are five different modes for responding to conflict situations – **Competing** (or Aggressive), **Accommodating** (Conceding), **Collaborating** (Cooperative) **Avoiding** and **Compromise**. It's important to understand your own conflict style and also the tendencies or natural style of your counterpart(s). Knowing this will make you more effective in preparing for and conducting a negotiation. The best negotiators are able to use the different styles and choose the most appropriate one for each type of negotiation.

Competing (I win, you lose)

Competing style negotiators are usually assertive and uncooperative, and some people view negotiation as a game they have to win. They use 'hard' negotiation tactics, which often leaves one party feeling very satisfied and the other side feeling that they have no choice but to agree. The problem with this approach is that the relationship between the two parties is often permanently damaged. The person asking for something may receive it, but the second person probably feels taken advantage of and perhaps angry and resentful. If it was a reluctant agreement, the person who conceded is unlikely to complete the work quickly or with a positive attitude.

When using a Competing style individuals may pursue their own needs at the other person's expense, often using whatever power and tactics they can think of, and they can be aggressive. Whether it's their ability to argue, their status or the fact that the other person is weaker than them, they simply want to win. Competing means standing up for your rights and defending a position you believe in. However, Competitive negotiators may not necessarily or purposefully want to cause suffering (losing) to the other party. It could just be a by-product of their competing behaviour.

Negotiators use this behaviour when they need to get results quickly, but if you are always using this style people will soon learn and not want to negotiate with you.

I recommend that if you are negotiating with a Competing type behaviour person, you should use a blended approach of the different styles as appropriate. A person who prefers this type of negotiating may also be more interested in 'winning' rather than reaching an agreement.

Word of warning: Appeasing Competitive negotiators does not create goodwill as they may perceive you as weak and demand more concessions. Restate your position firmly, using strong language such as 'we need...', 'we require...' etc. Remember never to reward bullies by conceding when you know and feel you shouldn't – remain strong and stand up for your rights.

Accommodating (I lose, you win)

The opposite approach to competing is 'Accommodating', which is unassertive and cooperative. This is when one person or party simply agrees to what the other person wants whilst neglecting their own wants and needs, which means they sacrifice something.

This tactic is often the result of wanting to keep relationships friendly and to avoid conflict. It might mean Accommodating parties have selfless generosity or charity, or they may obey an order when they prefer not to or concede to another person's point of view. The end result, however, is that they lose control to the other person or party. Again this may leave one person/party feeling resentful that they have let themselves down.

The relationship that Accommodating style negotiators have with other people is very important to them and they believe that the way to win people over is to give them what they want. Accommodators are usually very well liked by their colleagues and opposite party negotiators.

As repairing the relationship is critical to these types of negotiators, if they have nothing else that would benefit the other side after conceding some things then they feel they are in a weak position and believe their best option is to give in gracefully. At this point an Accommodating negotiator should remind the other person/party what they will both stand to lose. If you both intend to work together in the longer term, then refocus the negotiations on the longer term.

Word of warning: It is almost always a bad idea to use the 'Accommodating' style when negotiating against 'Competing' styles as they will take it as a sign of weakness to be taken advantage of. If you always use the Accommodating style you could be perceived as a 'doormat' by others.

Collaborative (I win, you win)

Collaborative (also known as win–win) is both assertive and cooperative. These are negotiations where all parties show respect and concern for everyone's point of view/needs and wants. They aim for mutually satisfying outcomes and are often best for everyone concerned, where everyone is left feeling happy and satisfied. 'Win–win' is where all parties feel they have benefited somehow even though they may have had to find a fair compromise. The main difference is that this style takes time, and collaborative negotiators who are willing to invest time and energy to find innovative solutions to problems, know that they will feel positive about the end result and it will be more valuable.

Collaboration is the best style to use in negotiations as you will need to understand the feelings and deeper interests or motivators of all negotiators. The advantages are that it achieves mutual satisfaction for both parties, builds trust, gains commitment and they can continue their relationship.

Many people confuse 'win–win' or the Collaboration style with the Compromising style. However, the Collaboration style is about making sure both parties have their needs met, with as much mutual value created as possible through innovation. Collaborative profile negotiators are adamant that their important needs must be met – and they acknowledge that the other party has needs that must be met too. Compromising is when one or both of you will 'lose' some things.

Collaborative negotiations are based on trust, relationship and creativity. Your questions need to explore options, build consensus and test boundaries.

Questions you could ask in the collaborative style are:

- Under what circumstance would you consider...? (powerful question)
- What if...?
- What is your primary issue with...?

- What is your main objective?
- Do you have flexibility with...?

Avoid (I lose, you lose)

Avoiding is unassertive and uncooperative – the opposite of the Collaborative style. People who habitually use this style really dislike conflict and they neither pursue their own concerns nor think about the other person's needs. Rather than talk directly with you about the issue, 'Avoid' styles may try to sidestep it, postponing an issue until a better time or simply withdrawing. The Avoid style can be a typical reaction to the Competing negotiators. You can use the Avoid style when the value of investing time to resolve the conflict outweighs the benefit or when the issue under negotiation is trivial to both parties.

Sometimes there is just not enough at stake to risk a difficult conflict situation and it is sometimes better to allow people to calm down and take a break and resume later when you are feeling more reasonable and rational. At that point an Avoid style is likely to be the most pragmatic alternative.

The Avoid style is useful when you find yourself in a negotiation where you are unprepared; it allows you to either avoid the meeting or avoid discussing the issues until you have had the chance to prepare properly.

> One way to use the Avoid style of negotiating is to say: 'If you want an answer from me right now then I will have to say no; if you can wait then it may be a different answer.'

Word of warning: The Avoid style of negotiators are frequently seeking to avoid conflict; however the fact that they have avoided the discussion or meeting may cause the other party to be frustrated and even resentful, which can cause even more conflict than they were trying to avoid in the first place.

Compromise (I win some, you win some; I lose some, you lose some)

Compromising is moderate in both Assertive and Cooperative behaviours. This style is about finding a solution that can be mutually accepted and partially satisfies both parties. This is what most people think of as a negotiation. Compromising often involves splitting the difference, usually resulting in an end position about halfway between both parties' opening positions. Both parties win and lose – but make sure you win and lose the right things. Meeting halfway can reduce the strain on relationships.

If you are not familiar with negotiation tactics and do not prepare well, then you may bluff your way through the discussions and end up compromising. If the outcome of the negotiation is critical, then you should not compromise on things that you absolutely must have.

Compromising style negotiators give up more than Competitive negotiators, but less than Accommodating negotiators. This style addresses an issue more directly than avoiding but does not explore it in as much depth as Collaborating.

Word of warning: One of the problems with Compromising is: if you make concessions without good reason then the other party may assume that you will make more concessions without the need for a clear and strong rationale. Calculate before the negotiation where you can compromise and the reasons for doing so. Compromises cheat both sides out of innovative solutions so remember to think about using the Collaborative style instead by making it safe to explore options together. Invite the other side to join you in 'what if' scenarios to explore possibilities.

Only compromise when you have a strong rationale for doing so, and when you are receiving something back in return. Stay with the problem or opportunity for longer. Don't give in so easily to the temptation of splitting differences until you've explored other alternatives.

Applying a negotiation style

To apply a negotiation style work through your list of goals and aims, taking into consideration what concessions you decide you could make before the negotiation begins. Decide which approach is the best for the issues you face: Collaborate, Compete, Compromise, Avoid or Accommodate.

Each of us is capable of using all five styles and some people use some modes more than others. Your negotiating behaviour is a result of both your personality/behavioural style and the requirements of the situation you are in and whether you are feeling stressed as then you will revert to your natural style. Be prepared to pause the negotiation and be ready to revert to another style when necessary and appropriate.

The key skills of a negotiator

Your mindset as a negotiator is just as important as the techniques, tactics, tools and soft skills required that are used throughout the negotiation process. Below are some key skills you should learn to be an effective negotiator:

- Remain positive and confident in your skills whilst keeping your desired outcome in mind. Think of a Collaborative or win–win outcome.

- Simply think of negotiations as conversations that you are good at.

- Make sure you are negotiating with the right person/party – many negotiations happen with the wrong person and much time can be wasted.

- Become a trusted negotiator – if you want to have high-level negotiations with high levels of trust it is important to assess character, competence and whether the other side are empowered to make decisions. You have to be able to trust each other.

- Remember you need to maintain effective working relationships after the negotiation has ended. You need to anticipate how people will feel about a proposal you make and how they are likely to react, and you must have the ability to offer concessions without losing sight of your own goals and objectives.

- Master the ability to reinforce the content or meaning of what you are saying with your physical actions, demeanour, intonation and delivery style; this improves the effectiveness of the point you are trying to make.

You need to use influencing and persuasive communication skills so you can get your point across effectively and passionately without raising your voice or letting your emotions take over. You also need excellent active listening skills to be able to understand and glean all the information you need in order to read the other negotiator's body language and not only hear what they are saying but be able to 'read between the lines' and know what they are not saying! Using the right language and body language play a huge part in effective negotiations. By listening attentively, you show the other party that you respect and value them and that you are interested in their needs.

The stages of a successful negotiation

Stage 1 Before the negotiation   Preparation
Stage 2 During the negotiation   Opening statement
Stage 3 During the negotiation   Discussion (including tactics)
Stage 4 During the negotiation   Bargaining
Stage 5 Agreement and action plan   Closing

Before the negotiation – preparation

When it comes to effective negotiation tactics, thorough and meticulous preparation is key. Not only will you gain the upper hand over the other person/party with the knowledge you acquire, it will also build your confidence, enabling you to gain your desired outcome. Remember a good case does not guarantee a favourable result but a bad case will definitely lead to disaster.

Establish the problem

It is essential to establish and identify what the problem or issue is before you start to negotiate, and to agree on the problem with the other party. Often arguments occur because you and the other person are discussing different issues and it's just a misunderstanding or miscommunication. Look for differences in priorities and probe into motivations – uncover your own true needs as well as your counterpart's true needs. You should repeat the problem in your own words and ask if it is accurate. You should say things like:

- 'It seems to me you feel that...'
- 'It sounds like you are saying that...'

If the other party does not agree with your restatement of the problem then you should ask questions to elicit information about it. You could say:

- 'Can you explain it to me another way (or in more detail) and perhaps give me examples?'
- 'How is this problem affecting you?'
- 'How would you like us to solve this problem?'

Once you have identified the problem or issue, then do the research and decide on how important it is.

Information gathering

Information gathering requires research and analytical skills with the ability to draw relevant conclusions and produce documents to support your case. It also includes decision making and discretionary skills as you need to decide on the information you require and what you might disclose to the other party.

For example, if you are negotiating a salary rise, to help your case you may wish to research current market offerings in your industry and geographical area and cost of living expenses, or produce survey results or gather information from recruiting agencies and cut job advertisements out of the newspapers or print them off the internet from such sites as LinkedIn etc. If you find many jobs are paying less than what you are asking for, you would of course withhold this information and only produce those jobs that are offering more.

There are many situations where you will need to gather information before you negotiate and you can do this by research and asking questions.

Questioning skills

Good questions vs bad questions

Can you tell the difference between the various types of negotiation questions? How often can you tell when the other party are using questions in order to get a 'fight or flight' response?

Asking questions the right way is both an art and a science. Ask the question the wrong way and the other person/party might become defensive and withdraw from the negotiation or the question may make them angry. Ask it the right way, and the person might talk so you get all the information you need. We need to learn how to ask questions to get vital information, and we need to think about how to ask questions to get the other party to talk.

Effective/useful questioning skills ('good questions')

To be a successful negotiator, you have to know the wants, needs and motivators of the other party. The easiest, quickest way to uncover this information that you can use to your advantage is through skilful questioning from all possible angles and perspectives. With practice, you will find yourself asking better questions and gaining increasingly valuable information.

You should ask questions to help guide your thinking to help you force them to address your concerns and any potential holes in their proposal. Questions will help you to know when to adjust your personal negotiation style to best fit your counterpart's psychological tendencies, strengths, weaknesses and objectives; find out their behavioural and personality style; gain their opinion (indicates you are interested in what they have to say); gain information; get the conversation back on track; find out what their goals are and reduce tension. The right questions will allow your counterpart(s) to dismantle their own argument through realization – this will also help maintain rapport. Asking them questions will encourage them to reciprocate and explore your ideas at depth so you can get all your points across.

Types of questions

- **Closed** and restrictive questions where the answer will be brief or with a yes or no reply. This type of question is useful for obtaining a specific piece of information, directing a conversation to a desired area or gaining commitment to a definite position.

- **Open-ended** and expansive questions reveal much more about your counterpart's objectives, needs, current situation and behavioural style. Open-ended questions often start with the words what, where, when, why, who and how; for example 'How did you arrive at that conclusion?' Be careful with the 'why' questions as it may put the other party on the defensive if worded wrongly. However using the '5 Whys' questioning technique may be beneficial. The 5 Whys is a management interrogative technique used to explore the cause-and-effect relationships underlying a particular problem. The primary goal of the technique is to determine the root cause of a problem by repeating the question 'Why?' Each answer forms the basis of the next question. (Children are also very good at this technique!)

  Again you need to use your judgement on whether the 5 Whys is right for your situation.

- **Probing** questions, where you dig deeper to find out more information and keeping digging deeper until you get the answer you require. For example: 'Help me understand …'.

When you use challenging questions with would/could/might, it stimulates new neural pathways to explore, discover and innovate and look for possibilities.

- o What **would** it take for you to…?
- o What action **could** you take to…?
- o What **might** happen if we …?

Avoid using should/must/have to as they cause disagreement and conflict.

- **Open-opportunity** questions invite the person to participate and offer their views; for example 'What do you think of this option?'

- **Leading** questions are those where you try to guide the person to your point of view in an influencing and persuasive manner. For example 'With everything I have just said in mind, don't you think it is the best way of working for both of us?'

    Another form of a leading negotiation question is to simply let the question tail off, which invites the other person to fill in the blanks. For example 'After we provide those documents that you asked for, you will…?'

- **Flattery** questions are effective because they are both complimentary and they make the other party feel good. They will therefore respond well and the result is that you can elicit information from them. For example 'As I know you are an expert in delegating and always deliver on time, could you please delegate these smaller pieces of work so that we can concentrate on this bigger piece together?'

- **Emotional sensor** questions – there may be times when you sense that emotions may be rising and at this time it would be a good idea to address a possible issue that might upset the negotiation by simply checking out how the other person feels about certain issues. For example 'How do you feel about what we have discussed so far?'

'Bad' questions

These are types of questions that can be counterproductive to negotiations, being perceived as confrontational and possibly inducing negative emotional responses. The other party may be put on the defensive or your question may cause them to respond aggressively or emotionally, which will in turn bring the negotiations to a close or at least set you back.

- **Aggressive**: Certain kinds of question can result in you appearing to be too pushy, especially when used at the wrong stage of your negotiation. For example: 'You are not trying to bluff your way out of this are you?'

- **Loaded questions**: These carry an assumption and are worded in such a way that the respondent who answers the question admits to accepting that assumption. This style of question puts the person on the hot seat regardless of how they respond, and therefore in a very defensive position. A loaded question is really two questions phrased as one. The loaded question assumes that the first answer must be true; otherwise why would someone phrase it that way? For example: 'I notice that you are on the internet a lot; do you speak on Twitter, LinkedIn and Facebook most of the time?'

- **Emotional trigger questions**: Certain questions may trigger a powerful emotional response, particularly when posed with a hint of arrogance or insult. By using this type of question you will not elicit any information you need and will probably stop the negotiation process. For example: 'Do you think I should waste my time on this ridiculous proposal – it's not been thought about properly has it?'

- **Impulsive question**: Speaking before you think. Always think – then ask, not the other way around.

- **Innuendo questions**: These questions could be perceived in different ways and may even imply a threat. For example: 'Are you in a position to concede on these points now or do you want to take it further?'

It is true that some of these types of questions may elicit the response you want; remember, however, what kind of brand or reputation you want to express and consider whether these questions will get you what you want in a durable and long term way. Think about the consequences and what kind of relationship you will have after the negotiations.

Objectives

You need to identify your objectives and priorities and know at what point you will walk away. Winning at all costs to get the best result rather than reaching a compromise will often bruise egos and make any future negotiations difficult or even impossible.

Most negotiators have three basic positions when they are in talks. Decide on what your ideal and best outcome is, your realistic and satisfactory outcome, and your acceptable minimum bottom line – ie your fallback position, the one you can live with.

The negotiation itself is a careful exploration of your position and the other person's position, with the goal of finding a mutually acceptable compromise that gives you both as much of what you want as possible.

Expected outcomes

What outcome will people be expecting from this negotiation? What has the outcome been in the past, and what precedents have been set? Clearly structure the outcome desired by both parties by writing it down (see Resource 7, which can be downloaded from www.suefrance.com before you do this), consider what you need (the essentials) and what you want (the desirables – intend to have, nice to have). Think about and understand what will happen if you cannot reach an agreement. Brainstorming possible outcomes could lead you to solutions that you had not even considered before. Be clear on what you won't compromise on and what your 'walk away' strategy is.

Team negotiations

Consider whether this will be a team negotiation, and if so consider who should be the participants. How the two sides populate their teams will usually have an impact on the outcome. Among other things you should try to keep people out of the negotiation who tend to inflame the situation. If you are negotiating in teams then you should also research the participants of the other team and understand who and what you are up against, why they were included and what role within the negotiating team they are likely to play. Understanding the other team's individual profiles and why they were selected gives an indication of the areas their team leader feels are important or the areas they feel require some expertise. Roles for team negotiation include: lead negotiator and the only person allowed to speak unless the lead negotiator requests them to speak; note taker; person to write down other team's body language and what they have noticed; observer (for an overall view and paying attention to details made); you can also have an advisor – an expert eg in artificial intelligence.

Make sure the whole team are well briefed and work well together as one team.

Facts or assumptions

When preparing, separate the facts from assumptions by understanding what you know about the situation and what you assume to be true. Validate your facts and make sure your information is current. Assumptions need to be tested, validated or discarded. Incorrect assumptions can damage an otherwise successful negotiating strategy. Don't set yourself up for failure by relying on an invalidated assumption because you like it or it helps your case.

During the negotiation ensure everyone is aware of the issues to be discussed and uncover any new issue that needs to be addressed. If new information is provided or the issues change, then it is advisable to take a break to reflect or regroup with your team if necessary.

Make sure you have a plan to deal with the outcome whether you win or lose for both short- and long-term benefits. As a negotiator, you will want to make sure what you are saying is the best way to get across the intent and that you are being heard. The best way to do this is to practise.

Relationships

Clarify the relationship – what is the current real and perceived business and personal relationship, and what is its true value to your and your organization's future? You must cautiously determine what could be lost in any negotiation and at the same time keep the goal in mind. Think about the history of the relationship. Could or should this history impact the negotiation? Will there be any hidden issues that may influence the negotiation? How will you handle these? Think about the consequences of winning or losing this negotiation – both for you and the other person.

Consider who has what power in the relationship. Who controls the resources? Who stands to lose the most if agreement isn't reached? What power does the other person have to deliver what you hope for? You may need to build relationships with key people before the negotiations – people who can help you with your information gathering.

If you are negotiating on behalf of someone else, you may need to get their agreement on what you have planned. At this stage you will need to have clarity, be assertive, capable and have influencing and persuasive skills to put your case forward both for the agreement and for the negotiation itself.

Values and beliefs

Values and beliefs determine how you and the other party view the world and how you prioritize your life, decisions and actions. In order to be successful in negotiation and start from a position of strength, you need to understand your own value to the other party from their perspective. You must also understand what you value about them too. During preparation, tailor your questions to the possible interests, needs and values of your counterpart. The other party's beliefs can also present fears, anxieties and concerns that you can use to your advantage throughout the negotiation process. Your goal is to dissect these value and belief patterns, determine the influence they have over the other party's decision-making ability and develop an appropriate strategy on how to use this information to your advantage throughout the negotiation process.

Pre-negotiation tactics

A pre-negotiation tactic could include an informal meeting to elicit information; using the grapevine, but better still your own ears and eyes (but be aware of wrong information from third parties); using the devil's advocate and looking at it from a neutral position and projecting yourself in your counterpart's position. You will then have further information to be able to predict counter-claims and schemes by the other party; consider possible concessions of both parties and thereby be prepared to respond to arguments and better able to decide on a 'fall-back' position. Sending out an agenda pre the meeting with your opening statement can set the expectations of your counterpart and thereby 'anchor' (see under tactics) your suggestion. You could also have a pre-negotiation meeting to decide on the agenda and the framework of the negotiation and where and when it will take place and whether it would be face-to-face or via an online platform or by telephone. Being able to see the other person is preferable as it gives you the opportunity to watch their facial expressions and body language.

Determine the ideal location for the negotiation, which should not be held in the other party's office as that gives them psychological power. To make it fair, ideally, the negotiation should be held in a neutral place. Factors that you should consider when setting up an effective location for the negotiation include room location, time of meeting, layout of chairs and tables and environmental factors such as: privacy, noisiness, crowded conditions and frequent interruptions.

The time of negotiations is also important. Human beings are always in some part at the mercy of their 'biorhythms' which cause the body and the mind to function differently at different times of day. Ideally you want to negotiate after a good night's sleep and in the morning when you are most alert and able to think clearly. Neither do you want to be hungry but at the same time you don't want to be feeling sluggish after a big meal. So choosing your time and place is important to be able to be the most effective negotiator.

During the negotiation – opening statements

The first few seconds

When meeting the other person/party, you should seek to create the desired impression right from the start. (Read Chapter 2 on 'Relationship management' and Chapter 3 on 'Compassionate communication' in *The Definitive Personal Assistant & Secretarial Handbook*, 3rd edition).

Agenda

Set and agree an agenda to keep the meeting structured, the dialogue focused and moving forward to a win–win conclusion. Agree on what is negotiable and what is non-negotiable. For example when negotiating for a new job, a non-negotiable may be that you have to leave every Tuesday and Thursday at 17.00 as you are attending University part time for the next two years.

Depending on the length of the negotiation you may want to incorporate breaks. Breaks can be used to reboot your brain, to check information with colleagues, to discuss what has been put on the table, discuss tactics, to have some refreshments, to get some fresh air, collect your thoughts and simply for a bathroom break.

Hidden agendas

People can have hidden agendas, which are the personal and private goals and objectives that affect the way we negotiate. Hidden agendas are likely to be different for each person and even for co-negotiators on your own team.

To uncover hidden agendas:

- Ask questions to get the other person's needs and wants, and then ask follow-up questions designed to cross-check or validate previous answers. Question the responses if you feel it necessary as it is important to understand not only the words being used but the meaning behind them so you truly understand the message of what you are being told. So look for the vagueness as well as what they are emphasizing.

- Make sure the message and the non-verbal body language, gestures and facial expression are congruent with each other; if they are not, ask more questions.

Who goes first?

The right time to put your offer is after you have prepared well and gathered all the information you need. Once you have a firm grasp of your own value to them and what the other party values then you should open first. If you open first, then you are showing a lead and forcing the other person to follow. You are also 'anchoring' your proposal (see tactics). It is not always possible to go first; eg when buying a car there will be a price already on it and therefore the 'anchoring' has already been done and you have no choice than to respond to the 'anchor'. If you put a good case, then you may make it more difficult for them, forcing them to try to counter your early initiative. Ask for more than you really want and more than you expect to get – if you don't ask you don't get and you won't know unless you try. If you start high you can always come down but if you start low you have nowhere to go! Having said that, be careful of pitching too high and not allowing the other party to move – this may happen if a principle is at stake. This is your judgement call!

State your case and your needs and make it clear what you want from the other person.

If you open second, then you have the opportunity to respond to whatever the other person says after gleaning as much information as you can from them. This is the preferred tactic of a hostage negotiator.

Listen to their case

In a negotiation, information really is power. There are many reasons to actively listen in a negotiation. The first stage is to listen without interrupting as that shows respect, and your interest will get the other party to give you more information. You can 'pause' them to paraphrase back what you have heard and you can ask them for clarification, but keep these interruptions to a minimum. This can be difficult especially when you are longing to respond to some of the things they are saying. However if you plunge straight into a debate, you may miss some very useful information. To paraphrase, state your non-judgemental impression and then pause to give them the opportunity to correct your understanding by using such phrases as:

It seems to me you are saying ...

It sounds like you are saying ...

I get the impression that ...

It looks like ...

I sense you are ...

I feel as if ...

Then probe for understanding

When they have made their case, you can then ask deeper questions to probe for further information. Explore their proposal not only to find out more but asking questions helps create an illusion of control for them!

Ask probing questions to draw out more information such as:

- How do you see that working?
- What concerns you about ...?
- What options have you considered for...?

However, if you think they have left out areas that you might have expected them to cover, it may be because they are not comfortable talking about this. In this case sustain a gentle approach of interest, curiosity and general inquiry. If you make it sound like an inquisition, they may well stop talking. Your goal is to make it easy for them to tell you more about their situation.

When your proposal or offer is countered, you have the following options: you can accept, reject, or counter back, sit back and do nothing, or ask for a break to consider the terms.

You may find you have to re-evaluate your position and be creative to find solutions. Experienced negotiators read the signals from the other party quickly and accurately. Instead of just giving in you can try trading: 'If you could do this for me then I could do your task quicker and be able to spend a bit more time on what you are asking me to do.'

Separate the people from the problem

If you were to meet these people in a social setting they would probably be entirely different, so concentrate on their behaviours not the person.

Discussion (including tactics)

Make sure that you share information at the same level of detail and do not give too much, or you could be exploited. There is a balance to get right – you can't give too little as this may stop the negotiations.

Let them concede first if possible but be prepared to concede and use your concessions wisely and ask for reciprocation. Begin conceding your 'nice to haves'/low priority but which are high value to them and at the same time seek high value items in return. All movement should be realistic and within your plan.

If you know in advance of a demand that you are willing to concede, link it to an issue where you require movement from the other party and also remember the Law of Reciprocation. If you concede something they will feel obliged to concede something also, and if they don't offer a concession then ask for one. This is known as a 'give–get' negotiation and will be more of a win–win outcome. However, you have to remember that giving away too much too early can leave you with a poor hand to play in the rest of the negotiation, and it could signal to the other party that your 'gift' (a concession that they have not had to work for) is just a taster of bigger and better things to come!

Similarly, if the other party offers you a 'gift' be cautious, as they may be trying to lure you into reciprocation, obliging you to give back something of greater value in return. So keep in mind the value of the item being given and the relative value to both sides.

You can proactively vary your emotions from 'stunned' to 'relaxed' depending on the context of the situation. You can make the 'unimportant issues' essential, then concede them at a later time with hesitation, making the other party believe they won a big battle and leaving them feeling satisfied.

Make logical arguments

Intelligent people will not be easily convinced by the use of emotional persuasive tactics. However, if you present them with a logical argument that breaks down your point of view into facts, statistics, business plan and data that they cannot disprove, then you will effectively win them over to your way of thinking.

Words are a critical component of the communication process. Sometimes they are so very important, that a few ill-thought-out words can spell your doom and break down the negotiation at a moment's notice.

Here are a few words that have negative or weak connotations and that you should refrain from using throughout the negotiation process as they could possibly ruin your chances of attaining a favourable outcome.

- 'Hope...'
- 'Can't...'
- 'Try...'
- 'But...'
- 'Should...'

Phrases to avoid and power phrases to use instead:

Phrases not to use	Power Phrases to use
yes but ...	yes and ...
you make me feel ...	when you ... I feel ... because ... I prefer ...
calm down	I think I understand, can I paraphrase to check...
you said ...	it seems to me you are saying ...
Are you serious?	that's interesting – why would you say that?
I totally disagree!	I see it differently, however I want to understand your point of view better – tell me more
what's wrong with you?	yhat's interesting – why would you do that?
how could you possibly think that?	that's interesting, tell me more
No problem	You're welcome – I know you would do the same for me (and nod whilst saying it)

Develop and maintain rapport

Your next objective is to first develop and later maintain a strong rapport with your counterpart. This is done in several ways involving the process of mirroring and matching, by observing the other party carefully, taking notice of their facial gestures, body language and the verbal language they persistently use. Match and mirror their body language and language ie words used, tone of voice, pace of voice, intonation (all of which can be used to build relationships over the telephone) in order to build relationships at a deeper level. You can even match their breathing to help build rapport.

Echo tactic

When your counterpart is talking and you want them to say more or expand on what they are saying, repeat the last one to five words or phrase of what they just said. This makes you focus and understand what they are saying and helps them to link their thoughts. Be silent for at least five seconds to let the echo tactic work its magic. It encourages the other side to say more and then you learn more about them, their wants and needs and gain insights into their thinking. It buys you time to consider the other party's latest offer and prepare a well-thought-out response. It creates a sense of similarity and understanding which facilitates bonding and trust and helps the other party to negotiate in good faith.

Match beliefs, values and habits

You can match the beliefs, values and habits that make up their personality, characteristics and behaviours. In order to connect with them at a deeper level, you must show that you are 'like them' in at least some ways. Consciously matching their beliefs and values will show the other party that you stand by the same principles that they believe in.

Acknowledge your understanding as they speak by nodding your head and making short verbal remarks. If they see that you are willingly considering their side of the story, then they will be more open and accepting of your perspective. Be clear that you are only nodding to show understanding of their point of view – not to agree with them.

Think in solution-oriented ways using 'chunking up' and 'chunking down'.

'Chunk up'

When you can't see eye-to-eye with the other party and you begin to feel that problems are getting in the way of your negotiations, decide to 'chunk up' (get to the bigger picture) by seeking common global interests that you and the other party share. These interests will help you establish areas of common ground that you can agree upon and therefore work from in order to reach a favourable outcome. A 'chunking up' question would be: 'How does this fit into the plan we've been following?'

An example of 'chunking up' would be when one person wants to buy cheaper copier paper and the other person thinks it would give a poor impression to the clients. You could ask: 'What would cheaper paper get for us?' and 'What would a good customer impression get for us?' The answers might be 'cost savings' and 'more sales', respectively. One more 'chunk up' by asking 'What do "cost savings" and "more sales" mean to us and our company?' and the answer would be 'We would make more profit.' Then both parties can address the problem with a common goal.

'Chunk down'

When you can't see eye-to-eye with the other party and you begin to feel that problems are getting in the way of your negotiations, decide to 'chunk down', seeking common agreement in the detail that you and the other party share. You may not see the same solution, but there may very well be certain aspects of this solution that you both acknowledge and can agree upon. Identify these aspects and work on re-establishing rapport and finding common ground. A 'chunking down' question would be: 'How does this affect the way I report my work?' taking you down to a particular detail. To chunk down further you may ask 'What are examples of this... ?'; 'What specifically... ?' or 'What else... ?'

Anchoring tactic

Anchoring is a very powerful tactic and is mainly in our unconscious mind so we don't even realize when we are doing it to people or when it is done to us. I will explain anchoring in the literal sense so you can understand the psychological meaning – anchoring is where you drop your anchor into the water and it brings the ship to a complete stop and movement is minimal once the anchor has been dropped. In negotiation there is a psychological process involved in anchoring. When we negotiate, we can become 'anchored' to a specific amount or plan of action, the anchor establishes a reference point and then we filter all new information through that framework, instead of seeing it objectively, distorting our perception and skewing our judgement. Make anchoring work for you by stating your expectations and outcome first in the opening statement or in a letter or agenda sent out pre-negotiation then any movement in negotiation is minimal from that starting point. Your counterpart will be unconsciously anchored to the statement. If you can get them to nod to this it enhances their anchoring!

We are all susceptible to this so make sure you are not being anchored by your counterpart! Even professional negotiators can fall foul of this technique. To check if you are being anchored, make sure you remember the anchor tactic and fully assess your opinions and decisions and take your time making decisions with an open mind. Ask yourself: 'Am I relying too heavily on the first piece of information?' Our unconscious minds find it difficult to ignore anchoring but you can reduce it by considering reasons why the anchor doesn't fit the situation well and search your memory for all the reasons and arguments against the anchor. The strategy of deliberately thinking the opposite negates the anchoring effect because it activates the prefrontal cortex (the thinking, logical, rational part of your brain). As nodding embeds the anchor even more, shaking your head in a 'no' fashion as if you were rejecting it, helps to remove the anchor and when you hear the anchor later you move further from it.

Your challenge is to avoid being anchored by what you have already heard or seen so proceed as if the anchor was not dropped.

Delaying tactics in order to build tension

Deferred response – get the other party to repeat what they have asked for and then compare the first and second statements. If there is a discrepancy between the two, you can say 'I am sorry I don't quite understand...'.

Priming tactic

Priming effect is a suggestion that we receive at an unconscious level and that influences our thoughts and behaviours. It is the art of prompting people to think a certain way and we are able to influence people's behaviour without their realizing. You are more likely to get what you want if they feel it is their idea. It works by using associations made in our subconscious mind because our brains look for shortcuts and easy ways of operating. Even the use of a single word – like 'keep' instead of 'lose' – in our opening statement can unconsciously influence the conscious choices people make. Studies show that using words of cooperation means you can reach agreements faster with more satisfaction. If we want to have a collaborative negotiation then we should use collaborative words such as respectful, fair, ethical. We can use the word 'we' instead of 'I' making it feel like both parties are on the same side. We can sit at a 45 degree angle rather than sitting opposite (depicting confrontation) for a priming of collaboration.

WARNING!

- Consider whether you have been primed by your counterpart!
- Think before you speak – or you might say something that changes the entire conversation in the wrong direction!

You can prime yourself to give a good performance. Expectations drive behaviour – if we expect to give poor performance we will – change your expectations to be positive and change your outcomes.

Using time as a negotiation tactic

Time is a valuable commodity to us all and is often overlooked as a tactic that can be used in negotiations.

You can extend the time originally allocated in order to settle or force a resolution. If the issue is a minor irritant for the other party, being openly willing to take more time in order to make an agreement may motivate the other party to agree/concede/settle rather than waste additional time negotiating.

You can shorten the time allowed to come to an agreement. If the issue is a minor irritant for you, being openly willing to walk away leaving the matter unsettled may motivate the other party to settle rather than risk losing the opportunity. This is especially effective if you have other options and the other party does not.

What if ... tactic

Use the 'language of possibility' to test interest and introduce concepts and make them realize what could possibly happen or what they could possibly get. This can be used at the beginning when exploring possibilities or at the end to say 'What if I do .... will you agree to the whole deal?'

For example: 'What if the company pays for my University fees and I promise to stay with the company for at least three years and use my skills for the company?'

Our brains are wired more strongly to avoid losses than to obtain gains – we feel worse about losing £50 than feeling good about finding £50. We even feel loss when we do not gain as much as we expect to.

We can use 'What if' for 'What if we don't do ...? This is what we will lose' eg if we don't offer any incentives, we won't get anyone to sign up and we will lose revenue.

Therefore: Be careful of taking risks to avoid losses.

Be careful of acting unethically to avoid losses.

Silence as a negotiating tactic

Imagine that everyone is gathered around a table, the stakes are high, tension fills the air as the other person lays out a detailed counter-proposal for your consideration. Everyone is waiting for your reaction, expecting a response.

Doing nothing causes a 'void' of silence. Often the other person will feel compelled to fill the void. Your silence is sending the message that you are not entirely happy with the proposal. If the other person offers to improve or modify the proposal or if they become otherwise uncomfortable with the silence, they may signal that they have the room to negotiate further. Negotiation necessitates that you have the patience and confidence to be still. If the other party perpetuates a long silence then you should simply wait and let them break it.

If ... then tactic

This tactic is based on the idea that most people never give up anything without getting something in return. 'If ... then' is about making an offer that is contingent on specific conditions.

IF you give me X, **THEN** I will give you Y.

If...then' plans use your subconscious mind to help you think quicker and help you stick to your prepared decisions.

For example:

If they offer my minimum, **then** I will ask for my maximum.

If we cannot come to a satisfactory agreement, **then** I will walk away with my best alternative to a negotiated agreement (BATNA).

Cognitive biases

Before engaging in a negotiation, it is important to understand some of the common cognitive biases that could affect you and the opposite party during the negotiation.

There are over one hundred cognitive biases so I am discussing just a few relating to negotiation. Conscious bias means we make associations without being aware we are doing it and they are not easy to identify. Biases are mental shortcuts that influence our preferences, what we pay attention to and create deeply embedded attitudes. For example, we might have gender stereotypes about women who we think of as likable, nurturing, non-assertive and men as competent, aggressive, protective which all play a large role in influencing negotiation outcomes.

Check your own biases by checking your assumptions and perceptions and change the internal narrative you are telling yourself. If you are in a conflict negotiation, ask yourself what part have you played in this and what can you do to change it? Think about whether you need to slow down the negotiation process to really understand what is going on in your brain and how it is affecting the negotiation.

In-attentional blindness

In-attentional blindness is our tendency to see, hear and experience only that which we are focused on, and we are blind to other obvious factors that are not the focus of our attention. This means that important information is overlooked and this could result in ineffective decisions. During a negotiation, parties are so focused on their positions/perspectives/goals while processing multiple issues and complex information that inattentional blindness could make even the most expert negotiators miss key information for effective resolutions.

Confirmation bias

I discussed confirmation bias in Chapter 3 on 'Developing emotional intelligence' but it is worth mentioning here too as it often goes hand-in-hand with in attentional blindness. Confirmation bias comes from a sense of self-protection and a desire to confirm what you believe is true and right – we hardly ever look for things that prove us wrong. When we're confronted with complex information, we're likely to focus on information that is favourable to us. When we encounter neutral information, we interpret it in a way that is favourable to us. The more time we spend on gathering and interpreting information that strengthens our perspective, the more likely we will believe our preconceptions. We only see what we look for.

When in a negotiation, we often analyse the situation purely from our own perspective. To engage in an effective negotiation and to neutralize the confirmation bias, it is important to be aware and understand that we do not see the complete picture. It becomes necessary therefore to analyse the situation both rationally and psychologically from your counterpart's perspective, so that effective and realistic decisions can be made.

Reactive devaluation

This is a cognitive bias that occurs in a negotiation when a proposal or concession is devalued simply because it originated from an adversary or someone you do not like and are therefore more likely to reject their proposal because of your bias against the person offering it. This bias can occur irrespective of the quality of your counterpart's proposal or concession.

It would be useful to reflect on the true reasons why you don't want to accept an offer (you could be causing problems for yourself by acting against someone else). Similarly, when you have offers to make at a negotiation, you might want to consider if you are the best person to make that offer to the other side.

Relationship bias/affinity bias

We tend to be attracted toward and like people whom we know well and with whom we share similar interests. The stronger our relationship with another person, the more likely we are to believe them when they tell us something. The weaker the relationship, the less likely we are to believe them. However, the relationship may have little to do with the accuracy of the information.

The relationship bias relates to the affinity bias where we tend to warm to people who are like ourselves and in negotiation are more likely to trust them. Ask yourself: 'Am I being overly trusting of the information from this person whom I feel an affinity with?'

Don't rush the negotiation process

Sometimes we rush negotiations too quickly and we fail to identify potential opportunities for agreement that could benefit all parties involved. In such instances it is better to walk away from the negotiation to gather your thoughts, and then step back into the negotiation at a later time with more clarity and 'ammunition' that will help you attain a favourable outcome.

Face-to-face negotiating behaviours that should be avoided by ethical and effective negotiators:

- unclear proposals;
- too many points in their arguments;
- attacking and defending.

Face-to-face negotiating behaviours that should be used by ethical and effective negotiators:

- asking questions;
- building on other's ideas;
- expressing feelings;
- testing understanding;
- summarizing.

When the negotiation comes to a standstill

When you face a seemingly insuperable problem in the negotiation say: 'Under what circumstances would you be prepared to give way on this?' In salary negotiations where they are not budging say: 'Under what circumstances would you be willing to give me a raise?' This will force your employer to spell out the criteria necessary to giving you a raise.

If you are stuck in deadlock and lack an effective way to negotiate differences leaving a huge impasse, you can bridge the gap by appointing a facilitator/mediator to ensure that both sides understand the data correctly, reconcile any cultural differences, remind you of your shared goals, clear up misunderstandings and enable everyone to speak freely and move on with the negotiation to a win–win outcome.

Bargaining

Past bargaining can determine the issues for future bargaining but if no precedent exists then power decides. Bargaining should be fair and once an offer is made it should not be withdrawn unless it was clearly stated when negotiated that it is only a provisional measure. Information given in confidence should not be used publicly.

Find common ground

If you both agree on some smaller points early on, neither side will want to jeopardize the progress made, encouraging a deal that benefits you both. Begin negotiations with what the parties agree on, then move to an issue where you are close to an agreement and finally work on the tougher issues once you have got to know your counterpart better. When you have got into a pattern of thinking in terms of shared interest and have a momentum then you have a positive dynamic for a win–win outcome.

Know what your 'best alternative to a negotiated agreement' (BATNA) is and write it down. This is not your bottom line but an alternative course of action you can take in case you cannot come to an agreement in your negotiations. It gives you more power because you do have an alternative and therefore greater flexibility and more room for innovation than if you have only a predetermined bottom line. You would then know the consequences of what happens if an agreement cannot be reached (it's like a safety net) and you know that you are able to walk away from the negotiation, which gives you more power when negotiating.

Tactical ways of saying 'no'

Instead of saying 'no' you could say:

- 'I'll see what I can do.'
- 'Maybe.'
- 'I'll ask.'
- 'I'll find out.'
- 'I need to ask my boss as s/he has more authority than me.'

Knowing your 'walk away' point

Do not negotiate if there are unrealistic demands being made at any stage as you must avoid having to concede substantial amounts unnecessarily. Walking away avoids raising false hopes that would make it difficult to satisfy later, and by not negotiating under these circumstances you will stamp your personal authority and professionalism on the situation. You should simply give a clear and honest 'I cannot agree to these terms', stating a suitable explanation and reasons with empathy for the other person's situation.

Let the other party know that you mean what you say but are still leaving the door open for them to reopen the discussion if they wish to concede on your 'walk away' issue. It is important to never re-evaluate your 'walk away' during the negotiation.

If new information is presented at this point, take a break to consider the information and take time to process it. It is easy to convince yourself to change your 'walk away' position if you can see that the negotiation will not come to a suitable conclusion for anyone. Remember, the reason for developing 'walk away' positions before the negotiation was to prevent you from being pressured into conceding on critical issues.

This is an instance where, unless the other party reconsiders, you will be far better served strategically in the future by looking for another way of accomplishing your goal, or indeed possibly building new relationships.

Tactic to get closure

If there is only one problem standing between failure and agreement and you are able to make a concession, then make it as long as it is a minor one and doesn't compromise your position. If there are two problems, maybe you could both agree to compromise.

Timing is important when reaching an agreement, as the time to conclude is when there is a collaborative not a confrontational atmosphere so you can preserve your relationships.

Agreement and action plan

The art of negotiating is most required when you are presented with an offer that is acceptable. The dilemma is in knowing whether it is the best you can do and whether it is time to stop negotiating and accept the terms.

Some people feel they have to win every deal and every point, which is not a good way to negotiate. If you want to develop relationships and come up with creative solutions then you must understand that you may need to be prepared to lose some battles to win the war.

Holding out for a lost cause is not only against your best interest but also makes you seem stubborn and foolish. Know when to give in on a point and, if it is not a 'walk away' issue and you know what you have previously decided you can concede, then concede graciously. It does not do any harm to ask what they can concede in return and continue to negotiate.

At the end of negotiation find ways to make the other person feel good about something. For example compliment the other person's performance, professionalism or knowledge. Indicate your appreciation that the other person was personally involved in working things out. Ease back from the transaction discussion to a more personal level of conversation.

Indicate that you appreciate how the other person was able to be flexible and help solve the situation. Indicate that he or she has won some loyalty on your part. Try to give the other person a reason to be pleased with more than just the terms of the agreement.

Once you have reached an agreement it is time to evaluate how the process has worked. If you have only achieved some of your objectives try to set a date to review what has been agreed and revisit outstanding points. In any negotiation you want to reach a deal that is acceptable to all involved. When you master the art of negotiation a relationship can be enhanced by the experience.

Unless what has been agreed is immediately summarized and noted, the two parties may leave the discussions with different interpretations of what their agreement really means. The final note taking and summary is therefore a vital part of every negotiation. The final agreement should include all necessary points for implementation, be clearly understood and should not be expressed in ambiguous terms.

Make the final agreement public and put the action plan in writing with both parties signing it. If implementation is to be gradual then specific time limits should be agreed and follow-up meetings may be required to monitor the progress.

Finally, good relations between all parties have hopefully been maintained and the negotiators have ended on friendly terms.

Summary

Negotiation is how we succeed in life. It applies to everything we do, and the better we are at it, the better results we can achieve. Understanding the way our brains work is crucial to understanding how we communicate with people. Language, prejudice, biases, preconceptions and emotional intelligence all fall under the category of neuroscience within negotiations.

To be an effective negotiator you have to be able to think of all possible outcomes for yourself and the other party. The other party has to be able to trust you and if you are always calm it translates across all cultures, creating clarity and credibility. You need to be in control of your language and tone of voice thereby keeping your reputation intact. You need to be able to develop durable agreements with creative solutions. You need to be likeable because if the other party can't help but like you it has an impact on them and on the negotiations.

To be an effective negotiator, you need to use your emotional intelligence (read Chapter 3), understand change management and resilience (read Chapter 10) and be able to motivate yourself (read Chapter 2).

When you are asking questions to get information you need to evaluate the circumstances of your negotiation – you want the other party to work with you and not against you. It is important to think about how to best use your communication skills to get the right results including using anchoring and priming tactics. The manner in which you ask your questions can have a powerful bearing on the results of your negotiation so remember to 'think before you speak'.

Negotiation is complex and uses many skills requiring discipline, patience, and an understanding of yourself, the other party as well as the subject matter and the circumstances of your negotiation. It is a gentle balancing act that must be carefully planned from before the negotiation starts to allow both parties to walk away with a win–win agreement.

Being able to effectively negotiate with your boss for a salary raise, a promotion, time off, skills training, or greater responsibility is vital for career growth. Taking into consideration this chapter with a well thought out strategic approach, you can make a persuasive case for yourself and have a successful outcome.

Great leaders are great negotiators and now that you are an effective negotiator you should be able to recognize situations where negotiating could help you in your leadership role. Maybe it will enable you to lead discussions; negotiate on artificial intelligence and what will be most helpful in your role; negotiate teamwork; and avoid conflict. You could negotiate hiring an assistant so that you can reduce your workload. This might even be the time to renegotiate your job description and redefine your roles and responsibilities within the organization. Remember: if you don't ask you don't get and practice makes perfect! Like any skill, the more you practise, the more intuitive it will feel and the more flexible and adept you will become under pressure. Be pleasant, persistent but not demanding and have fun!

Change, resilience and brain power

10

There are many drivers of organizational change including:

- technological developments including artificial intelligence;
- economic downturns and challenging trading conditions;
- growth opportunities including diversification, new markets and mergers;
- competition;
- social media;
- customer or supplier pressures;
- legislation;
- strategic shifts and reorganizations;
- sustainability and responsible business – corporate social responsibility;

The Covid-19 pandemic resulted in huge organizational change as many people started to work from home full time who previously thought it was highly unlikely they would ever do so. The pandemic showed that people can change and change quickly. However, this was only doable due to technology. Technology is driving further change and fundamentally the way businesses operate and the way people work.

Whether we realize it or not we communicate about change all the time and it is your responsibility to do it more consciously and intentionally as it is important to be a change agent and help your bosses become change champions.

Organizations need to introduce and manage change to achieve their vision, mission and strategic objectives whilst at the same time maintaining the commitment of their employees and ensuring the business continues as usual. It is the role of the assistant to aid these objectives.

Success depends on being resilient, positive and engaged while this rapid and accelerating change constantly turns our world upside down. This chapter is about explaining what exactly 'change management' is and how you can help it happen for yourself, your boss and your organization in a productive and less stressful way. It will help you change your limiting beliefs to empowering positive beliefs to enable you to accept change and achieve the best possible outcome for yourselves and others. You will learn how to use empowering questions to foster positivity and get rid of negativity for yourself and your teams.

You will learn the 'SixEss Threat/Reward Model', which helps you minimize threat and maximize reward feelings in the brain.

The chapter will help you think what you can do and say to help yourself and others through an effective and smooth change process, which leads to being more in control and calm and accepting, and therefore more motivated and successful. It will give you ideas on how to be a leader of change whether it is actually your project or not. You will learn theories of change management and what change acceptance means, whilst understanding the emotions of change that people can go through at each stage. It emphasizes that, after change, something better comes out of it and our understanding and positive attitude towards change will help us get there much quicker and with much less pain! The whole process of change can be perceived as an exciting opportunity instead of something to dread or shy away from. This chapter will help you understand and adopt that perception.

What exactly is 'change management' and how can you help it happen effectively?

Change management is a structured approach for ensuring that changes are thoroughly and smoothly implemented, and that the lasting benefits of change are achieved.

The focus is particularly on people and how they, as individuals and teams, move from the current situation to the new one. The change in question could range from a simple process change to major changes in policies and procedures as well as mergers and acquisitions that are sometimes needed if the organization is to achieve its highest potential, and sometimes indeed survive!

Change does not happen in isolation – it impacts the whole organization (system) around it, and all the people touched by it.

Change your view of change

When we think of change it quite often makes us feel fearful, negative, alone, apprehensive and in a state of stress as it flags up uncertainty and our brains treat uncertainty as a threat! If we could change our view of change and always think of it as something exciting that will stretch our minds and offer new opportunities, we will start to view it as something that can 'open doors' for us. Be full of optimism and enthusiasm and think of it as a challenge and therefore motivating and satisfying; life would be much more hopeful, positive, happier and less stressful. So here is how we are going to do it!

Understand how your brain works

Psychological safety

The way we conduct change management plans and the words we use can make a difference to how people respond to change. When we feel psychologically safe, the brain generates emotions such as excitement, trust, happiness that enables us to collaborate, be creative, problem solve and be highly productive, which all help towards successful change management plans.

To try and force a plan through will create a threat response, anxiety, distrust and a negative atmosphere. Even though you may think you know the change is for the best and believe everyone will just have to get used to it, you must consider the way people think to make it a smooth and easier transition for the benefit of the organization and its employees. A change management approach based in neuroscience helps engage the hearts and minds of those who need to change. They will not only be able to accept the change management plan, they will also be willing to accept it.

How to use neuroscience knowledge of threat and reward feelings in the brain to help you collaborate with and influence others

The brain responds with either a threat or a reward feeling in many different situations due to its primary responsibility to keep us safe. It constantly scans people's behaviours and what they say, as well as the environment, to identify and respond to threats. Understanding how the brain's threat and reward networks lead us to move towards (rewards) and away from (threat) situations is the key to applying neuroscience to your toolkit of communication and influencing skills.

Reward response: Our brain looks to identify opportunities and reward, which is when we release feel good hormones such as dopamine, endorphins, serotonin, oxytocin etc and we then have a feeling of trust and are able to use our prefrontal cortex. We then able to think better, make informed decisions, problem solve, have more insights and creative responses, are able to rationalize and become far more engaged, productive and efficient. As dopamine is an addictive hormone, we seek ways to be 'rewarded' again.

Threat response: When we feel threatened, either physically or socially, whether real or perceived, our sympathetic nervous system is activated, our amygdala wakes up, we release adrenaline and cortisol (stress hormone) and we either want to fight, flight, freeze or flock (go and find allies to talk to). We do need some adrenaline and cortisol to give us the 'oomph' but too much is detrimental to our health and shuts down our prefrontal cortex and we literally cannot think properly. We therefore become disengaged and less productive as it blocks our creativity, reduces our ability to solve problems and makes it harder to communicate.

I have created a model to help with understanding how to minimize threat and maximize reward:

'The SixEss Threat/Reward Model':

Survival	Be aware of how our survival system works and that our natural instinct for survival depends on our ability to make predictions (which are not always correct) to keep us safe. Our brain looks for threat five times more than it looks for reward as the primary goal of the brain is to predict where and how we can avoid threats. Understanding this means we can take control of our knee jerk reaction of fight, flight, freeze or flock and use our more responsive prefrontal cortex which allows us to rationalize, take control of our behaviour and make well thought out decisions resulting in more effective outcomes.
Self-rule	The brain values choice and has a reward feeling when we feel in control and have autonomy over decisions and our work. When we do not feel in control of our own destiny and whether the threat is true or imagined, we feel stressed and have feelings of threat.

Sociability	Social connection, a feeling of belonging and engaging in effective interpersonal relationships and a sense of feeling safe with others are important and motivating factors for success. When meeting people we weigh them up to see whether they are a 'friend' or a 'foe'. The pain we feel from social anguish such as rejection, being ignored and not getting 'likes' and being trolled on social media activates the same areas of the brain as being physically hit, which illustrates how important social relationships are to human beings.
Social standing	Social pain or perceived social pain could be a feeling of being belittled, ignored or rejected and social acceptance or your status and social standing is about how important and respected we feel in the eyes of others.
Silos	When people work in silos and lack diversity and inclusion it creates cynicism, resentment and feels extremely unfair and therefore we have a threat response. However, when we feel respected, valued and are being treated fairly it turns on the brain's reward circuit as fairness satisfies a basic human need. We have a threat feeling or reward feeling depending on whether you feel you are being excluded ie in the 'out group' or included ie in the 'ingroup' respectively. In organizations we need a unified focus, collaborative teamwork and a feeling of connection and belonging to the organization as a whole. When you have a fair and inclusive working environment you create trust.
Sureness	We like to feel sure and certain of what the future holds for us which produces a reward state. When the brain detects ambiguity and uncertainty we are less able to predict and therefore feel the threat response.

Many people accidentally create a threat response in others; therefore remember 'The SixEss Threat/Reward Model' and always strive to create a reward response in your own brain as well as in the brains of others. When you affect people positively by giving them the feeling of reward you are more able to influence them for more positive outcomes. Remember to think when interacting with others: 'Is what I am about to do or say likely to elicit a threat or reward response?' Get to know the people you work with so you can better understand what they find rewarding and what threatens them and treat them as individuals. For example, you could ask a colleague to give a presentation to the leadership team and they may think of it as a reward and be delighted to be asked; whereas another person may find it a threat and want to run away.

'The SixEss Threat/Reward Model' can be used in many areas of human relationships both at work and personally. Teach this model to others including your boss. As an example, I will explain how to use this model to help support and positively influence change management initiatives.

Each element is on a continuum and actions and words can either cause an 'away from' ie threat response or a 'toward' ie reward response.

Behaviour causing
threat feelings 'away from' state

Survival

Not understanding the process of change, and in particular change that is forced upon you, and how the brain treats change as a threat and that the threat response is easily triggered as the brain treats threat as critical for our survival.

Understanding the 'Change Curve Model' and the 'journey' you will go on will help you keep control of your feelings or at least 'ride' them and be better able to survive a change management process knowing that the outcome will be positive and at the very least that you will be able to accept and work with the outcome. People experience what they expect to experience so manage expectations of yourself and others and make sure expectations are positive.

Self-rule

Taking away any decision-making privileges and/or control in aspects of the change management process and simply telling people what to do.

Allow them to have choice and use their discretion and judgement (even if limited). If you cannot give full autonomy, then at least give a perception of it but never micro-manage.

Sociability

Fostering internal competition and stopping people from socializing in the workplace.

Make sure everyone has the opportunity to communicate with each other to develop relationships and trust with a view to collaboration. Encourage regular communication and relationship building by whichever channel is available and suitable.

Social standing

Whenever you disrespect or rebuff people's ideas and solutions especially when witnessed by others. Reducing responsibilities of their role without consultation and/or distributing part of their role to other people.

Show respect by genuinely considering contributions, giving praise openly in meetings. Consult individuals on their workload and ask whether they need help and if so, what suggestions do they have. Provide opportunities for learning and enhanced responsibility wherever they feel they have the availability and capability to take more on.

Silos

Allowing silos to form and cliques to develop, leaving individuals out of certain meetings. Regularly choosing your 'in-group,' the ones you favour for certain tasks, will be deemed unfair and will cause a rift between people and teams

Make everyone feels included and listened to and part of the 'in-group'. Encourage collaboration and cross divisional/cross cultural teamwork. Treat people fairly, never show favouritism or exclude anyone without a full reasonable explanation and transparency. Follow the policies of the organization on equality, diversity and inclusion.

Sureness

People will feel unsure when they have not yet experienced the new changes taking place. Having a lack of clarity, goals, expectations and appearing to keep secrets will add to their uncertainty and threat feeling.

Provide a sense purpose with clear goals, expectations and transparency and a vision for the future. Boost their confidence of their capabilities.

Learn to spot threats in others early so you can learn to influence feelings of reward. Practise self-awareness and understand the roots of your own emotions and use your emotional intelligence to be better able to manage yourself. Creating long term change requires regularly repeating the new ways of thinking and working to deepen the new neural pathways until they become a habit or routine.

Change your beliefs – become a change optimist!

Through extensive research, Ariane de Bonvoisin (author, entrepreneur and an expert on change) has created the nine 'Principles of change' that really work and that seem to be true of all people who are good at navigating the twists and turns of life. Use them, and you will be on the path to becoming a change optimist, one who understands that from even the most difficult change, something good will come (it always does!). Read the nine Principles below and think about which ones apply to you and which ones you will endeavour to use more fully!

People who successfully navigate change...

Principle 1:   Have positive beliefs.

Principle 2:   Know that change always brings something positive into their lives.

Principle 3:   Know they are resilient, strong and capable of getting through anything.

Principle 4:   Know that every challenging emotion they feel is not going to stop them and will guide them to positive emotions that help them feel better.

Principle 5:   Know that the quicker they accept the change, the less pain and hardship they will feel.

Principle 6:   Use empowering questions and words, think better thoughts, and express their feelings.

Principle 7:   Know they are connected to something bigger than themselves.

Principle 8:   Are not alone. They surround themselves with positive people who can help, who have the right belief and skills. They create an environment that supports their change.

Principle 9:   Take action. They have a plan and know how to take care of themselves.

We can help the change process by changing attitudes from avoidance to acceptance and from resistance to resilience. The ability to deal with change is at the heart of what it is to thrive as a species; as Charles Darwin put it: 'It is not the strongest of the species that survive, or the most intelligent, but the ones most responsive to change.'

When change is introduced, each employee's filter of the world, their past experiences, values and belief systems will produce a different perception and attitude towards that change. You cannot see or measure attitudes but you can see and measure the response towards change.

For example:

- Instead of thinking 'Why is this happening to me?' think 'What new opportunities will this provide?'

- Instead of thinking 'How will this affect me?' think 'What problems will this solve?'

- Instead of thinking 'We have always done it this way,' think 'There could be a better way – what would it look like?'

- Instead of thinking 'Who is doing this to us?' think 'How can I help make this process to manage change easier for myself and everyone?'

Feelings are contagious – when someone around you is feeling negative, it can make you feel negative. Similarly, when someone is positive and passionate about something, it can have an inspiring effect, motivating everyone else to be positive and passionate. Change management should consist of making it enticing, exciting and perceived as an opportunity so that others want to be a part of it. When you feel ownership of change and feel a part of it, your attitude will improve.

Our reactions to 'being changed' also depend on what the change is.

Change a limiting belief – NLP technique

This is a neuro-linguistic programming (NLP) technique that creates an empowering belief using submodality differences between a useful and less useful belief. It will help you stop your limiting beliefs from becoming self-fulfilling prophecies. Remember you have full control of choosing which beliefs you want to retain. The example below is about changing a limiting belief to an empowering and positive one, but the approach has many other applications.

Visual submodalities

For example, think of a picture about a situation or limiting belief that you have. Then, if you currently think of the picture in black and white, change it to a colour picture; if you think of it as dull then change it to a bright picture; if you think of it as near then think of it as far away and so on.

It's simply a matter of changing how you see the picture right now to make it different. If it's a picture of something you would rather get rid of, then make it duller or further away; if it is a belief you want to enhance then make it brighter, nearer, more colourful and so on. You can vary the size of each image; its positions/locations in your mental space (mind's eye) – left, right, top, bottom; the change may involve movement – for example whether it is still, a slideshow, video, movie, looping; it may be two or three-dimensional; framed or unframed; convex or concave; shape – clear/fuzzy/ any specific shape to it; style – picture, painting, photo, poster, drawing, 'real life'.

Auditory submodalities

With sounds you can change the volume to either loud or soft, or coming from a particular direction; mono or stereo; clear or fuzzy noise; pitch low or high; fading in and out; voice – whose and how many; other background sounds.

Kinaesthetic submodalities

How you felt/feel; is there a texture to it; sensation; pressure; temperature?

Use empowering questions to change beliefs – NLP technique

There is a lot in NLP about how you use language, and one of the most powerful areas is how to ask questions of yourself and others; for example, 'What is the one thing I can change about my thinking that will give me the best benefit right now?'

Ask yourself (and others) questions with the appropriate structure and voice tone, as that can help change our state and focus. While questions have an impact on us in different ways, consider the different internal impact of asking:

Why does this sort of thing always happen to me?

What can I learn from this so it will never happen to me again?

One leads us to focus on negative states and strategies that haven't worked, while the other leads us to focus on empowering states and strategies that have worked. You can use questions to improve parts of your life, and the impact of asking these type of questions repeatedly is likely to significantly affect how you feel and what you achieve.

Here are some examples of questions you could think about. In this technique we're using empowering questions to direct attention towards useful states, resources and actions.

What can I do to help others succeed?

What am I going to do to enjoy my day today?

What is the most useful thing I can do right now?

What do I need to do to get better at [specific area]?

What is the most effective way I can move forward?

What is going to be the most fun and going to move me forward today?

What am I going to start doing today, which in starting will help me succeed?

What am I going to stop doing today, which in stopping will help me succeed?

What am I going to continue doing today, which in continuing will help me succeed?

What is [name the person] doing so that s/he achieves things and how can I replicate it?

How good do I want to be at this, how can I get there in the quickest and most fun way?

How can I become more passionate about helping others to succeed?

How am I going to enjoy improving what I do?

How can I achieve more with less effort?

Who can help me with this?

You will be able to think of many more positive empowering questions that suit your situation. Write them down and ask yourself several questions every day – remember to leave a pause after each question to let the question resonate throughout your mind and body. Keep revising these questions every two weeks or so. You will also find some questions to think about in Resource 4, 'Coaching questions', in the section about this book on my website: www.suefrance.com.

A tip on self-talk

Add short phrases at the end of negative self-talk to change your mindset. Try saying it in different tones of voice and see what works for you.
For example add the phrase: 'Well for this second it might be true but not anymore.' Therefore if you say 'I am a complete fool,' it will become 'I am a complete fool, well for this second it might be true but not anymore!'

Leading change

Martin Luther King did not simply say, 'I have a very good plan,' he shouted,

I have a dream!

It is imperative as a leader to provide passion and a strong sense of purpose if you want to aid change through an effective transition.

Today's business world is highly competitive and to survive is to reshape to the needs of a rapidly changing world. Customers and clients are not only demanding excellent service, they are also demanding more. If you do not supply it, your competitors will.

Bill Lucas (author and speaker) suggests if you are leading change in your organization you should:

- make connections to the experiences of those with whom you are working so that you can build on a shared past;
- take time to make the case, dealing with difficult issues openly and acknowledging the feelings of those involved;
- actively engage people in creating the future;
- provide a compelling alternative vision and show how it is the best course of action;
- be a role model for the change you would like to see, so that people can see you walking the talk;
- minimize uncertainty and, once you have allowed enough time for reflection, take action.

Although each individual will have different and personal responses to change, people often show their attachment to the team and the way teams bond by joining in a uniform response and the majority way of thinking ('group think'). Although each person in that group might want to do something different, the need to belong to a group is strong and often sways individuals to follow the rest of the team. Therefore our response towards change is sometimes influenced by personal history and sometimes by the social situation.

When you are defining your change management objectives and activities, it's very important to coordinate closely with the wider team – the other stakeholders such as project managers, executive managers and the HR department. Find out who is responsible for identifying change agents and organizing the training and development plan etc.

Once you have considered the change management objectives, you will also need to consider the specific tasks. It is a question of working out what will best help you meet the change management challenge and how to work alongside other people and their projects' activities and responsibilities.

If you are not making changes and in particular embracing new technologies, artificial intelligence, social media, apps, tools that provide collaborative and better ways of working, saving time, energy and effort in the long term as well as challenging yourself, you will become outdated and irrelevant!

> It is only when they go wrong that machines remind you how powerful they are.
>
> Clive James

In addition to being an expert in tools such as Microsoft Office or G-suite, you have to be proficient in a myriad of different systems and new technology that appears on a daily basis, especially as many people are hybrid working from home and office. This may mean becoming an expert on Teams, Slack, Evernote, Hootsuite, OneNote, Zoom to name but a few. Taking the time to fully understand technological tools and artificial intelligence (and perhaps being involved in bringing it into the office) makes you relevant in today's world of work. We all need to change with the times and the evolution of the way we work and the ability to troubleshoot for your boss and colleagues is a must have skill.

Employees often resist change as it is the brain's natural reaction. It is our survival instinct and our brain is trying to keep us safe. Colleagues can become negative and complain when change is mentioned causing decreased morale, demotivated employees and a debilitating atmosphere resulting in a less productive and less efficient workforce. When employees resist change and change initiatives fail, it causes problems.

People will not choose to change until they know how to do it so help your boss create a change management plan by answering: Who? What? Where? When? Why? and How?

Six keys to a successful change management plan:

- Involve everyone concerned from the beginning.
- Show the bigger vision.
- Advocate that change is a process and take it step by step.
- Allocate enough resources.

- Build a powerful change leadership team and include people to get their buy-in.
- Communicate, communicate, communicate.

Change and emotions

People get comfortable performing tasks and processes in a particular way. They are within their 'comfort zone', and you often hear people say 'But we always do it this way.' This comfort provides people with the security of feeling that they are in control of their environment. They know what they are doing and it's human nature to want to stay within our comfort zone. Some of the things that cause them to fear change include: a dislike of a disruption in their lives; they don't want to look foolish if they cannot grasp the new procedure or new ways of working; their jobs may become harder, at least for a little while until they get used to them; and there is a feeling of loss of control. In some cases there may be a fear of redundancy too.

Resisting 'what is' (negative thoughts about what the situation is)

Remember to keep your power – the opposite of resisting 'what is' is accepting 'what is', ie accept the things we cannot change and change the things we can. Make friends with your fears and realize the difference between real and perceived fears and don't allow the imaginary and emotional fears to hold you back. Don't spend your time and energy wishing things were different and the challenges were not there, simply focus on what needs to be done and take the first step. Taking the first step is powerful because if we want to change the future we need to act and once the first step is take the rest follows easily!

The Japanese have a term called *Kaizen*, which means continual improvement. It is a never-ending quest to be better, and you become better by changing. Standing still allows your competitors to get ahead of you and could be the start of a possible demise.

Theories of change management

There are many theories to help us through change, and one of the most important ones that I would like to bring to your attention is the 'Change Curve', which explains explicitly the emotions people go through at four different stages of the change process. Understanding this process is extremely useful for everyone. It shows that, whatever emotions you are going through at the different stages, you will come out the other end accepting, happy and sometimes even delighted. Even if people are made redundant you often hear them say 'It's the best thing that ever happened to me – the job I've got now is much better than the last one and it suits my needs more.'

Understand the emotions of change using the 'Change Curve'

Ensure that people involved and affected by the change understand the change process and have access to help and support during times of uncertainty and upheaval. Assess the training needs driven by the change, and plan when and how these will be implemented. Identify and agree the success indicators for change, and ensure they are regularly measured and reported on.

The Change Curve Model attributed to psychiatrist Elisabeth Kubler-Ross, resulting from her work on personal transition in grief and bereavement, is a popular and powerful model used to understand how people will react at the different stages of change. Understanding this helps you to get through change easier and helps you to help others by making sure they have the help and support they need.

The model describes the four stages most people go through as they adjust to change.

Stage 1: Change is first introduced

People's initial reaction may be shock or denial. Once the reality of the change starts to hit, people tend to react negatively. Even if the change has been well planned and you understand what is happening, this is when the reality hits and people need to take time to adjust. People need information, need to understand what is happening, and need to know how to get help. It is critical that they are communicated to often and at the same time make sure that this doesn't overwhelm people: they'll only be able to take in a limited amount of information at a time. But make sure that people know where to go for more information if they need it and ensure that you take the time to answer any questions that come up.

If you ask people's opinions they will feel involved. Engaging people in dialogue rather than simply telling them what is going to happen ensures that information is shared. It also encourages people to be creative and to possibly come up with solutions that may not have been thought of, especially ones related to their own area of work. They know it better than anyone else. Such dialogue sends out strong messages about the respect you have for them and provides space where feelings can be shared.

We all like certainty and knowing where we stand. Much of the resistance to change may be due to a lack of clarity. The role of the leader is to offer a clear vision or a set of possible routes. Clearly state the advantages and disadvantages of the different courses of action. Create a vision for the future, maximize face-to-face communication and reiterate everything several times.

When decisions need to be taken, leaders must be seen to be taking them. Sometimes this involves painting a picture of what will happen if the changes are not made.

Stage 2: People start to react to the change

People may at first feel concern, anger, resentment or fear. They may correctly identify real threats to their positions and may resist the change actively or passively. They may feel the need to express their feelings and concerns, and vent their anger. This stage is the 'danger zone.' If this stage is badly managed, the organization may descend into crisis or chaos. Therefore this stage needs careful planning and preparation. As someone responsible for change, you should offer an empathetic ear, allowing people to approach and speak openly to foster trust and openness. Prepare for this stage by carefully considering the impacts and objections that people may have. Make sure that you address these early with clear communication and support and by taking action to minimize and mitigate the problems that people will experience. As the reaction to change is very personal and can be emotional, it is often impossible to pre-empt everything, so make sure that you listen and watch carefully during this stage or have mechanisms to help you get information so you can respond to the unexpected.

For as long as people resist the change and remain at Stage 2, the change will be unsuccessful, at least for the people who react in this way. This is a stressful and unpleasant stage. It is much healthier to move to Stage 3 where pessimism and resistance give way to some optimism and acceptance.

It is important to realize that people's reaction to change can be extremely negative and it may even affect their health. Be careful not to simply believe that people are being stubborn; change may affect them negatively in a very real way.

Stage 3: People stop focusing on what they have lost and explore possibilities

At this stage, people start to let go, and accept the change. They begin testing and exploring what the changes mean, and so learn the reality of what's good and not so good, and how they must adapt. This is the turning point for individuals and for the organization. You then start to feel you are on the way to making a success of the change. Individually, as people's acceptance grows, they'll need to test and explore what the change means. They will do this more easily if they are helped and supported, even if this is a simple matter of allowing enough time to adapt. Leaders should facilitate involvement in the change and encourage employees to offer their suggestions. Leaders will recognize when this stage begins because employees will complain less and focus more on optimizing the solution.

As the person managing the change, you can lay good foundations for this stage by making sure that people are well trained, and are given early opportunities to experience what the changes will bring. Be aware that this stage is vital for learning and acceptance, and that it takes time. Don't expect people to be 100 per cent productive during this time, and build in contingency time so that people can learn and explore without too much pressure.

Stage 4: People not only accept change but also start to embrace it

People rebuild their ways of working. Only when they get to this stage can the organization start to reap the benefits of change. This is where the changes start to become second nature, and people embrace the improvements to the way they work. As someone managing change, this is where you will start to see the benefits of your hard work in making the change transition as smooth as possible. Your team or organization start to become productive and efficient, and the positive effects of change become apparent.

Remember to celebrate success when appropriate! People will at the very least have been uncomfortable and everyone deserves to share the success. Also, celebration may pave the way to make things easier for future changes.

With knowledge of the Change Curve, you can plan how you'll minimize the negative impact of the change and help people understand and adapt more quickly to it.

Kurt Lewin's Change Management Model

Lewin, a physicist as well as social scientist, explained organizational change using the analogy of changing the shape of a block of ice. If you have a large cube of ice, but realize that what you want is a cone of ice, what do you do? First you must melt the ice to make it amenable to change (unfreeze). Then you must mould the icy water into the shape you want (change). Finally, you must solidify the new shape (refreeze).

By looking at change as a process with distinct stages, you can prepare yourself for what is coming and make a plan to manage the transition. To begin any successful change process, you must first start by understanding why the change must take place.

This model states that there are three stages of change. It describes how you generally have to 'break up' the current state of things in order to make improvements, using the concept of 'unfreeze–change–refreeze'.

Unfreeze

Resistance to change should be minimized. This entails the management detailing what the consequences of any change would be for all stakeholders, and also outlining what would happen if change did not take place.

> Lewin stated: 'Motivation for change must be generated before change can occur. One must be helped to re-examine many cherished assumptions about oneself and one's relations to others.'

To prepare the organization to accept that change is required, it is necessary to break down the existing status quo before you can build up a new way of operating. The key to this is developing a compelling message showing why the existing way of doing things cannot continue.

To prepare the organization successfully, you need to start at its core – you need to challenge the beliefs, values, attitudes and behaviours that currently define it.

This first part of the change process is usually the most difficult and stressful. When you start cutting down the 'way things are done', you put everyone and everything off balance. You may evoke strong reactions in people, and that's exactly what needs to done.

Old ideals and processes must be tossed aside so that new ones may be learned. Often, getting rid of the old processes is just as difficult as learning new ones due to the power of habits. During this part of the process you may need to provide some coaching as people are unlearning and need emotional support to break the old habits.

The transition from unfreeze to change does not happen overnight: people like to take time to embrace the new direction and participate pro-actively in the change. A related change model, the 'Change Curve Model' described above, focuses on the specific issue of personal transitions in a changing environment and is useful for understanding this specific aspect in more detail.

Changing

After the uncertainty created in the unfreeze stage, the change stage is where people begin to resolve their uncertainty and look for new ways to do things. People start to believe and act in ways that support the new direction.

In order to accept the change and contribute to making the change successful, people need to understand how the changes will benefit them. Not everyone will fall in line just because the change is necessary and will benefit the company. This is a common assumption and pitfall that should be avoided.

This period also requires emotional support as there may be confusion, overload and despair, but there will also be hope, discovery and excitement. This period requires coaching and possibly training as people are learning new things.

Unfortunately, some people will genuinely be harmed by change, partic-ularly those who benefit strongly from the status quo. Others may take a long time to recognize the benefits that change brings. You need to foresee and manage these situations.

Time and communication are the two keys to success for the changes to occur. People need time to understand the changes and they also need to feel highly connected to the organization throughout the transition period. When you are managing change, this can require a great deal of time and effort, and hands-on management is usually the best approach.

When the changes are taking shape and people have embraced the new ways of working, the organization is ready to refreeze.

Refreezing

The new processes are now intellectually and emotionally accepted. What has been learned is now actually being practised on the job. It is repetitive practice that will create new habits.

The refreeze stage also needs to help people use the new changes all the time, and ensure that they are incorporated into everyday business. With a new sense of stability, employees feel confident and comfortable with the new ways of working.

The rationale for creating a new sense of stability in our ever-changing world is often questioned. Even though change is a constant in many organizations, this refreezing stage is still important. Without it, employees get caught in a transition trap where they aren't sure how things should be done, so nothing ever gets done to full capacity. In the absence of a new frozen state, it is very difficult to tackle the next change initiative effectively.

As part of the refreezing process, make sure that you celebrate the success of the change – this helps people to find closure; thank them for enduring a painful time and help them believe that future change will be successful.

Mission and vision statements are a well-structured way of helping you to communicate what the change is intended to achieve, and to motivate everyone with an inspiring, shared vision of the future. (See the suggested mission statement for professional assistants in Chapter 4 on 'Leading effective office based and virtual teams to success').

Ongoing change is a part of everyday life and you need to learn to be agile and adapt on a daily basis in order to stay relevant and optimized. Strategies to help you embrace change are:

Be aware: Be proactive and observant, keeping eyes and ears open not only in work but in the wider world, look for new trends, new ways of working, new technology and keep informed with an open mind.

Prepare yourself: Do your research, embrace, learn, make plans, be flexible and collaborate with others to make sure you are not reinventing the wheel.

Embrace and visualize: Be excited about new ways of working, look for opportunities, be aware of obstacles and see yourself overcoming any obstacles and looking towards a bright future and career.

Bring others with you: Share your thoughts, ideas and feelings and build on them working together. Encourage and motivate each other.

Be resilient: Resilience is the ability to overcome challenges and turn them into opportunities, bounce forward from adversity, connect with others successfully and discover your workflow.

Resilience and brain power

Resilience can be defined as the ability to respond wisely and flexibly to adversity, be it small daily stressors or unexpected traumatic events. Research shows that we can change our brains to become more resilient to the ever changing 'VUCA' (Volatile, Uncertain, Complex, Agile) world, causing stress inducing experiences and challenges.

Resilience is important because:

- It drives success in change.
- It prevents you from feeling overwhelmed.
- Helps you to view challenges as a way to learn.
- Keeps you positive.
- Encourages you to reach out to new experiences.
- Helps you strive for personal and professional growth.
- It leads to better psychological well-being and health.
- Helps you to focus on priorities and what really matters.
- Enables effective behaviour.
- Increases happiness at work and home.
- Increases life expectancy.
- It's the armour you need for modern life and it can protect you from mental health issues.

Ask yourself the following questions to help create clarity and find out whether it is really the way you want to think, feel and act:

- Am I reacting to this situation on purpose?
- Did I **decide** to feel this way?
- Is this how I want to be perceived?
- Do I want to define myself as someone who reacts to people and certain situations this way?
- How is this working for me – is it helping me create the life I want and is it effective?
- Would I teach or recommend this reaction to someone I care about?

It is likely that you want to do something about your faulty thinking and here are some factors to help contribute towards building resilience:

Social: Having positive relationships, having a good support network, being considerate of others and having time to build trusting relationships both at work and home.

Physical: Getting enough sleep, eating a well-balanced diet, exercising, listening to music, dancing and simply enjoying life.

Mental: Having self-awareness, having a positive self-image, being able to control your mood and feeling in control overall, understanding your brain.

The art of living a happy and resilient life includes practising the following habits that resilient people display: be big picture focused and don't worry about less important things; broaden your perspectives and see things from different points of view – challenge your thinking and your assumptions; never think of yourself as a victim – be confident you can handle situations and recover quickly; take time to reflect, recharge your batteries and learn from experiences; be able to put a positive spin on challenging situations; be willing and able to change your approach and plans rather than being fixated on one outcome or one way of doing something.

Resilience is finding a new way to behave when the old way is no longer available to you

Understanding the Change Curve, explained above, will help you be resilient and more in control of your emotions. Knowing you will thrive in the end is empowering. Taking control and feeling in control is an important element of feeling resilient so look at your workload and your relationships and write down what you **can** control and what you **can** influence and don't waste your time and energy on things that are outside of your control.

Use your brainpower to foster resilience

Agile brainpower is the most powerful mental health resilience tool we have. Understand how your brain works best; how to make it stronger and make it work for you instead of against you!

Building your brain and brain agility is about having access to all different brain regions at the same time; it's about being able to be expressive and receptive, rational and emotional, logical and creative. It helps you to move away from getting stuck in that survival mode and back into the cognitive thinking areas of the brain by intentionally creating neuroplasticity – growing your neural pathways. It's also about activating your **parasympathetic** nervous system so it slows your heart and breathing rates, lowers blood pressure and promotes digestion which enables our body to enter into a state of relaxation and relaxation leads to recovery and resilience. The more time we spend in a parasympathetic state, the healthier we become. Your cognitive, social, emotional and intellectual functions improve when you brain build.

The following suggestions will help you build your brain, gain an agile mindset and activate your parasympathetic nervous system which is crucial for a healthy mind and body and to help prevent human error:

Mindfulness based resilience can help you to stay focused and productive no matter what is happening by giving your brain a 'power rest' to reboot it. Neuroscience and clinical research have demonstrated the amazing effects that mindfulness has to help people to develop resilience, focus, calm and clear thinking. Mindfulness is about training the mind to pay attention in the present moment, and non-judgementally.

Practise the following exercise for at least three minutes each day and as often as you need it:

Sit comfortably with your eyes closed, both feet flat on the floor, hands on your lap and your back supported by your chair. Notice the sensations of breathing whilst you breathe in through your nose to the count of six and out through your mouth to the count of eight, keep on counting throughout the exercise. Notice your feet on the floor, notice your hands on your lap, notice where you are tense in your body and relax your muscles. You will have thoughts coming into your mind so **acknowledge the thought** and imagine a bright blue sky and put your thought on a cloud and watch it fly away until it disappears. Do the same to every thought and keep on counting your breaths in and out. Keep doing this for three minutes then return to what you were doing and notice the difference.

Exercises for the brain

Physical exercise, whether you are swimming, jogging, walking, using the stairs instead of the elevator, etc, not only exercises your body – you are also exercising your brain and that is key to resilience. It stimulates neuroplasticity – the growth of new neural pathways and new connections.

It releases chemicals that are known to improve mood and lessen depression. When we are feeling stressed, we release cortisol (stress hormone). We need a certain level of cortisol, but too much is detrimental to our health – exercise dampens the release of cortisol and its impact on heightening stress. Exercise aids recovery because it releases the hormones we need to help us feel happy. It enhances the growth of neurons and promotes the repair of brain cells. Endorphins produced whilst exercising help you concentrate and feel sharp.

You can also practise mindfulness whilst exercising: by noticing the sensation of your feet hitting the ground, the rhythm of your breathing and the feeling of the wind on your skin etc. Adding this mindfulness element and really focusing on your body and how it feels as you exercise will enable you to interrupt the flow of constant worries running through your head, allowing you to become more resilient.

We can use the knowledge that the left hemisphere of your brain controls the right side of your body and the right hemisphere of your brain controls the left side of your body to help increase neuroplasticity, leading to resilience.

Change your mindset

Mind your language! Check your internal dialogue and reframe how you think. When we think negatively, our emotions and behaviour will be negative. For example use positive calming words such as feeling cautious instead of feeling dread; feeling excited instead of nervous and alert instead of feeling tense etc.

Non-dominant hand activities – You can build your neuroplasticity by using the opposite hand for writing than you normally do, so if you are right-handed try writing with your left hand. It is an effective way to enhance your cognitive capacities and build your resilience. Also doing such things as holding your cutlery in the opposite hands, brushing your teeth with the non-dominant hand, putting your keys in your other hand when opening the door, switch the hand you use for your computer mouse etc. Yes, you will find it hard but that is when you will create new neural pathways.

Change your routines – Brain activity declines when tasks become routine and automatic so changing your routines increases levels of brain activity in several distinct areas of your brain, for example: driving a different route than you normally would when you go places and using your own maps in your mind rather than relying on satellite navigations systems; walking to places taking different routes; sitting at a different seat at the table; wearing a watch on the opposite arm; folding your arms in the opposite way etc

Gain new knowledge! This is about deliberate, intentional and deep learning – not just scanning information without absorbing its meaning. Feed the brain regularly with new and challenging information that is well digested and deeply understood by reading articles, industry magazines, look at what your bosses read so you can understand their world better; take some professional studies and continually learn for the sake of your health and cognitive, emotional and intellectual abilities including resilience. Deep and deliberate learning will calm an anxious mind, help you to refocus and help you become highly resilient.

You can do it right now with my book! Take the information you are interested in – read, learn and choose what you want to think deeply about, make notes on it, highlight information, draw mind maps in order to really understand it to the point where you could give a lecture on it, have a really great discussion about it, take an exam in it or prepare and give a podcast on it, all of which would be good measures of how well you understand and how much brain building you are doing.

Continually gaining new knowledge with deep and intentional learning benefits your entire body and brain. It:

- changes how the brainwaves flow in your brain;
- changes how the connections occur within the different areas of your brain, making more connections across the two hemispheres;
- increases the flow of good hormones;
- changes your stress response for the better;
- improves your cardiovascular and immune function;
- increases resilience.

To be successfully resilient, visualize you are a winner and do not allow circumstances to push you down. You need to have pertinacity; be proactive in your intentional, deep learning, practise the habits of resilient people, take control of what you can and create the life you want.

Summary

Understanding the different models of change including 'The SixEss Threat/ Reward Model' will help you reduce the threat feeling and promote a reward feeling in yourself and others. The Change Curve, in particular, allows you to understand and know what to expect emotionally at the different stages, will help you in your personal and professional lives. This chapter and will help you to help yourself and others to have a smooth and painless transition through any change; adopt the right attitude, help and encourage others to understand the process, and realize that with hindsight all change can be extremely worthwhile. Helping yourself, your boss and colleagues through the change process will prove your skills as a strategic business partner and you will enable the achievement of goals and objectives that are aligned with the ever evolving business strategy.

I hope you now perceive the process of change as something to be excited about as change brings opportunities and progression. Being at the forefront of change is much more empowering as it gives you a feeling of being in control, so get involved, lead change and help others.

Continually practise the skills of change management as well as developing your brain's agility and resilience as they are vital for career success and for future proofing your role and should be an integral part of every assistant's journey. The assistants who are resilient and quick to adapt, willing to trailblaze and lead change are the ones who will survive and thrive.

Remember to be an agile leader of yourself, your boss(es) and your teams and be a strategic support keeping abreast of the mission, vision and goals of your organization and promote and lead change management. Create, maintain and develop your internal and external networks. Continue to have ongoing 'intelligent conversations' that lead to self-awareness and understanding what is required of everyone to make the organization and everyone in it successful. Understand different personality styles to enable excellent communication, influencing and negotiation skills and motivate others as well as yourself. Keep abreast of all new technology and artificial intelligence etc and discover ways in which you can use it to help you reach your goals and make your job interesting as well as challenging. Take on projects that stretch you and take you out of your comfort zone to aid your growth as well as enabling the strategic direction of the organization. Coach and mentor others and be coached and mentored to continually learn, discover more about yourself, resolve problems, find solutions and continue to develop yourself and others. Understand how your brain works and take action to grow and improve it; keep control of it and be highly emotionally intelligent and resilient.

Throughout this book I have given you tips, techniques, methods, tools and models to help you navigate, adapt and flourish in your roles. Remember to optimize your brain power, keeping it healthy and under your control. Reward yourself and celebrate every success, large or small. I wish you every success in your careers and life.

INDEX

Italics denote information within figures or tables.

Lightning Source UK Ltd.
Milton Keynes UK
UKHW050200101121
393612UK00006BA/20